Multicultural Counseling

Multicultural Counseling

Toward Ethnic and Cultural Relevance in Human Encounters

John M. Dillard
Texas A&M University

Nelson-Hall nh Chicago

LIBRARY OF CONGRESS CATALOGING IN PUBLICATION DATA

Dillard, John M.
Multicultural counseling.

Includes bibliographies and index.
1. Cross-cultural counseling—United States.
I. Title.
BF637.C6D54 1983 158'.3 82-24651
ISBN 0-88229-714-7, cloth
ISBN 0-88229-830-5, paper

Manufactured in the United States of America

10 9 8 7 6 5 4 3 2

The paper in this book is pH neutral (acid-free).

To my sons
Scott Maurice Dillard
and Brian Milton Dillard

"... increasing communication across ... [cultural and ethnic] lines to destroy stereotypes, to halt polarization, to end distrust and hostility, and to create common ground for efforts toward common goals of public order and justice."

Contents

Preface

THIS BOOK FOCUSES ON the problems faced by individuals from diverse ethnic and cultural backgrounds who live in the United States. It proposes the use of nontraditional intervention strategies in addition to traditional, middle-class counseling strategies. Chapters devoted to individual ethnic and cultural groups include suggested counseling approaches and practical exercises that apply to each group.

It is my hope that this text will stimulate the reader to conceptualize ethnic and cultural factors; to become aware of ethnic groups' perceptions of mental health and mental illness; to recognize acculturative variations and behavior; and to see the need for bilingual and bicultural counseling and culturally relevant counseling approaches.

Part One of this text serves as an introduction to the issues of cross-cultural counseling. Part Two focuses on the social and psychological factors of various ethnic groups, discusses the problems encountered, and suggests counseling strategies. Part Three presents a communicative counseling model, and Part Four draws conclusions and offers methods for improving counselor training and counseling practices.

Intended for instructors as well as graduate and undergraduate students, this text is also appropriate for interested laypersons and participants in preservice and inservice training workshops who seek to attain greater understanding of the diverse ethnic clients who seek counseling assistance. This book may be used as a primary or as a supplemental text.

In the preparation of this book, I am indebted to several people who assisted me greatly. My sincere appreciation goes to Leslie Miller, Grace B. Chisolm, and Susan S. Walker, who read drafts of each chapter and offered significant suggestions for improving the manuscript. I also express my gratitude to Lynell Barnes, Deborah R. Boone, Theresa Y. Nasalroad, Janice Smith, and Gail Johnson who were helpful in typing major segments of this manuscript.

Part One

Multicultural Counseling in a Pluralistic Society

The major goals of counselors and other mental health professionals have been to help change a client's behavior by positively increasing personal growth or self-awareness. This has usually been done through the use of counseling techniques based on Anglo middle-class values. The goals of most counselors, like the goals of most counselor-education programs, reflect the values and standards of the majority society. Educational programs, in particular, reinforce these cultural values and standards. Student counselors usually subscribe to mainstream values and are expected to continue them in practice. Consistent with this belief, ethnicity has been defined as "un-American," and ethnic and original attachments have been thought of as almost disfunctional by counselors and counselor educators.

The ethnic and cultural movements that emerged in the early 1960s and 1970s were destined to have a significant effect on many counseling programs. These movements influenced many counselor educators and psychologists to reexamine their counseling and psychological theories and the relationship of these theories to ethnic and cultural pluralism in the United States, and increasing numbers of professionals are being asked to work effectively in settings that involve cultural and ethnic pluralism. As a result, many counselors and psychologists now acknowledge significant ethnicity and varying degrees of socialization among individuals within American society; counselors are becoming aware of the ways in which cultural characteristics are often used to deny individuals and groups adequate social services. Since ethnicity plays a valid role in any pluralistic society, skilled counseling professionals also need to be able to communicate effectively with clients of diverse cultural groups.

A multicultural philosophy is winning a place in the counseling and psychology programs of many institutions, yet many of these programs and practices are not consistent with the general philosophy of multicultural counseling, a philosophy emphasizing permeation of overall programs and practices. Some programs address this area in isolation in programs designed only for minorities.

Multicultural counseling is based on a concept of cultural pluralism. Cultural pluralism involves the recognition of various cultural and ethnic groups within the United States, including each group's anthropological, sociological, economic, and political relationships. This concept exceeds mere observance of the presence of multicultural and ethnic groups; rather, it fosters an equal presence by suggesting respect for human diversity. There is an urgent need to permeate mental health programs with multiculturalism. The development of sensitivity to a culturally diverse community in an increasingly interdependent society has opened the door to a significant task for counselor educators—that of recognizing and respecting the concepts of multicultural human services.

We must examine and accept our similarities and differences as members of a society. Our similar socialization processes, values, and aspirations may assist in the reduction of the nation's division of mental health services. Multicultural human services will allow us to make better decisions concerning ourselves as individuals, group members, and citizens.

1

The Counseling Relationship and Cultural Diversity

MANY STUDENTS AND PRACTITIONERS remain unaware of the shortcomings of traditional and theoretical modes of communication in cross-cultural relationships. Some critics argue that traditional notions, which emphasize a monocultural or a general counseling approach to everyone, disregard cultural differences. Several issues concerning traditional versus multicultural counseling will be discussed in this chapter. This general discussion is intended to aid in understanding subsequent chapters, which contain discussions of cross-cultural communication in specific groups.

THE COUNSELING RELATIONSHIP

Counseling can be defined simply as a helping relationship (Carkhuff, 1969; Brammer, 1973). This relationship consists of the counselor, who provides assistance to a client (or group of clients) seeking to resolve a concern; the client, who may come from any of our numerous diverse cultural and ethnic backgrounds in the United States, and who seeks counseling for one or more reasons. One client may voluntarily seek assistance, while another may come reluctantly after being compelled to do so by the courts. Some may initially resent the idea of counseling and experience unpleasant feelings toward themselves and the counselor as well; others may come eagerly to the counseling relationship. Regardless of the client's reason for seeking assistance, the subsequent relationship is serious and purposeful.

Communication is the core dimension of any counseling relationship (Ivey, 1977). Without communication between the counselor and the client, there can be little, if any, progress toward resolution of the problem. The counseling relationship is a communicative process that operates as a sequence of events occurring over a period of time. The counselor and the client mutually respond with two-way verbal and nonverbal behavior (Beir, 1966; Hansen, Stevic, and Warner, 1977). Within this process, the counselor, a culturally skilled communicator, teaches the client effective communicative skills that enable him to explore, understand, and take action on this understanding of himself. The client is helped to identify areas of conflict, make objective judgments about his problem and himself, and develop improved methods to independently control the situation in question (Egan, 1975).

The client and the culturally skilled counselor must share in the relationship. Communication between the counselor and client is a reciprocal relationship—the behavior of one affects the behavior of the other (Loeffler, 1970). For example, a statement of communication by the client is a response to as well as a reinforcer of the counselor's last statement and a trigger for the counselor's next statement.

CLIENT: Uh, so what are we supposed to do here?
COUNSELOR: What would you like to do?
CLIENT: (Silence) You know all about it, anyway.
COUNSELOR: Only what I heard from your teacher; only her side of it; only as she sees it. How do you see it?

The counselor's assistance is only as effective as his communication—especially where intercultural barriers exist. A client may use many words to transmit his concerns to the counselor, but the feelings and emotions behind the words—the nonverbal signals—convey a more accurate picture of his problem. Examples of nonverbal communications include facial expressions, spatial distance from the counselor, and posture. Also important in communication are such things as tone of voice, rate of speech, and grammar. The client may feel he has successfully transmitted his message when the counselor receives and responds to it. A message is considered communicated when the counselor accurately understands the linkages between the words and feelings:

CLIENT: (Angrily) I'm not sure how I feel!
COUNSELOR: It sounds to me as if you're damn angry.

The counselor in this example is showing awareness of the total content of his client's response. For the counselor to receive and respond to the words alone suggests to a client that he has not made his messages clear and again has been misunderstood.

The communicative process also requires the counselor to transmit his thoughts and responses clearly to ensure that the client understands his message. Mutual understanding is needed for the relationship to progress. How well the client and the counselor understand each other determines to a great extent the client's sense of freedom in the process, that is, with mutual understanding, the client may feel less inhibited and thus be able to explore an area of concern, choose material appropriate to himself, feel secure in a safe environment, and choose available alternative forms of action (Carkhuff, 1969; Hansen, Stevic, and Warner, 1977).

In the cross-cultural counseling relationship, both counselor and client rely heavily on cross-cultural verbal and nonverbal communications. The quality of the communication determines the effectiveness of the assistance.

Communication, though, takes on added dimensions when there are cultural and ethnic differences between the counselor and the client. Each participant brings to the counseling setting a spectrum of ethnic and cultural characteristics that influence behavior (Sue, 1977; Ridley, 1978). The counselor should be aware that what is culturally appropriate behavior with one client may be inappropriate with another. For example, direct eye contact may be appropriate with an adult

Chicano male, but not with an adult Chicano female. Thus, the culturally skilled counselor must know how to apply basic cultural skills of each culture (in addition to the communicative, qualitative, and focus skills discussed in detail in chapters 9 and 10) when dealing with clients from that culture. Such skills are important in providing required assistance to the culturally different client (Ivey, 1977). This cultural competence on the part of the counselor facilitates the communicative process. It is essential that special consideration be given to any counseling relationship where cultural or ethnic differences exist between the counselor and the client.

Culture frequently causes difficulty in communication because of the changing nature of cultural values. For instance, assertive behavior among Anglo women was once unacceptable, but it is increasingly acceptable today. Sharing personal mental-health problems outside the family, once virtually prohibited among most Chinese Americans, is now more acceptable. As cultural values change, so do the difficulties in communication (Porter and Samovar, 1976, p. 6)

A Call for Cultural Diversity

The problems that some ethnic minorities encounter in counseling, psychotherapy, and other helping relationships now have been heavily researched and documented, yet research literature continues to tell the story of ineffective communication, ignored value differences, ethnic and cultural stereotyping, high attrition rates, and the insensitivity gap between ethnic minority poor and middle-class Anglo groups. Despite innovative programs of the 1960s and a deluge of professional journals calling attention to the problems of ethnic minority individuals, many counselors, psychotherapists, and other professionals remain ineffective in providing human services to ethnic groups.

Since the 1960s, numerous books, journal articles, workshops, conferences, and major policy statements have presented such concepts as "multiethnic," "multicultural," and "cross-cultural." Emphasis was placed on cultural pluralism as an essential human relations reform in the counseling fields. In 1973, the American Association of Colleges for

Teacher Education (AACTE), for example, adopted a strong and forceful multicultural statement, which, in part, reads:

> To endorse cultural pluralism is to endorse the principle that there is no one model American. To endorse cultural pluralism is to understand and appreciate the differences that exist among the nation's citizens. It is the continuing development of a society which professes a wholesome respect for the intrinsic worth of every individual. Cultural pluralism is more than a temporary accommodation to placate racial and ethnic minorities. It is a concept that aims toward a heightened sense of being and of wholeness of the entire society based on the unique strengths of each of its parts. [p. 3]

The AACTE's position is shared by a 1977 special issue of *Personnel and Guidance Journal* in which the concepts of multicultural counseling and cultural diversity receive strong support. Also, there is a suggestion for massive implementation of these concepts into counseling relationships. Despite all this, though, definitions of multicultural counseling are not always clear, even among its proponents.

MULTICULTURAL COUNSELING

Multicultural counseling has become a fashionable concept among some counseling practitioners and writers (Dillard, Kinnison, and Peel, 1980; Dillard, 1980). This concept has been suggested as the basic vehicle to assure consideration of cultural diversity between the counselor and client. It is necessary to define *culture*, *assimilation*, and *acculturation* before discussing what is purported as multicultural counseling.

Literature is filled with definitions of culture. In their extensive examination of this concept, Kroeber and Kluckhohn (1952) present more than one hundred meanings. One rather practical and relevant description of culture is provided by Porter and Samovar (1976):

> . . . culture refers to the cumulative deposit of knowledge, experience, meanings, beliefs, values, attitudes, religions, concepts of self, the universe, and self-universe relationships, hierarchies of status, role expectations, spatial relations, and time concepts acquired by a large group of people in the course of generations

> through individual and group striving. Culture manifests itself both in patterns of language and thought and in forms of activity and behavior. These patterns become models for common adaptive acts and styles of expressive behavior, which enable people to live in a society within a given geographical environment at a given state of technical development. [P. 7]

Culture, therefore, includes, among other factors, shared belief systems, behavioral styles, symbols, and attitudes within a social group. These group attributes help to differentiate one group from another. Even as a culture's uniqueness is apparent, though, its similarities with other cultures are also present. These similarities help to maintain interdependent relationships among cultures.

A culture may refer to a dominant culture (e.g., Anglo middle-class) and its subcultures (e.g., southern culture and youth culture). Each subculture contributes to the dominant culture. One may be a rightful member of more than one culture simultaneously—that is, one may be a Westerner, a female, and an intellectual.

Assimilation and acculturation are broad concepts linked to the sociocultural context of human interaction. Acculturation, the loss of ethnic identity through adoption of dominant social and cultural norms, is a necessary step in the assimilation process. Assimilation is a slow process in which ethnic minorities and immigrants attempt through acculturation to merge into a dominant society. Gordon (1964) maintains that there are seven stages within the assimilation process: (1) assimilation that includes behavioral and cultural acculturation; (2) structural assimilation that includes cliques, fraternal groups, certain church groups, and basic institutions; (3) marital assimilation that includes acceptance of interethnic or interracial marriage; (4) identification as part of the dominant society; (5) positive attitudes with the absence of ethnocentric biases; (6) nondiscriminatory behavior; and (7) absence of value and power differences.

Research results suggest that many ethnic minorities and immigrants to the United States are at the acculturation stage. That is, they are attempting to adjust to the cultural and behavioral patterns of American society. At the very least, acculturation involves the adoption of and adaptation to behavioral and cultural patterns—such as values or life-styles—of one or more dominant cultural system. There are few empirical data to support the notion that ethnic minorities, generally, have been assimilated into American society. Therefore, the focus is on the influence of acculturation.

Bogardus (1949) maintains that acculturation may be expressed in at least three overlapping types. The blind process of acculturation, for example, occurs when individuals of various cultures who are in close proximity exchange goods and services, incidentally adopting cultural patterns from each other in a hit-or-miss manner. A second type of acculturation is one that forces or imposes cultural patterns, behaviors, or beliefs upon ethnic minorities and immigrants. Most group members of the imposing cultural system tend to believe that their own beliefs, patterns of behavior, and customs are superior to those of other cultural systems; thus, all other cultural characteristics are considered less than desirable while all of their own cultural characteristics are perceived as strongly desirable and necessary. Force or imposition acculturation is founded on the concept of ethnocentrism. The third type of acculturation uses democratic process. Individuals view with respect the history and strengths of each other's cultures. Social and psychological patterns of any culture are perceived as equivalent to other cultures unless empirically demonstrated to the contrary. As a general principle, culturally different individuals are neither forced nor coerced to accept cultural patterns that differ from their own. Democratic acculturation allows a person, over a period of time, to choose freely to change to the cultural patterns of other groups.

All three types of acculturation probably function in American society. Many individuals, particularly ethnic minorities (including many Southern Appalachian Anglos), are compelled to endure economic and social constraints that prevent their penetration of a dominant middle-class, Anglo society. These individuals are likely to experience less psychological stress should they experience blind or democratic acculturation rather than the imposed cultural patterns of an ethnocentric society. While many persons of an ethnic minority do not sanction adoption of and change to other cultural patterns, most persons realize the necessity of attempting to attain such dominant Anglo cultural patterns (e.g., fluent English and educational excellence) in order to facilitate their social acceptance and entry into this society. These patterns are prerequisites to the acquisition of adequate economic needs such as employment and housing.

Literature indicates that there is a relationship between mental health and acculturation. Individuals or groups of individuals undergoing sociocultural change are likely to encounter various degrees of psychological discomfort (Berry & Annis, 1974). Individuals may experience psychological stress as a result of antecedent factors, such as changes in levels of linguistic, perceptual, or cognitive behaviors. According to Berry and Annis (1974), some psychological stress factors are usually present as a function of acculturative influences.

The following chapters in this book will treat acculturation as a significant factor in personal development. The extent to which acculturation affects an individual's behavior is an important consideration for multicultural counselors who are interested in providing effective services to ethnic minorities.

Multicultural counseling, then, may be defined as a one-to-one helping relationship between the counselor and the client when the two are of dissimilar cultural and/or ethnic backgrounds. Examples of this relationship are Black counselor-Anglo American client; American Indian counselor-Vietnamese American client; Chinese American counselor-Chicano client; Anglo counselor-Appalachian Anglo client; and Chicano counselor-Black client. The key difference between multicultural and traditional counseling rests with the counselor's awareness of the client as a member of a cultural and/or ethnic group. The counselor is equally aware of his own cultural and ethnic background and what he brings into the relationship that affects the client's behavior. Application of this awareness is demonstrated in counseling goals, skills, personal attitudes, and behaviors adjusted to increase the client's personal growth.

The concept of multicultural counseling suggests that *all* cultural groups should be included under the umbrella of multiculturalism, yet the unlimited scope of multicultural counseling may not lend itself to reaching that goal, which is advanced by many professionals such as DeBlassie (1974); Pedersen, Lonner, and Draguns (1976); and Sue (1977). Therefore, many professionals suggest that the central aims of multicultural counseling should be limited to those ethnic/cultural groups that have been victims of discrimination and oppression because of their unique characteristics. For purposes of this book, the focus of multicultural counseling will be on those groups that experience discrimination and the psychological effects of acculturation in the United States. This is based on the belief that such terms as *prejudice, discrimination, alienation, acculturative stress,* and *image conflicts* are commonly shared among these diverse cultural groups, which include American Indians, Chicanos (or Mexican Americans), Southern Appalachian Anglo Americans, Chinese Americans, Black Americans, Vietnamese Americans, and Puerto Rican Americans.

Issues Concerning Cultural Pluralism and the Counseling Relationship

To attain a sound basis for multicultural counseling as a vehicle for cultural pluralism, it is necessary to become aware of some key issues in counseling culturally and ethnically diverse populations. The following questions will be considered, and pro and con arguments will be presented. (1) Is the concept of counseling monocultural or multicultural? (2) Can counselors provide clients with effective assistance if they are viewed as more alike than unalike? (3) If the counselor has effective communication skills in one culture, should he acquire them in another? (4) Is it necessary that the ethnic identity of the counselor and the client be identical? (5) Do counseling theories help to perpetuate disregard for cultural diversity in counseling practices?

Is the concept of counseling monocultural or multicultural? A major goal of counseling is to provide effective assistance to individuals in need of counseling services. Persons seeking help require various treatments based on various cultural, ethnic, and personal backgrounds. The clients may come from any group—Puerto Rican, Black, Chicano, or Mexican American, Amish, female, lower class, or middle-class. Most counseling professionals are members of the Anglo cultural and ethnic group. Thus, there are many counseling relationships where the participants are culturally and ethnically different. Cultural differences are likely to exist even in situations where the professional and client are of similar ethnic backgrounds. These differences are present by the nature of the counselor's educational and professional training, which may include a different set of values and behavioral styles than those of his client. As all subcultures share similar behavioral characteristics, each culture has its own uniqueness. In a counseling relationship, cultural differences usually have significant impact on the effectiveness of the communicative process. In many cases, the counseling relationship may be considered a multicultural or cross-cultural enterprise.

A counselor might argue, though, that counseling is monocultural or culture-specific because his professional assistance engages members of only one cultural group—for example, the psychiatrist whose professional assistance is so expensive that only middle-class Anglos can afford his services. Because American society consists of many subcultures, other counselors contend that people are generally the same regardless of their cultural or ethnic background, that is, the culture-bound counselor sees all individuals as more alike than different.

Can counselors provide clients with effective assistance if they are seen as more alike than unalike? The tenor among some professionals in the counseling field has been that counseling is basically the same for most individuals (Vontress, 1971). This position suggests that all clients who seek assistance, regardless of their ethnic affiliation, share more commonalities than differences. A counselor who assumes that he can provide effective assistance to individuals across ethnic boundaries without changing his one-model approach is either unable or unwilling to recognize his client's cultural and ethnic differences (Pedersen, 1976). This side of the issue is synonymous with the "melting pot" theory—"We are all human beings."

Other professionals in the field such as Vontress (1971, 1976); Stewart (1976); Pedersen, Lonner, and Draguns (1976); and Ivey (1976, 1977) suggest that effective assistance to the client will emerge only as the counselor recognizes and respects the commonalities *and* differences that each client brings to the counseling relationship. Should the counselor consider that all clients are the same, he runs the risk of having difficulty communicating, and thus, of not providing effective assistance.

Clients are essentially the same to the extent that they all engage in certain basic activities most of their lives. The different approaches to these activities are what make them different. Some of these differences—learning styles, language, and speech patterns—frequently hamper the communicative process. Thus, awareness of the diversities and the reasons behind them help the counselor avoid many obstacles that negatively influence communication in the dyadic relationship.

If the counselor has effective communication skills in one culture, should he acquire them in another culture? The individual who has communicative skills in a particular culture can be referred to as a culturally skilled counselor. This person is cognizant of his own attitudes, values, self-worth, and ethnic and cultural identity. He is communicatively effective both verbally and nonverbally within one culture. Some would contend, then, that the culturally skilled counselor has no need whatsoever to learn additional communicative skills. This assertion would be especially true should this counselor's clients be drawn from his own cultural group.

Others would view the culturally skilled counselor as one who has limited skills that cannot meet the goals of multicultural counseling. Cultural variations within a diverse culture such as American society require the counselor to communicate effectively with clients across cultural and ethnic boundaries, particularly as more minority-group members seek help. Traditionally, many minority members have been excluded from therapeutic assistance for such reasons as: (1) lack of financial resources, (2) "wrong" ethnic or racial affiliation, (3) lack of accessible facilities, (4) lack of awareness of service location, and (5) lack of awareness of the purposes of the services. Within recent years, increased educational opportunities and socioeconomic gains have become visible among ethnic minority members. A newly emerging segment of the population has straddled the threshold of middle-class status; for example, many Blacks can now afford therapeutic assistance. Hence, it becomes even more than ever important for the counselor to recognize that the counseling relationship is becoming (however slowly) a pluralistic milieu. To provide adequate assistance to clients in an ever-changing society, the traditional counselor must consider becoming the multicultural counselor.

Is it necessary that the ethnic background of the counselor and the client be identical? There are opposing arguments that surface regarding the significance of ethnic and cultural identity within the counseling relationship. Several professionals explicitly state that the counselor must be of the same ethnic background as the client to assure effective assistance (Phillips, 1959; Brown, 1973; Johnson, 1974). For example, Brown asserts that the counselor of one group, such as an Anglo American, cannot be sensitive to the special problems and life-styles of ethnic minorities such as Blacks, Chicanos, and American Indians. Johnson contends that the Anglo-American counselor is usually not as able to communicate such intangible concepts as sincerity, warmth, and empathy to Black clients as is the Black counselor. Phillips likewise concludes that different ethnic and cultural identities in the counselor-client relationship may give rise to counselor ethnic hostility, a poor relationship, and ineffective assistance. Hence, these and other advocates strongly suggest that the counselor can effectively assist the client only if the counselor and the client have similar ethnic and cultural experiences.

Others such as Bell (1971), Vontress (1971), and Williams and Kirkland (1971) suggest that ethnicity may be important in the therapeutic relationship but that ethnic identity between the counselor and the client should not be a prerequisite for effective assistance. Brown (1973) contends that ethnic characteristics such as skin color and hair style, which may prove helpful in establishing initial rapport, are insufficient for effective counseling.

Lewis, Lynch, and Munger (1977) conclude that counselor-client ethnic identity may have little, if any, relation to the counselor's effectiveness in the relationship. It is unrealistic to assume that all Chinese-American counselors, for example, must fully understand Chicano culture and behavior to effectively counsel Chicanos.

Overall, though, to effectively work with persons of different cultures, counselors need to understand the social and psychological forces that affect their clients' verbal and nonverbal behavior in the therapeutic milieu. There are many social and psychological factors that shape the behavior of clients of various cultures who seek our assistance. These will be discussed in Part Two.

Do counseling theories help to perpetuate disregard for cultural diversity in counseling practices? This question centers on whether or not counseling theory influences the practitioner's application of monocultural or general approaches that intentionally or inadvertently ignore ethnic and cultural variations. Monocultural approaches derived from traditional theories assume that all persons are the same since all persons are human beings. Some professionals (Gunnings, 1971; Patterson, 1971; Franklin, 1971) support the conclusion that traditional theories are one of the major culprits contributing to the counselor's insensitivity to and nonconsideration for ethnic and cultural diversity in practice. According to Gunnings (1971), Patterson (1971), Franklin (1971), and Smith (1973), many traditional theorists—Freud, Jung, Adler, Fromm, Horney, Rank, Reich, and Sullivan—are outdated and culture-bound and do not lend themselves to therapeutic, multicultural practice. As Gunnings explains:

> They [traditional theorists] are looked upon as being the knowledge base from which many methods of counseling are taught. Yet as I look at this eminent list I fail to find a black [a Puerto Rican, a Chicano, an American Indian, or an Asian American] or one who has done an in-depth work with blacks [or other ethnic minorities]. These theorists cannot speak to the

> frustrations, intimidations, and experiences of blacks [and other ethnic minorities] since there is no linkage between the theory and actual life styles of blacks and [other ethnic minorities]. [P. 100]

Patterson corroborates Gunnings' contention that these traditional theorists have class and culture limitations. The practitioner who adheres solely to his training, where his counseling programs relied exclusively on traditional theories, will undoubtedly apply these theories across cultures in therapy, however inappropriately. Thus, it can be concluded that traditional counseling philosophies may indeed influence the counselor's assistance.

There are others, however, who suggest that theories have little, if any, effect on the modality of a monocultural assistance in practice. Theory alone is not the culprit; the counselor assumes the ultimate responsibility for a theory's application. Recognizing the limits of some theoretical models, Jones and Jones and Smith support the notion that counseling theories are universally applicable. Jones and Jones (1972) contend: "The principles of counseling, which are practical and ideal, are universally applicable to all people in Western culture, black and white, and probably to people everywhere" (p. 195). Smith (1973) takes a similar stance regarding counseling theories and their relevance to ethnic groups: "Almost all of the theories have some point of relevance for [ethnic and culturally different clients]. What the theories mainly provide are conceptual frameworks or maps for outlining how behavior is acquired and modified. This is the strength of most counseling theories" (p. 68). Counseling theories are viewed with some degree of validity across ethnic and cultural lines; however, disregard for variations in practice still prevails.

Both Smith (1973) and Jones and Jones (1972) contend that omission of ethnic and cultural differences in practice (inadvertently or not) is the responsibility of the practitioner. Smith advocates that this omission may likely be the practitioner's "misapplication" of counseling theories in practice with a culturally different client. From a slightly different perspective, Jones and Jones contend that the act of omission of the ethnic and cultural factors is a function of the practitioner's culture-bound, middle-class orientation. Jones and Jones proffer:

> Thus the courageous counselor, when faced by a black or other minority person, often finds himself at a total loss. If he applied the basic acceptance of counseling and were willing to listen receptively, interaction might conceivably take place, but instead he attempts to project his innate middle-class orientations on the client. The cultural barrier becomes an immediate block to communication. The client perceives that he is not being heard or understood and mentally withdraws. [1972, p. 196]

In short, the struggle between—and sometimes among—the issues continues. Although cultural variables are gaining some consideration in counseling settings, many culturally different clients still must wait until practitioners shed their fettered, ethnocentric behavior to obtain equitable assistance. Until all issues in question are resolved, little can prevent preferential treatment of middle-class, Anglo clients over lower-class, ethnic minority clients.

Dispelling Counseling Stereotypes

Cultural variations in the therapeutic setting are frequently plagued by images and perceptions persons hold about each other. While the counselor recognizes that cultures vary, difficulty in communication seems to emerge when perceptions and images are distorted, grossly exaggerated, and generalized. Stereotypes or attitudinal sets are actually labels wherein certain characteristics are ascribed to persons based on the group with which they are affiliated (Porter and Samovar, 1976). Such stereotypic behavior on the part of the counselor impedes the communicative process of the counselor-client relationship. Porter and Samovar's (1976) conclusion supports this statement:

> Stereotypes and prejudices work in various ways to affect our communication. By predisposing us to behave in specific ways when confronted by a particular stimulus and by causing us to attach generalized attributes to people whom we encounter, we allow stereotypes and prejudices to interfere with our communicative experiences and to limit their effectiveness. We spend

> our time looking for whatever reinforces our prejudices and stereotypes and ignore what is contradictory. (P. 13)

The unfairness of such perceptions is addressed more directly to counseling professionals by Smith (1977) who contends:

> Stereotypes are the conventions that people use for refusing to deal with each other on an individual basis. Although it is difficult to face the idea that counseling stereotypes have been created and nurtured by the behavior(s), fears, good intentions, and incompetencies of counselors, it is something that the profession must face. [P. 390]

Counselors and psychologists must begin by examining the roles, values, perceptions, and images that influence their therapeutic encounter with the culturally different client. Since it follows that stereotypes or attitudinal sets emerge as a result of limited factual information concerning cultural and ethnic differences and similarities, one purpose of this book is to attempt to pull together information on various cultural groups to facilitate the counselor's awareness of the needs of the culturally different client.

SUMMARY

The preceding pages have examined the counseling relationship as a basic communicative process providing effective assistance to the client. Mutual understanding between the counselor and the client is a prerequisite to effective counseling. Acute disparities are compounded when the middle-class counselor attempts to communicate on a monocultural basis with a client of a different background. According to Wittner (1970), the "worker functioning in his congenial cultural situation and inexperienced in the ways that cultures differ is more prone to impose his idealized values on this type [of client] rather than just expose them" (p. 9).

Since humans live in a multicultural society, it is only natural that many counselors will experience cross-cultural interactions in therapeutic encounters. Numerous factors concerning various cultural groups merit special attention from counseling professionals and require specialized knowledge. Discouragingly, however, little unbiased information is available about the unique characteristics of these groups. For instance, the special aspects that should be considered in the counseling relationship of Chicanos, Southern Appalachian Anglos, and American Indians must be enormous; yet these groups are underrepresented in professional literature. The paucity of understanding that frequently reflects the availability of information on the part of the counseling professional can jeopardize the psychological well-being of the culturally different client. The tragedy of this situation is that many culturally different clients are being provided assistance primarily on the premise of counseling as an art with little relevant scientific foundation. What is needed is a reservoir of unbiased information concerning different cultural groups and individuals on which professional practitioners can base their assistance. Part Two attempts to provide some of this information.

Exercises

A. The following are some statements about ways people feel regarding contacts with members of different cultural and ethnic backgrounds. Rate your feelings about each statement by using the following scale:

1—strongly agree
2—slightly agree
3—slightly disagree
4—strongly disagree

1. Most illegitimacy is found among ethnic minority groups.
2. In larger cities, the natural divisions of cultural groups into different living areas should be respected and left alone.
3. I would support my child in an interethnic marriage.
4. Busing children for integration has proven to be an effective procedure.
5. After being denigrated for so many years, Black people have a right to strike back.
6. Separate but equal facilities in education are not realistic.
7. Reverse prejudice is a growing concern of Anglo people.

8. No one of any cultural or ethnic background needs to be unemployed if he really wants to work.
9. If a Puerto Rican family moved next door, the value of property would decrease.
10. In business, the quota for minority employment should be maintained but not exceeded.
11. Although a number of Black Power movements exist today, most Black people are still apathetic and lazy.
12. Everyone should be able to live together peacefully, regardless of their ethnic differences.
13. American Indians have a great deal of difficulty communicating with other cultural groups.
14. My child is permitted to play with any child regardless of ethnic or cultural background.
15. Certain ethnic or cultural groups need not be included in private clubs.

B. In each of the following situations, discuss the issues involved, the social implications, and the possible solutions.

1. Two women with comparable qualifications have applied for the same position with a small business firm. One woman is Chinese and one is Puerto Rican. What considerations and additional information would assist you in deciding whom to hire?

2. Two fifteen-year-old females have been arrested for possession of drugs. One female is Chicano from a broken home where the mother is on welfare. The second female is American Indian, with a similar family situation. What is a likely or realistic outcome of this situation? What conditions could be altered to provide a meaningful and lasting societal adjustment for these females?

C. Listed below are several groups of people. For each one, write down the first three descriptions that come to your mind.

- Militants
- Lower-class people
- Puerto Ricans

- Southern Appalachian Anglos
- The Elderly
- Upper-class people
- American Indians
- Chicanos
- Blue-collar workers
- Black Americans
- Vietnamese Americans
- Politicians
- Minors (under eighteen years)
- Professionals

Analyze and discuss your responses with the group. Tally the most frequent and least frequent descriptions for each, and discuss the frequency of differences and similarities among your responses.

REFERENCES

American Association of Colleges for Teacher Education. *No One Model America*. Washington, D.C., 1973.

Beier, E. G. *The Silent Language of Psychotherapy*. Chicago: Aldine Pub. Co., 1966.

Bell, A. L., Jr. "The culturally deprived psychologist." *Counseling Psychologist*, 1971, *2*, 104–7.

Berry, J., and R. C. Annis. "Acculturative stress." *Journal of Cross-Cultural Psychology*, 1974, *5*, 382–405.

Bogardus, E. S. "Cultural pluralism and acculturation." *Sociology and Social Research*, 1949, *34*, 125–29.

Brammer, L. M. *The Helping Relationship: Process and Skills*. Englewood Cliffs, N.J.: Prentice-Hall, 1973.

Brown, R. A. "Counseling Blacks: Abstraction and Reality." In C. F. Warnath and Ass. (eds.), *New Directions for College Counselors*. San Francisco: Jossey-Bass Pub., 1973, 163–72.

Carkhuff, R. R. *The Helping and Human Relations*, vol. 2. New York: Holt, Rinehart and Winston, 1969.

DeBlassie, R. R. "The Counselor and Cultural Pluralism." *Educational Leadership*, 1974, *32*, 187–89.

Dillard, J. M., L. R. Kinnison and B. Peel. "Multicultural Approach to Mainstreaming: A Challenge to Counselors, Teachers, Psychologists, and Administrators." *Peabody Journal of Education*, 1980, *57*, 276–90.

Dillard, J. M. "Multicultural Counseling and the International Student." *Journal of International Student Personnel*, 1980, *1*, 3–8.

Egan, G. *The Skilled Helper*. Monterey, Calif.: Brooks-Cole, 1975.

Franklin, A. J. "To Be Young, Gifted and Black with Inappropriate Professional Training: A Critique of Counseling Programs." *Counseling Psychologist*, 1971, *2*, 107–12.

Gordon, M. M. *Assimilation in American Life*. New York: Oxford University Press, 1964.

Gunnings, T. L. "Preparing the New Counselor." *Counseling Psychologist*, 1971, *2*, 100–101.

Hansen, J., R. Stevic, and R. Warner. *The Counseling Relationship*. Boston: Allyn and Bacon, 1977.

Harper, F. D. *Black Students: White Campus*. Washington, D.C.: American Personnel and Guidance Association Press, 1975.

Ivey, A. E. "Cultural Expertise: Toward Systematic Outcome Criteria in Counseling and Psychological Education." *Personnel and Guidance Journal*, 1977, *55*, 296–302.

Johnson, R. "What a Difference a Black Counselor Makes." In R. Johnson (ed.), *Black Agenda for Career Education*. Columbus, Ohio: Educational-Community Counselors Ass., 1974.

Jones, M. H. and M. C. Jones. "The neglected client." In R. L. Jones (ed.), *Black Psychology*. New York: Harper and Row, 1972, 195–204.

Kroeber, A. L. and C. Kluckhohn. *Culture: A Critical Review of Concepts and Definitions*. New York: Vintage Books, 1952.

Lewis, M. H., M. L. Lynch, and P. F. Munger. "The Influence of Ethnicity on the Necessary and Sufficient Conditions of Client-Centered Counseling." *Journal of Non-White Concerns*, 1977, *5*, 134–42.

Loeffler, D. "Counseling and Psychology of Communication." *Personnel and Guidance Journal*, 1970, *48*, 629–36.

Patterson, C. H. "Counselor Education for Black Counselors

and for Counseling Black Clients: Comments." *Counseling Psychologist,* 1971, *2,* 112–13.

Pedersen, P. "The Field of Intercultural Counseling." In P. Pedersen, W. J. Lonner, and J. G. Draguns, eds. *Counseling Across Cultures.* Honolulu: University Press of Hawaii, 1976, 17–41.

Pedersen, P., J. Lonner, and J. C. Draguns. *Counseling Across Cultures.* Honolulu: University Press of Hawaii, 1976.

Phillips, W. "Counseling Negro Pupils: An Educational Dilemma." *California Journal of Educational Research,* 1959, *10,* 185–88.

Porter, R. E. and L. A. Samovar. "Communicating Interculturally." In L. A. Samovar and R. E. Porter (eds.), *Intercultural Communication: A Reader, 2d ed. Belmont, Calif.: Wadsworth Pub. Co., 1976, 4–24.*

Smith, E. J. *Counseling the Culturally Different Black Youth.* Columbus, Ohio: C. E. Merrill Pub. Co., 1973.

Smith, E. J. "Counseling Black Individuals: Some Stereotypes." *Personnel and Guidance Journal,* 1977, 55, 390–96.

Stewart, E. C. "Cultural Sensitivities in Counseling." In P. Pedersen, W. J. Lonner, and J. G. Draguns, eds. *Counseling Across Cultures.* Honolulu: University Press of Hawaii, 1976, 98–122.

Sue, D. W. "Counseling the Culturally Different: A Conceptual Analysis." *Personnel and Guidance Journal,* 1977, 55, 422–25.

Vontress, C. E. *Counseling Negroes.* Boston: Houghton Mifflin, 1971.

Vontress, C. E. "Racial and Ethnic Barriers in Counseling." In P. Pedersen, W. J. Lonner, and J. G. Draguns, eds. *Counseling Across Cultures.* Honolulu: University Press of Hawaii, 1976, 42–64.

Williams, R. L. and J. Kirkland. "The White Counselor and the Black Client." *The Counseling Psychologist,* 1971, *2,* 114–17.

Wittner, J. "Intracultural Communication: The Dilemma and Some Possible Solutions." *International Association of Pupil Personnel Workers,* 1970, *14,* 9–16.

Wylie, R. C. *The Self-Concept.* Lincoln, Nebraska: University of Nebraska Press, 1974.

Part Two

Before the Encounter— Entering Behavior

Many practitioners and educators ignore the importance of cultural variables that surround both the counselor and the client as they begin their therapeutic work. These counseling professionals have long practiced what amounts to impressionistic guesswork, disregarding significant information and facts pertaining to their clients' cultural and ethnic differences. Research has demonstrated, however, the significant impact of such variables on the outcome of the encounter. Each participant brings to the therapeutic milieu a variety of background experiences and values that influence the communicative process, e.g., self-perception, values, attitudes, social-class role, and cultural and personal identity. This unique set of psychological factors is learned behavior, shaped through cultural interaction with society. Both clients and counselors are bound by the psychological and social factors that influence all behavior.

In stating that psychological factors are learned behavior, we mean that both psychological and social attitudes are acquired from our relatives and associates and the experiences that they have encountered. These experiences may have included such factors as prejudice, poverty, powerlessness, slow social mobility, assumed inferiority, or inadequate educational opportunities. Although each generation's experiences vary, they still directly affect the eventual cultural identification of the immediately following generation and even of several generations in the future.

Clients undergoing counseling as well as other individuals often adopt some generational and cultural behaviors while modifying others as they face new situations. The attitudes manifested through their behavior (their values, educational and social achievements) are a means to adapt to their surroundings and survive. The psychological and social behaviors discussed in Part Two are characterized as situational behaviors rather than as strictly cultural or ethnic characteristics. For example, the responses of a group of Chinese Americans may vary with situational changes in the same manner that the responses of these same persons may differ when these individuals encounter new situations. Counselors and clients alike will be affected by this situational behavior.

Most counseling professionals, however, are Anglo-Americans and of middle-class socioeconomic status. Their attitudes are reflections of their ethnic inheritance. Research suggests that professionals' experiences are often based on stereotypes that can impede communication. A faulty communications set-up can easily influence the counselor's perception of a situation—she thinks she understands a client's motivation; however, her understanding is based more on a stereotype of that client than on his actual conversations with her. Her perception of the reality of the client's situation is thus faulty. Hence, to align perception with reality, this counselor must sensitize herself to factual information pertaining to cultural behavior. Counselors can then best assure adequate assistance across cultural lines by allowing each client's needs to dictate counseling strategies.

The chapters in Part Two include discussion of some of the social and psychological factors related to situations encountered by American Indians, Mexican Americans, Southern Appalachian Anglos, Black Americans, Chinese Americans, Vietnamese Americans, and Puerto Ricans. Except for American Indians, there is no significance to the order in which each group is presented. We choose to discuss American Indians first as a tribute to America's original settlers.

Each chapter includes discussion of social characteristics, basic counseling concerns, suggested counseling strategies for each ethnic group, and practice exercises for the reader.

2

American Indians

In the early 1960s, increased attention was directed to various cultural and ethnic groups. As did other cultural groups, American Indians demanded their equal place within the American social system. They sought human dignity, self-identity, and self-determination. Much progress has been made. For instance, assertive court efforts by many American tribes have recently been responsible for redistribution of and payment for portions of land confiscated by the United States government. A large number of American Indian issues remain unresolved. For example, although attention has focused on the problems of American Indians—poor health, failure to be assimilated into the American culture, unemployment, and poverty—and numerous writers have brought these unfavorable conditions to the public's attention, much data still remain unreported. Counseling literature is still sparse, for instance, and we actually know very little about present-day American Indians.

Social and Psychological Characteristics

Defining American Indians

Since certain privileges and obligations are extended to this group alone, the first consideration is to determine who are considered American Indians. Faherty (1974) cites from the 1958 Federal Indian Law two central qualifications used as rule-of-thumb guidelines: (1) some of the individual's ancestors lived in America before its discovery by the Europeans, and (2) the individual is accepted as an Indian by the legally constituted Indian community in which he lives (U.S. Department of Interior, 1958, pp. 4–12). The legal definition of "American Indian" remains unclear. Legal considerations tend to be more politically and socially than biologically oriented, and cases often reach resolution through personal opinions, administrative decisions, and other irrelevant enactments. Further, more individuals whose parents were both American Indians can disengage themselves from their tribal ties and legally assume non-Indian status. Conversely, tribes can accept and legally declare individuals as American Indians who possess only the slightest American Indian ancestral background (Faherty, 1974).

Attempts to define American Indians then are obscure and confusing. First, such attempts to identify any cultural or ethnic group often focus on the image that is most characteristic of that group, thus heightening the risk of continued stereotyping and creating new myths or perpetuating old ones. Second, no agreement has been reached on single labels ascribed to American Indians across all tribes. There is no group sanction of an identifiable term for all American Indian tribes. Many American Indians maintain that a single label groups them altogether without regard for tribal differences. A single label suggests the existence of one American Indian culture; yet American Indians come from numerous and varied tribes. There are approximately four hundred recognized tribes in the United States, and each tribe has its own distinct culture (Youngman & Sadongei, 1974).

Today, common labels include *Indian, American Indian, Alaska Native, and Native American,* and *New Indian.* The first two terms are perhaps the most popular among members of these cultural groups. The term *Native American,* in vogue in the 1960s and 1970s, now tends to be used interchangeably with *Indian* and *American Indian.* The term *Alaska Native* refers collectively to Eskimos, Aleuts, and Alaskan Indians.

New Indian—referring to the new generation of university-educated Indians who publicly advocate Red power and Indian self-determination (Steiner, 1968)—is the term least preferred by older American Indians.

The term *American Indian* will be used throughout this book except where names of specific tribes are substituted. It correctly delineates all cultural groups who are members of the approximately 400 recognized tribes, and is the most frequently accepted term among the many tribal members. Support of this term also is illustrated by its use in professional literature: *Indian Voices*, 1970; Boutwell, Low, and Proffit, 1973; Attneave, 1973; Youngman and Sadongei, 1974; Faherty, 1974; and Croft, 1977.

Location of American Indians

According to the 1980 United States Census, the American Indian population increased from approximately 760,000 in 1970 to 1,361,869 in 1980. The latter figure does not include approximately 56,000 Eskimos and Aleuts in Alaska, collectively referred to as Alaska Natives. Some unofficial estimates put the American Indian population much higher, at about 15 million, a figure that includes all those American Indians who have not joined the popular movement to make their Indian heritage known (Johnson, 1975).

The members of this minority population are heavily concentrated in the Southwest, North Carolina, Oklahoma, and Alaska. California has the largest number of American Indians found in any state (198,095), followed by Oklahoma (169,297), Arizona (152,610), New Mexico (104,634), North Carolina (64,519), and Alaska (56,326).

In 1970, the total urban American Indian population was approximately 340,000. Slightly more than 40 percent of this group lived in the West, 25 percent in the South, 20 percent in the North Central region, and 10 percent in the Northeast. California had the largest urban American Indian population (67,000), followed by Oklahoma (48,000). The 1970 Census also showed New York City, San Francisco–Oakland, and Oklahoma City with minimum populations of 10,000, while Los Angeles had the highest concentration, nearly 28,000.

Ever since the Civil Rights Movement, a significant goal of American Indians has been to attain their rightful place in the technological and urbanized American society—despite the fact that this is a world they see as both alienating and ever-changing. To this end, in spite of the data presented above, it is imperative that counseling professionals acquire current statistical, cultural, and factual information pertaining to American Indians' social and psychological behaviors.

Social Value Characteristics

Social or interpersonal interactions are reflections of belief systems or value characteristics. Values are communicated verbally and nonverbally. Characteristics of American Indians' value systems and social behavior have been variously delineated in counseling literature. In a psychosocial examination of the value orientation of the Hopi tribe, Aberle (1951) cited six basic values expressed within this cultural group: (1) strength, embracing self-control, intelligence, and wisdom; (2) composure, good judgment, or tranquility; (3) obedience to the law comprising unselfishness, responsibility, kindness, and cooperation; (4) peacefulness or nonaggressive behavior; (5) health; and (6) preservation or protection of all living species (pp. 95–96).

Bryde (1972) suggests a basic list of general differences in value orientations between reservation-oriented American Indians and non-Indian Americans. These value differences are supported in data reported by Spang (1965), a member of the Cheyenne tribe. Spang found that the reservation-oriented Indian placed great emphasis on values incompatible or counter to those of the American non-Indian. The American Indian values a system that is present-oriented versus the future-oriented system valued by non-Indians; lacking in time consciousness versus time consciousness; giving versus saving; respecting of age versus emphasizing youth; cooperative versus competitive; and at harmony with nature rather than in conquest of nature (p. 5).

A more specific set of values is provided by Zintz (1969) in his comparison of Pueblo American Indians and Anglo Americans. While there are some commonalities among the values held by the Pueblo and those held by the reservation-oriented Indians, Zintz notes additional values contradictory to those held by Anglo Americans. For example, Pueblo Indians value anonymity as opposed to individuality, submissiveness as opposed to aggressiveness, and humility as opposed to the Anglo value of personal glory.

It is important to understand, as Locke (1973), half Sioux and half Chippewa, rightly contends, that while values are common to all American Indians, many values are tribal-specific. For example, the Sioux place great value on generosity in the form of sharing with fellow tribe members, yet this trait is not valued by the Chippewa, who call it "institutional give away," or by the Plains Indians or other tribes of the Southwest. These latter groups exhibit other behaviors to exemplify their generosity. The Southwest tribes strive to maintain a reserved nature, while the Plains Indians try to develop openness and instant acquaintances (Youngman and Sandongei, 1974).

Yet, there are general characteristics common among all tribal groups, such as "tribal loyalty, respect for elders, reticence, humility, avoidance of personal glory and gain, giving and sharing with as many as three generations of relatives, an abiding love for their land, attribution of human characteristics." These characteristics have also been delineated by Spang (1965), Zintz (1969), and Bryde (1972). However, the "giving and sharing" concept may not be a shared value, as Locke (1973) has suggested.

The value system of a tribe may not be shared to an equal extent by all its members. Thus, it is dubious that one can accurately assign a value on the basis of the individual's role or assign a role on the basis of a value. For example, White (1970) researched the values of lower-class Sioux in Rapid City, South Dakota. The results suggested that they value the most preferred or ideal values; their behavior, however, was associated with different intracultural factors which were situationally dependent.

Characteristics of American Indians can be better understood when combined with discussion of other factors (socioeconomic, religious, familial, educational, linguistic, discriminatory) that reflect social and psychological behavior. For instance, the socioeconomic situation of an urban American Indian may impel him to communicate behavior different from that of a rural American Indian. The lower-class, rural American Indian who has not been assimilated into the dominant society, and who is inadequately educated, may possess the traditional values of his tribe, yet a counselor must not rely on those without first examining the individual values of the client.

Socioeconomic Characteristics

In 1970, most American Indians remained predominantly rural; however, there is a trend toward urbanized living. Figures show a 70 percent rural American Indian population in 1960, but only 55.4 percent by 1970 (Johnson, 1975). Rural American Indians have become overwhelmingly nonagricultural. Johnson (1975) contends that 89 percent of rural American Indians possessed nonagricultural residences in 1970, compared to 80 percent in the total United States population (p. 1). Recognition of these rural-urban factors may facilitate an understanding of American Indians' socioeconomic. Again, however, it must be stressed that no figures represent all members of any population.

The Bureau of Indian Affairs' 1973 statistics indicated that some reservations experienced a rate of unemployment as high as 57 percent. The Navajo, the largest American Indian reservation in population and in geographical size, had 35 percent unemployment and 21 percent underemployment, while the Umatilla had 57 percent unemployment and 9 percent underemployment.

In 1973, when the U.S. Department of Labor ranked reasons for joblessness on the reservations in order of importance, there was a high degree of agreement between respondents that unavailability of jobs was the greatest reason. Other reasons were lack of vocational education, lack of general education, and transportation difficulties. Alcoholism and lack of day care and supportive services were the least important reasons.

While unemployment (40 percent on reservations; 20 percent off) and poverty (48 percent on reservations) are widespread among American Indians, there are those who are on the middle and upper rungs of the socioeconomic scale (U.S. Department of Labor, 1977). For instance, in Oklahoma there are American Indians who are millionaires. Some of these have accumulated their wealth from oil profits; others are land owners (U.S. Department of Labor, 1977). There are also professionals, scholars, artists, and historians among American Indians.

Pepper (1973) summarizes some of the broad socioeconomic characteristics of American Indian cultures:

> The average life span of the American Indian is 44 years. The infant mortality rate is 53.7 deaths per thousand live births. The birth rate is 2.5 times higher than that of [Anglos], and the majority of Indians are under 20 years of age. The average yearly income per family is less than $1,500. . . . The unemployment rate is 90 percent of the Indian population. Ninety percent of the housing is substandard. Indian culture has the highest suicide rate in the nation and has a 10 times higher rate in the teenage bracket. Dispirited by poverty [and] rejected by an Anglo culture in which they often are unable and unwilling to compete, many Indians choose death or drink. There is a 60 percent school . . . dropout [rate] among children as a whole and 20 percent of Indian men have less than 5 years of schooling. The highest dropout rate occurs in grades 8 and 10. There are nearly a quarter-million Indian children in our schools today and about half of them are the responsibility of the . . . Bureau of Indian Affairs, with a greater majority of them unable to speak or to understand English.

Obviously, a combination of historic, social, economic, and cultural variables has contributed to the depth and persistence of poverty among American Indians. Lack of job opportunities, persistently low incomes, relatively poor educations, and lack of skills result in little chance for advancement above the poverty level. Moreover, prejudice and discrimination frequently hinder Indians' chances for upward mobility (Johnson, 1975, p. 7).

Religious Characteristics

Religion is an essential spiritual force in the lives of modern American Indians (Deloria, 1974); as a force, it has sustained them for centuries. According to Deloria (1974), many Anglos regard the ceremonials of American Indian religion as heathen practices that accomplish little and are a continuation of superstitions best forgotten. Significantly, though, American Indians persist in developing and maintaining a continued association with the spiritual forces that guide their lives. Many ceremonies have lost their importance as a result of changing life-styles or have been eliminated or forgotten. Recent attempts of American Indian activists to restore tribal ceremonies have underscored this dilemma. Traditional American Indians still believe in the presence of spiritual forces, but they are threatened by a changing environment—transportation, communication, and technology.

The Pueblo tribes are among those who adhere to traditional religious practices (Ortiz, 1969; Deloria, 1974). The life of many Pueblos hinges on the ceremonial. Many Pueblos practice traditional religious customs even though they are employed in modern jobs in an Anglo society. During ceremonial periods, outsiders (Anglos and other American Indians) are permitted to view only certain features of the ceremony. Deloria (1974) contends that the Hopi are the most traditional of the old Pueblos. The Taos tribe likewise adheres strongly to tribal religious ways. Traditional religious customs, especially those pertaining to healing ceremonials, are also strong among the Navajo. Navajo medicine men and women continue to practice ancient rites of healing for many tribal members. Early Anglo health services were rejected on the basis of cultural prejudice and ignorance related to religion and customs, although today the prejudice has decreased, and now many Anglo doctors work side-by-side with tribal healers in attempts to deal with health problems. The Apaches of New Mexico and Arizona also have strong religious customs. The high sense of tribal bond is related to religion. Religious songs are not shared with other American Indian tribes because the Apache "do not want the songs profaned by people who would not understand their meaning to the Apache" (Deloria, 1974, p. 251). Some Iroquois of New York practice ancient long-house ceremonies; others practice the Handsome Lake that began as a reform movement in the early part of the nineteenth century (Wallace, 1970). Their ceremonies consist of the use of masks and sacred wampum belts and the recitation of tribal legends and histories. The American Indian tribes of the northern plains have restored their traditional Sun Dance after several decades in which it was forbidden by the United States government. According to Brown (1953) and Deloria (1974), the Sun Dance consists of piercing the flesh of the dancers, fasting, and tolerating much pain.

Christianity has permeated the religious life of most tribes. For example, the Five Civilized Tribes of Oklahoma (Choctaw, Cherokee, Creek, Chickasaw, and Seminole) have high membership in the Baptist and Methodist denominations. These tribes have developed their own preaching and teaching leadership. Most of the Five Civilized Tribes' members tend to practice "fundamentalism in their theology and resemble the rural churches of Appalachia and the Deep South" (Deloria, 1974, p. 251). These tribes are not entirely Christian; medicine women and men continue to perform ceremonies and healings in traditional communities. Deloria (1974) states: "Considering the national rate of Indian acculturation, one might suggest that the Five Civilized Tribes have reached a proportion of traditional versus Christian religious beliefs that all other tribes will eventually approximate: 80 percent Christian, and 20 percent traditional" (p. 251).

The Native American Church or "the peyote religion" exists among some tribes in Oklahoma and the Plains states and with the Navajo in the Southwest (Howard, 1978). In its ceremonies, the Native American Church uses peyote—a hallucinogenic drug derived from the peyote cactus *(lophophora Williamsii)* that produces a mild psychedelic effect (Wax, 1971; Howard, 1978). The Native American Church has assimilated some aspects of Christian beliefs into its teachings. The religious ethics related to the practices of the Native American Church consist of family care, self-reliance, shared love, and avoidance of alcohol (Wax, 1971). Outsiders who express an interest are often invited to view or participate in the ceremonies.

The importance of surveying religions among American Indians is to recognize the many differences in religious beliefs. As with other ethnic groups, American Indians are not all alike in their religious values; therefore, counselors must carefully assess the religious values of each of their American Indian clients.

Family Characteristics

Poverty and other difficult socioeconomic conditions profoundly affect the social and psychological behavior of many American Indian families. There are also many family variations among American Indians, and knowing some family characteristics may facilitate understanding of the inter- and intracultural differentials that exist in social units.

Alfonso Ortiz (1970) contends that a sense of freedom exists among Pueblo families, that is, "there is very little need for parents to say 'Don't!' And there is very little need for children to ask, 'May I?' " (p. 12). Parental permission simply is not a cultural value. While each parent wants the best for the child, emphasis is placed on developing the child's freedom, responsibility, and autonomy. According to Youngman and Sadongei (1974), it is also considered inappropriate to discuss one's own accomplishments. Praise is welcome as it is earned, but it is usually provided without being sought. Disclosure of one's own strengths may appear as negative behavior. Many American Indian families do not place emphasis on individualism; cooperative efforts appear to have greater value than individual efforts. Sharing is encouraged not only within a family, but among many families. Possessions as well as duties are shared, and individuals develop a strong sense of belonging (Youngman and Sadongei, 1974).

Another characteristic of some American Indians, although not unique to them, is the social organization commonly referred to as the extended family. Attneave (1973) considers the extended family as a viable social unit. She further states that there may not be an automatic passage of a family role or clan membership from the parents to child but occurs after group consensus. Although the child may refuse this role, some degree of stress may accompany his or her refusal. This is a modern option usually not underscored but often practiced consciously or by default.

In the extended family, a great deal of attention is given to the children. Demongtigny (1970), a Chippewa, explains that a nuclear family might not exist initially. The children of one brother are considered the children of another brother. The mother is allowed to bear a child only every six years, to ensure proper rearing of that child. The father is responsible for teaching the child skills to earn a living, while the child acquires philosophy and religion, knowledge of how to live a good life, and the meaning of things in the world from the grandfather. Neither parent punishes a child. If parents feel that reprimanding is warranted, an uncle is usually given the responsibility of carrying out the task. It is believed that the mother's and father's effectiveness in teaching will be lost should they administer punishment.

These few examples indicate the many variations of familial characteristics among American Indians. Invariably, social values and economic conditions are closely related to family behavior. It is important that stereotypes be avoided, and that social values, economic conditions, culture, and environment be considered as they relate to specific families rather than to American Indian families in general. Knowledge of other dimensions of the family may provide insights that facilitate communication with the individual and his family in therapeutic relationships; the counselor may want to do client-specific research in this area.

Educational Characteristics

Social scientists suggest that schools are not meeting the needs of the American Indian student (Bass, 1971). The adage that "the first American, the Indian, is the last educationally" (Croft, 1977, p. 7) aptly describes the educational conditions of the American Indian. Croft (1977) contends that "there is general agreement that American Indians do not differ from other groups in inherited intellectual capacity, but that they are, nevertheless, seriously disadvantaged educationally" (p. 17). Some social scientists, such as Bass (1971), suggest that variations in family background account for more differences in scholastic achievement than do variations in school characteristics; yet, according to Croft (1977), "achievement of [ethnic] minority students depends more upon school factors than does the achievement of non-Indian students" (p. 18).

Research indicates that American Indian children are as intelligent and as able to achieve as other children (Havighurst, 1970a; Voyat, 1970; Montagu, 1974); however, such studies as Coombs' (1958) and Coleman's (1966) tell us that American Indian students score below their grade level on standardized examinations. They enter ninth grade about one grade level behind the national average; by the completion of the twelfth grade, they are three grade levels below the national average.

Coombs (1958) concluded that American Indian students in public schools, on average, have higher academic achievement than those who attend Bureau of Indian Affairs schools; however, Bass' (1971) research did not corroborate Coombs' conclusions. Bass studied academic achievement among American Indian high school students of four school types—public, on-reservation; public, off-reservation; federal, on-reservation; and federal, off-reservation. After statistically controlling for intelligence and achievement differences, he concluded that neither superior nor inferior academic achievement was present in any particular school type. There was, however, evidence of differences in individual schools.

Research further indicated that the academic achievement level of the public-school-educated American Indian student in Oklahoma is lower than the national averages. The achievement level for the American Indian student attending a Bureau of Indian Affairs boarding school is even lower. Research of the current and projected educational needs of American Indian students of Oklahoma revealed that parents of American Indian children place top priority on basic skill development for their children—reading, mathematics, and writing (McKinley, 1976). In spite of these findings, it is well-known that the quality of education varies within and between both public and Bureau of Indian Affairs schools. Variations can also be found among the students. Thus, individual American Indian student's academic achievement will most likely depend on such factors as personal abilities, home environment, and quality of teachers' instructions and school facilities, and parental interest.

The values of education held by Indian and non-Indian students were compared in a study by Boutwell et al. (1973). The investigators concluded that American Indian students tend to value education more highly than do their non-Indian counterparts; they relate enjoyment in life to education, while non-Indians in the study do not. The groups did not differ significantly in their estimation of the value of school training for meeting real life problems; nor did they differ significantly in their grade-point averages.

Educational characteristics of some American Indian adults and public school children, however, tell a different story. Pepper (1973) was cited earlier as reporting a 60 percent dropout rate among American Indian children. She reports, additionally, that 20 percent of the average American Indian children had not completed more than five years of schooling. Pepper further states that a large percentage of children attending Bureau of Indian Affairs schools are unable to verbalize or comprehend English. These percentages are indeed indicative of their low value for education. Such devaluation of education is derived from several sources, non-Indian teachers and insufficient instructional materials. It is little wonder why any of these American Indian students would not prize education when they can see only a few American Indian adults who have attained significant gains because of their educational achievement. Too, such students are likely to have a dislike for education and psychologically and physically remove themselves when their culture is not included in classroom instructions. Johnson (1975) reports that the average American Indian twenty-five years old and over is more than two years behind the United States population in median years of school completed.

While it is evident that many of the educational conditions of the American Indian warrant vast improvement, a stereotype that labels all American Indians as poorly educated must be avoided. Such a notion can only hinder communication. Progress has been especially notable at the college level. For example, Johnson (1975) maintains that 24,078 American Indians had completed one to three years of college in 1970. During that same year 12,198 American Indians had completed four years or more of college. Higher percentages of American Indians completed college in urban areas than rural areas. The counselor must realize that there are many American Indians who have completed higher education programs. Many American Indians are now attending professional schools, receiving training in law, psychology, counseling, engineering, and other fields (Johnson, 1975).

Language Characteristics

Present-day languages are varied among the American Indian tribes. There is no one American Indian language or dialect (Faherty, 1974). A historical account of what characterized the languages of early American Indians is provided by Faherty (1974):

> At the time of the first contact between Indians and . . . [Anglos], there was far greater linguistic and cultural diversity in the New World than in Europe. The number of distinct languages depends upon recognition of what constitutes a separate language. Some 200 languages have been claimed for aboriginal California alone. Anthropologists' estimates range from a conservative 200 to between 600 and 800 as the number of languages in use in the area that was to become the United States. [p. 242]

Many languages are used by different tribes even today. And while one member of a tribe may adhere to the official tribal language, another is likely to use both the English language and the official tribal language. Some American Indians speak little or no English, others communicate only in their tribal language and cannot read or write at all. Language differences among the various groups are emphasized by Youngman and Sadongei (1974). It will be helpful for counselors to realize that many uneducated Indians lack experiences in traditional counseling. For many, too, the use of the English language may not be as well developed as for those who are educated. Therefore, counselors should use the language that can be understood "in a literal and symbolic sense as well as a verbal" (Attneave, 1973, p. 196).

Furthermore, communication within the tribe is often highly developed and nonverbal. Some members scarcely use words in their daily routines, and learning is best accomplished through observation (Stillwell and Allen, 1966). Of the American Indians who leave the reservations and rural areas for urban surroundings, many are better educated than were Indians in previous times (Johnson, 1975), and English is normally their language.

The Navajo tribe present a good example of the language development trends of many tribes. Navajo children at the Rough Rock Demonstration School in Chinle, Arizona, are taught both Navajo and English languages (Billison and Platero, 1970). The children in some Navajo schools communicate only in the Navajo language in the early years of school. Only after they have learned to read and write in Navajo and are about eight or nine years old do they turn to English as a second language (Havighurst, 1974).

The language differences among American Indians suggest a bilingual approach to communication may be necessary for the counselor. Such an approach increases and facilitates understanding between two cultures, and it enhances cultural pride and self-respect.

Self-Concept

Much of human behavior is determined by an individual's evaluation of himself—his assessment of his importance, capabilities, worthiness, or success. The individual's self-concept changes when he encounters a new situation. For instance, an adult, American Indian male may feel important and proud among his tribal group on the reservation, yet he may feel weak, insecure, and unimportant on his job in an urban setting. Another American Indian may have a high self-concept in both situations. Self-concepts include personal judgments of worthiness of both external behavior and internal states (Wylie, 1974). The self-concept is influenced by social interactions with family members and friends and by situational determinants such as socioeconomic background, and educational and employment opportunities. Perceptions of others' assessments are vital; they may cause a person to view himself with either pride or shame. Outside factors weighed heavily on the self-concepts of American Indians in the early days of European settlement and continued even into the late 1950s. Outsiders viewed Indians as savage, nomadic, hostile, brutish, uncivilized, and as mentally, culturally, and religiously inferior beings. They were denied equal status as people and removed from their homelands to reservations. This greatly eroded Indians' self-images.

Today, however, studies paint a brighter picture of the self-concepts of American Indians. Martig and DeBlassie (1973) investigated the self-concepts of both Anglo and American Indian children using the Primary Self-Concept scale. Results indicated no significant differences between the two groups of students. Havighurst (1970b) and Lammers (1970) found similar results in their studies. However, American Indian males and females at the first-grade level saw themselves rejected by adults to a significantly greater degree than did first- and fourth-grade Anglo males. This investigation does not support Coleman's (1966) and Hathhorn's (1971) findings that American Indian children have lower self-concepts than Anglo children do. Martig and DeBlassie's findings also did not support Havighurst's conclusions that American Indian females seemed more self-critical than American Indian males. They concluded that first-grade American Indian males had significantly lower self-concepts than the fourth-grade American Indian females.

Trimble (1975) conducted an investigation on five reservations and in selected American Indian communities in Oklahoma in which he studied 710 American Indians from 10 to 80 years of age. Results suggested that the individuals viewed themselves highly (see results in figure 2.1). There are vast differences between early and contemporary research results regarding American Indians' mental health. It appears that when cultural variables of American Indians are considered, results are not as plagued with negative generalizations.

PROBLEMS IN COUNSELING AMERICAN INDIANS

In common with many other ethnic minority groups, American Indians have had to endure many of the socioeconomic ills of American society—unemployment, inadequate education, deteriorated housing, limited political power, poor communication skills, low income, low social status, and for some, rural reservations that are inadequate when compared

FIG. 2.1.
SELF-REPORT OF AMERICAN INDIANS' SELF-ESTEEM

Survey Items	Response Percentage Among 710 American Indians
I take a positive attitude toward myself.	88.5
I am satisfied with myself.	100
I am a useful person to have around.	100
I look for opportunities to better myself.	84.61
When I have reached a certain level in anything I do, I set myself a higher level and try to reach it.	73.1
I don't like to have the feeling I'm just standing still.	80.8
I have noticed that my ideas about myself seem to change very quickly.	73.2
In order to get along and be liked, I tend to be what people expect me to be rather than anything else.	57.7
I seem to have a real inner strength in handling things, I'm on a pretty solid foundation, and it makes me pretty sure of myself.	89.5
If I should die today, I would feel that my life has been somewhat to very worthwhile.	80.8
If I should die today, I would feel that my life has been completely worthless.	3.9

Source: Adapted from Trimble, J. E. "In sacred manner they are sending voices: partial results of a survey of the self-image of the American Indian." In J. W. Berry and W. J. Lonner (eds.), *Applied Cross-Cultural Psychology* (Amsterdam, Netherlands: Swets and Zeitlinger, 1975), p. 152.

to the facilities in our modern technological society. These extrapsychic factors (outside the individual) are considered high stress predictors that lead to personality disorganization that, in turn, leads to the need for therapeutic assistance. Another major extrapsychic stress source is the difficulty in adjusting to an unfamiliar urban society, to ethnocentric biases, and to discrimination.

Many of these factors hinder the American Indians' penetration of the social, economic, and political systems in mainstream American society. Yet there are those American Indians who realize that in order to lower ethnocentric barriers, they must identify with certain cultural values and patterns of mainstream American society. To complicate the issue, the identity of American Indians may be positioned along a continuum that ranges from their traditional tribal culture to the dominant Anglo culture. The diversity in value orientations among American Indians poses serious problems for counselors and other mental health professionals who attempt to provide effective assistance. The extent to which American Indians have been socialized to one culture or another and identify with a set, or overlapping sets, of value orientations are important dictates for culturally relevant counseling interventions.

American Indians and Acculturation

The American Indians' adaptation of and shift to dominant Anglo, middle-class beliefs and behavior patterns exemplifies psychological acculturation. This phenomenon occurs when an ethnic minority group or individual is in contact with mainstream American society. There are numerous behaviors that may occur as a result of acculturation; for example, there are changes in levels of linguistic, perceptual, or cognitive behavior. A shift in such behaviors of a group or an individual often leads to acculturative stress, a kind of psychological stress that emerges from acculturative influences (the individual's or group's response to sociocultural change).

The extent to which American Indians encounter conflict between their own cultural patterns and those of other groups is contingent upon their degree of socialization to one culture or another. According to Meyer (1974): "The stresses on Indian life today result from a variety of attempted solutions, ranging from rigid conservation and insistance on traditional values and life-styles to wide swings towards dominant culture that embrace acculturation, urbanization, and intermarriage. With the changes occurring within individuals and families at a rapid pace, mental health staffs increasingly see the casualties" (p. 44). Laurence French (1976) maintains that the dilemma of limited accommodation is perceived as a consequence of (Eastern Band) Qualla Cherokees' loss of their traditional heritage in one way and their inaccessibility to substitute Anglo culture in another way. Thus, the individual or group gravitates toward sociocultural nonstandards for acceptable behaviors and confused role identities. The Qualla Cherokee are torn between two opposing social systems, the traditional Cherokee and the dominant Anglo. Those persons who adhere to the traditional culture are referred to as traditional or conservative Cherokees. Some Cherokees who have acculturated the Anglo cultural system are perceived as middle-class or "Anglo" Cherokees. The third subculture of Qualla Cherokees are thought of as marginal Cherokees. Traditional or conservative Cherokees often speak their native language and generally have adjusted to reservation conditions. The middle-class or "Anglo" Cherokees are the most accepted by the Anglos. These Cherokees strongly accept and adapt to cultural behaviors and patterns of their Anglo counterparts. French (1976) contends that middle-class or "Anglo" Cherokees encounter personality disorders and maladjustments that are similar to those of middle-class Anglos. Marginal Cherokees, the largest of the three subcultures, often express themselves in overt, assertive behavior. Most are younger members who range from their teens to their late thirties (French, 1976). Marginal Cherokees seem to experience the greatest psychological conflict between their traditional culture and dominant Anglo cultural patterns.

Bryde (1972) maintains that American Indians in general—particularly the young, such as teenagers—endure a great amount of acculturative stress as they shift from traditional family socialization to the dominant Anglo culture. Inability to penetrate dominant Anglo social and political systems and a lack of adherence to traditional American Indian family values contribute to much of this acculturative stress. Liberman and Frank's (1980) research findings indicated that Miccosukee Indians' perceptions of their most stressful situations, i.e., change in family get-togethers, moving to a different reservation, moving to town, vacations, Christmas, changing to a new school, were probably produced by external forces that were alien to their traditional culture.

In conclusion, the extent to which American Indians acculturate cultural patterns of dominant Anglos may be related to their world views: how they perceive and interpret their associations with nature, social systems, various individuals, and world events around them. Their world views build for them psychological orientations that may affect how they perceive events, how they may behave verbally and nonverbally, how they make decisions, deal with information, and how they think. For example, marginal American Indians' world views might be that their existing problems, i.e., unemployment, inadequate education, deteriorated housing, and poverty, are caused by their inability to penetrate mainstream society's structure, but they feel helpless to bring about change. Some American Indians may perceive of themselves as capable individuals who can attain their goals should they be given opportunities. Others, such as those referred to as middle-class, may feel that they are in full control of their destiny and, thus, are self-accountable to the outcomes of their destiny.

Perceptions of Mental Health and Mental Illness

American Indians' levels of acculturation, however, will have a varying impact on their perceptions of mental health and mental illness. Perceptual variations of mental health and mental illness can also be observed within and between tribal groups as well. Traditional American Indians' attitudes toward mental health and mental illness also vary from those of the dominant Anglo society.

Traditional mental health practices among many American Indian tribes are linked to Western religions and to some Western mental health practices. According to Leighton and

Leighton (1941), significant elements of psychotherapy not readily recognized in the formal structure of the Navaho ceremonial are reeducation and analysis. For example, there is much communication between the Singer, or medicine man, and the patient and other persons, such as relatives and respected elders. Because the Singer often knows the habits and tendencies of the patient, he frequently provides sound, practical advice. In short, the Navaho religion provides a powerful suggestive psychotherapy that helps to alleviate states of anxiousness and helps the patient to tolerate his illness.

From the very beginning of the ceremonial, the Navaho religious ceremonial appeals powerfully to the patient's emotions. The Singer communicates reassurance, frowning on gossip as a means of coping with unpleasant topics. Emphasis is placed on health and strength, and instances when other persons were treated and cured through ceremonials are stressed. Other persons, such as relatives and respected elders, participate in the ceremonial by focusing their attention on the patient to bring their influence on the patient's illness. Their existence signifies strong unified forces that work toward the patient's well-being. According to Leighton and Leighton (1941), "There is the prestige and authority of the Singer assuring the patient that he will recover" (p. 521). This powerful assurance is communicated to the patient to suggest that he has the strength to deal with his misfortune. The patient focuses his thoughts on the Singer's instructions and considers the implications expressed in the prayers, songs, speeches, and implicit statements of the Singer.

In most Indian religions, there are also differences from Western views on therapy. Perceptions of mental illness and indigenous therapeutic practices among some Navaho are an example of the differences. According to Beiser and De Groat (1974), one Navaho Singer stated that he concentrates on the whole person, physically and psychologically. Some Navaho patients complain of being witched. Some of them have bodily symptoms that are accompanied by emotional disturbances. This phenomenon is referred to as *Tsadayah*. A person who experiences some form of personality disorganization or who is "out of his mind" is considered *Biniasdee*. Navahos believe there are several reasons for a person to be *Biniasdee*, but witchcraft is considered the usual cause.

Jilek and Todd (1974) state that Salish Indians' (from northern Washington and British Columbia) therapeutic activities focus on winter spirit dances. Initiation to these dances constitutes a healing process based on the therapeutic myth of neophyte death and rebirth. The new dancer "is made to regress to a state of infantile dependency to obtain his spirit power *(sye'wan)* and then group with it into a healthier existence." Thus, he has attained "a new Indian identity in the name-giving ceremony" (p. 351). Restructuring of the personality toward acceptable standards of the Salish Indian culture is attained "in the initiated passing through an altered state of consciousness as a result of collective and individual suggestion, psychic and physiologic shocks, and sensory deprivation, alternating with overstimulation" (p. 351). Modern spirit dancers perceive of the initiation as an instructional process that teaches physical and emotional well-being. Salish medicine men believe that individuals experiencing depression, anxiety, and somatic complaints, as well as behavioral and alcohol problems, are suitable clients for spirit dance initiation. The Salish medicine men diagnose psychological problems such as low self-concepts, discouragement, depression, existential frustration, and psychosomatic conditions as spiritual illnesses. The dances allow the alienated Salish Indian to reidentify with his aboriginal culture through initiation into spirit dancing.

The Apache Indians of the Mescalero Reservation (New Mexico) hold different perceptions of mental health and mental illness (Boyer, 1974). These Indians believe that all illnesses emerge as the result of actions that offend the supernatural powers, witches, and ghosts of the deceased. In the past, shamans (medicine men) were thought to be the only ones capable of defying these evil influences. The contemporary functions of Apache shamans are confined mostly to the treatment of psychogenic conditions.

These examples are only a few of the many perceptions of mental illness and mental health among the approximately 400 American Indian tribes in the United States. Carolyn L.

Attneave (1974) contends that traditional healers are viable sources of psychological assistance to American Indians; however, any one American Indian's identity with these and other traditional healing methods or with Western interventions will depend upon the extent to which he or she has acculturated the cultural patterns of middle-class, Anglo society. An individual's perceptions are also contingent upon his experiences with and attitudes toward non-Indian professionals.

Attitudes toward Mental Health Professionals

There is a lack of trust or disbelief in many non-Indian professionals and their treatment compared to indigenous therapeutic practices among medicine men and women. According to Jilek and Todd (1974), the contemporary use of medicine men and women rather than non-Indian counselors is strongly linked to the belief that the therapeutic effects of Western psychiatry and medicine are often insufficient in meeting specific needs of Salish Indians.

Another attitude among American Indians is that many professionals fail to take the time to learn about the various Indian cultures. Attneave (1974) maintains that many non-Indian mental health professionals do not have or take the "time to familiarize themselves with Indian people as people" (p. 54). Few undertake an in-depth examination of tribal life among American Indians. In failing to do this, these professionals cut themselves off from significant persons around them, such as, for example, mental health Indian paraprofessionals who are apprentices or practitioners of traditional tribe medicine. Because many non-Indian mental health professionals deny the value of the contemporary practice of traditional tribal medicine, few medicine men and women are used in conjunction with Western therapeutic interventions for American Indian patients.

In short, many American Indians' attitudes and perceptions toward non-Indian counselors and mental health professionals are based on realities they encounter when mental health services are used. Still, the reader should bear in mind that the degree of American Indians' socialization and acculturation will play a role in determining their reception of counselors and their behavior in the counseling setting. It behooves counselors to familiarize themselves with those American Indian cultures with which they will have contact; they should pay special attention to healing practices.

Cultural Conflict and Inadequate Mental Health Resources in Urban Areas

Most of the major cities in the United States have growing Indian populations (Barter and Barter, 1974). Barter and Barter state that although more than 35 percent of American Indians inhabit urban areas, they comprise less than 1 percent of the general urban population. As a result, they have been neglected in many urban programs. Although the goal of American Indians in urban areas is economic advancement, Barter and Barter (1974) note that migration to cities from reservations has not proven successful for many American Indians. High rates of unemployment and low earnings plague many urban-dwelling American Indians.

The 1970 census indicated an increasing trend toward urbanization of the American Indian, although that population officially remains predominantly rural. A variety of factors are prompting this urban movement—unemployment, poverty, the closing of reservations and reservation schools, an effort toward acculturation, or a reunion of families. An individual's ability to adjust to an urban environment is directly related to his background (Westerman, 1974). For example, the Indian who has been part of a semi-urban, transitional community on a reservation will make the move more easily than an Indian from a traditional section of a reservation, who may view the urban setting as alien to his way of life. The degree of adherence to tribal values is a major factor in adaptation to urban life.

Another factor is acceptance or rejection by the community that the American Indian enters. Westerman (1974) maintains:

> Border towns—urban communities that have grown adjacent to reservations—are notorious among Indians for the discrimination, often ranging to open hostility, that these communities exhibit toward Indians that move into them. The attitudes toward Indian residents affect their adjustment to a specific city,

> and perhaps to other urban areas where they may subsequently migrate. [P. 259]

Difficulties to adaptation grow from the non-Indian's difficulty in understanding American Indians' cultural values, as well as the American Indian's personal conflicts over urban living (Westerman, 1974). In addition, problems from which the American Indian sought to escape by leaving the reservation often follow him to the city. Problems dealing with bureaucracy, lack of education, poverty, and discrimination can only be extended into the urban environment. Those who have not acculturated the dominant Anglo cultural patterns or have not been assimilated into the mainstream of American society have returned to the reservations, particularly when government monies have been made available to tribal groups for employment.

American Indians bring a unique cultural heritage to urban areas, but their traditional values, according to Ablon (1971), are often incompatible with the non-Indian culture. Sometimes, they function in direct opposition to the competitive, capitalistic urban society. Ablon states:

> They tend to withdraw in the face of conflict. Indians traditionally have regarded the good person as one who shares his money and property with others. A man's reputation was based on what he gave away, not on what he kept. Budgeting and putting away resources for a later day for oneself is improper if others are in need. The functional time dimension is the present, thus the deferring of goals and gratifications that we take for granted in our future-oriented world is very hard for Indians to comprehend. [P. 203]

After moving to cities, Indians are often not only separated from their tribal culture but are at a loss regarding government benefits, particularly those pertaining to social services and medical care. In spite of the availability of sophisticated social services, such as counseling and other mental health resources, in metropolitan areas, access to medical care and assistance with emotional problems is often better on rural reservations (Barter and Barter, 1974, p. 41). For example, American Indian clients who live on rural reservations or in rural areas often may choose between traditional spirit healing and Western mental health interventions. In some tribal settings, the client may have received a collaborative arrangement of both traditional spirit healing and Western mental health interventions. More often, though, Barter and Barter (1974) contend that urban mental health facilities do not lend themselves to the tribal orientations of most American Indian clients. Furthermore, Indians often encounter barriers when seeking medical care and mental health assistance. Barter and Barter contend that many professionals at city- or state-supported urban facilities feel that Indian health is the responsibility of the federal government. In most cases, American Indians must struggle to satisfy local qualification criteria. Many Indians who seek assistance are frequently referred to the nearest federal Indian hospital, which is often far less accessible than local mental health facilities. The unique cultural background of urban American Indians continues to create problems for them. Many emotional problems that are observed among American Indians can only be reflections of stresses occurring as a result of social disorientation and profound economic deprivation.

Alcoholism and Mental Health

A great deal of literature suggests that alcoholism is a serious problem among many American Indians (Curley, 1967; Levy and Kunitz, 1971; Shore and Von Fumetti, 1972). In investigating the mental health of 348 Navaho Indians, Schoenfeld and Miller (1973) concluded that alcoholism was the major health problem on the reservation. Also, drinking among American Indian teenagers is frequent and is a major school problem.

Westermeyer (1974) contends, however, that even among American Indians who experience high rates of alcoholism, determining whether a specific problem is caused by alcohol or by other economic, social, historical, political, or cultural factors, is difficult. Westermeyer further explains:

> Alcohol problems are often associated in given individuals with such stresses as migration from the reservation to a non-Indian community; racial and ethnic prejudice; health impairment; unemployment or marginal economic status; outside interference by non-Indian social agencies in family and community affairs;

> and lack of control in his own community over the education of his children, law enforcement, religious institutions, and health and welfare resources. [P. 30]

It is probably accurate to say that alcoholism is frequently related to the many social problems found in American Indian communities; however, the association between alcoholism "and these problems is not a clearly causal one" (Westermeyer, 1974, p. 30). Hence, attention focused specifically on single cases of alcoholism without regard for its relationships to sociocultural problems will not help individual American Indian clients or prevent new cases of alcoholism within the Indian community (Westermeyer,1974).

Finally, with regard to the use of alcohol and alcohol related problems, there are significant variations among individual American Indians and within and between tribal groups. Therefore, statements pertaining to American Indians' use of alcohol should be directed at specific tribal groups, their location, time period, and conditions under which such behaviors are present. Shore (1974) advocates caution in interpreting alcoholism as an illness indigenous to Indian communities.

Education-Related Problems

The scholastic achievements of American Indians are generally below the national average. Wax (1971) and Howard (1978) observed a continual decline in performance as American Indian students progress to the higher grade levels. In the early grades, Indian students' achievements are comparable to those of other students, but Indians' achievement seems to decline during the intermediate grades (Wax, 1971). At least two basic factors may contribute to this decline: a refusal to engage in competitive activities and an unwillingness to interact verbally. Many American Indian students are reluctant to engage in an individual activity while under observation, particularly when the activity is viewed as an assessment of the student against his classmates. Howard describes their reluctance to interact verbally:

> As they go through school, Indian students participate less and less in verbal interaction. Sometimes the cause of this reluc-

> tance to interact verbally has been interpreted as a lack of familiarity with a tribal language, but this argument does not wash; the same failure to participate verbally has been observed in Indian students who are monolingual English speakers. It is, however, definitely tied to enculturation in traditional Native American modes. [1978, P. 73]

Another reason for the decline in achievement may be due to the fact, as Montagu (1974) contends, that textbooks do not contain references to factors with which American Indian students can identify. Most texts lack Indian language, traditions, folklore, or history. Indian youngsters assume, then, that these factors are insignificant; they study the Anglo culture and are made to feel ashamed of their own. They have little incentive to show interest.

SOME PRACTICAL COUNSELING CONSIDERATIONS

Though all social and psychological characteristics have individual importance in the counseling dyad, they attain greater significance when viewed collectively. Behaviors should be viewed as parts of a series of behavioral events because social and psychological characteristics function integratively. Values work in concert with one's socioeconomic status, self-image, and education.

Values also vary between Indians and non-Indians. Non-Indian counselors must deal with their personal values as they differ from those of their American Indian clients. These values will influence the communication process. By the very nature of a counselor's professional goals, he invades a private world, functioning from his own frame of reference rather than from the client's perspective. To provide effective professional assistance, though, a counselor must try to understand the client's behavior from the client's point of view. His behavior is determined solely by his own experiences.

Furthermore, the counselor must recognize that some social values indigenous to reservation-oriented American Indians are not held by those who have become acculturated. Spang (1965) advocates that the latter group is more likely to have concerns similar to those of the non-Indian than to his own group.

To work with an American Indian client, a counselor must understand the client's self-concept. In addition, he must develop his client's trust in his professional assistance because understanding and trust are essential to providing assistance. Some therapeutic methods may prove ineffective when a client perceives the counselor's efforts as probing into areas that should not concern an outsider. Spang (1965) and Trimble (1975) maintain that traditional therapeutic methods—client-centered therapy, psychoanalysis, and group therapy—do little to meet the needs of the American Indian client in a positive way.

The client-centered counselor will not be effective with some American Indian clients because some are (at least initially) nonverbal and passive (Spang, 1965) by Anglo standards. These clients may communicate verbally only when queried, and then, their responses may be short and direct, with no elaboration or qualification of their statements. Spang maintains that eclectic or directive counseling may be more effective with many reservation-oriented Indians. This author's group counseling experience with some American Indian university students in Oklahoma supports the effectiveness of this approach.

Kinship or adopted kinship is important to the American Indian in maintaining support and trust. Kin are much more frequently sought for assistance than are non-Indian counselors. Attneave (1973) says that in the network-clan, where the extended family is the primary living unit, individuals may communicate literally and symbolically in a language understood by all. She suggests that, if possible, the therapist should become a participant in the network-clan and should use the clan's methods of communication rather than relying on clinical methods. The therapist maintains her professional role by assisting the individual to solve his problems in his own context rather than by forcing an external solution upon him. Attneave believes that "these skills can be acquired by non-Indians who are genuinely interested and concerned" (p. 196). As mentioned earlier, disclosure of one's own strength or accomplishments is frequently unacceptable to some American Indians (Youngman and Sadongei, 1974). Thus, the counselor should be wary of citing credentials as he might be expected to do with Anglo clients.

To communicate to the American Indian client that he is understood and that the counselor can be trusted may well require going beyond the usual counseling setting. The counselor will have to demonstrate interest and concern through direct participation, when permitted, in those activities that are significant to the client. Such activities might include community projects, home visits, tribal ceremonies, and athletics.

Diagnostic approaches selected for use with American Indians are significant. Spang (1965) states:

> The counselor's use of techniques, primary tests, would have to be modified when used with Indian [clients]. Tests and instruments that have been validated on norms from another culture are not applicable "blankly" to Indian [clients]. It then behooves the counselor to modify the tests he plans to use, or to establish his own norms, or to construct his own tests and instruments . . . the Indian languages do not contain many of the concepts that the English language has.
>
> Also, the use of projective techniques must be modified. . . . Some of the responses given to the various items seem quite bizarre when they are interpreted in the non-Indian cultural orientation. However, when they are interpreted in light of their cultural orientation they become more meaningful and 'normal.' [P. 14]

It is not surprising that the medicine man is frequently sought by tribal members. The success of his treatments rests in the American Indian's feeling of confidence, trust, understanding, and belief in his methods. Gross (1978) argues that modern psychological interventions are not demonstrably superior to primitive methods.

SUMMARY

The social and psychological conditions discussed here affect the communicative behavior of the American Indian. It is imperative that a counselor recognize all of these factors—tribal customs, location (rural or urban), health, discrimination, unemployment in order to be successful. Counseling attitudes also must be adjusted to account for individual behavior variances.

EXERCISES

A. Each situation below is typical of one that might be encountered by an American Indian client who needs some form of counseling. Read each example and answer the following questions pertaining to it:

- What are the issues involved?
- As a counselor, what would you do?
- Role play and then discuss the situation in a small group.

1. Mary, a thirty-year-old, urban American Indian, is divorced and lives alone with her three children, ages six, seven, and eight. She is a third-year, full-time, undergraduate student and receives minimal financial support through a government grant for educational and family expenses. She maintains a 3.5 grade-point average. One of Mary's brothers, who is a thirty-six-year-old, who alternates between living on and off the reservation, frequently asks Mary for money. Reluctantly, she has given him money for some time. Now, however, she is questioning continuation of this practice.
2. Frank, a seventh grader, lives with his mother, father, three sisters, and three brothers. The family has recently migrated from the reservation to a large city with hopes of improving their livelihood. Frank's mother remains at home and cares for the children; the father is an unskilled laborer for a construction company. Although Frank's scholastic achievement scores indicate he is performing at his grade level, he does not participate verbally and avoids most competitive activities. His teachers have expressed concern that his behavior will negatively affect his scholastic achievement.
3. Calvin is twenty-three years old, married, and has two children, ages two and three. He lives on the reservation but commutes to work in a nearby urban area. He is often tardy for work, and is sometimes absent. It is reported

that he has been drinking heavily on those days when he is absent.

4. Patricia, a twenty-eight-year-old, is single and lives with her mother. Her father died about nine months ago; since then, she has attended at least five other funerals of close family relatives. Patricia has expressed feelings of fear and depression, including fear of the death of her mother and herself and a dispirited sense that life has little to offer her or her mother in the future.
5. Bill, a forty-eight-year-old, is unemployed and has a family of four, including a wife. Little work can be found on the reservation, and his wife berates him constantly for not providing sufficient food and clothing for his family.

B. This exercise is intended to help students become familiar with the feelings of an American Indian who is often faced with environmental problems. If possible, have the students form triads in which at least one member is ethnically different from the others. Ask one volunteer in each triad to role play his expectations of how a person of a particular American Indian background would act, think, and speak. The other two members of the triad should provide feedback. Then, have the groups discuss the following issues for ten to fifteen minutes:

1. Problems faced in urban environments
2. Unemployment and lack of career opportunities
3. Interethnic marriage, housing, neighborhoods
4. Education from preschool through college
5. Hereditary beliefs regarding intelligence, personality, motivation, and general health.

REFERENCES

Aberle, D. F. "The Psychosocial Analysis of a Hopi Life-History." *Comparative Psychology Monographs,* 1951, *21,* 80–138.

Ablon, J. "Cultural Conflict in Urban Indians." *Mental Health,* 1971, *44,* 199–205.

Attneave, C. L. "Therapy in Tribal Settings and Urban Network Intervention." In R. V. Speck and C. L. Attneave (eds.), *Family Networks*. New York: Pantheon Books, 1973, 192–210.

Attneave, C. L. "Medicine Men and Psychiatrists in the Indian Health Service." *Psychiatric Annals*, 1974, *4*, 49; 53–55.

Barter, E. R., and J. T. Barter. "Urban Indians and Mental Health Problems." *Psychiatric Annals*, 1974, *4*, 37; 41–43.

Bass, W. P. "Formal Education for American Indians." *Research and Development in Education*, 1971, *4*, 21–32.

Beiser M., and E. De Groat. "Body and Spirit Medicine: Conversations with a Navaho Singer." *Psychiatric Annals*, 1974, *4*, 9–10; 12.

Billison, S. and D. Platero. "Innovations in Education." In *Indian Voices: The First Convocation of American Scholars*. San Francisco: Indian Historian Press, 1970, 129–49.

Boutwell, R. C., W. C. Low, K. Williams, and T. Proffit. "Red Apples." *Journal of American Indian Education*, 1973, *12*, 11–14.

Boyer, L. B. "Psychoanalytic Insight in Working with Ethnic Minorities." *Social Casework*, 1974, *45*, 519–26.

Brown, J. E. *The Sacred Pipe*. Norman: University of Oklahoma Press, 1953.

Bryde, J. F. *Indian Students and Guidance*. Boston: Houghton Mifflin, 1972.

Bureau of Indian Affairs. *Estimates of Resident Indian Population and Labor Force Status; by State and Reservation: March 1973*. U.S. Department of the Interior, Statistics Division, Washington, D.C., March, 1973.

Coleman, J. S., et al. *Equality of Educational Opportunity*. Washington, D.C.: U.S. Government Printing Office, 1966.

Coombs, L. M., et al. *The Indian Child Goes to School*. Washington, D.C.: U.S. Department of Interior, Bureau of Indian Affairs, 1958.

Croft, C. "The First American: Last in Education." *Journal of Indian Education*, 1977, *16*, 15–19.

Curley, R. "Drinking Patterns of Mescalero Apache." *Quarterly Journal of Studies on Alcohol*, 1967, *28*, 116–31.

Deloria, Vine, Jr. "Religion and the Modern American Indian." *Current History*, 1974, *67*, 250–53.

Demontigny, L. "The American Indian Case: Modern Psychology and Child Development." In *Indian Voices: The First Convocation of American Indian Scholars*. San Francisco: Indian Historian Press, 1970, 219–46.

Faherty, R. L. "The American Indian: An Overview." *Current History*, 1974, *67*, 241–44; 274.

French, L. "Social Problems among Cherokee Females: A Study of Cultural Ambivalence and Role Identity." *American Journal of Psychoanalysis*, 1976, *36*, 163–69.

Gross, M. L. *The Psychological Society*. New York: Random House, 1978.

Hathhorn, J. R. "A Comparative Study of Factors Related to Post-High School Education Pursuits of Selected American Indians." *Dissertation Abstracts*, 1971, *31*, 4461A.

Havighurst, R. J. *The Education of Indian Children and Youth: The National Study of American Indian Education: Summary Report and Recommendations*. Chicago: University of Chicago Press, 1970a.

Havighurst, R. J. *The Indian Self-Image as Evaluated with Semantic Differentials*. Chicago: National Study of American Indian Education, 1970b (ERIC ED 044 217).

Havighurst, R. J. "The American Indian: From Assimilation to Cultural Pluralism." *Educational Leadership*, 1974, *31*, 585–89.

Howard, J. J. *North American Indian Culture*. Stillwater: University Extension, Oklahoma State University, 1978.

Indian Voices: The First Convocation of American Indian Scholars. San Francisco: Indian Historian Press, 1970.

Jilek, W. G., and N. Todd. "Witch Doctors Succeed Where Doctors Fail: Psychotherapy among Coastal Salish Indians." *Canadian Psychiatric Association Journal*, 1974, *19*, 351–56.

Johnson, H. W. *American Indians in Transition*. Economic Development Division, Economic Research Service, U.S. Department of Agriculture, Agriculture Economic Report No. 283, April, 1975.

Lammers, D. M. "Self-Concepts of American Indian Adolescents Having Segregated and Desegregated Elementary Backgrounds." *Dissertation Abstracts*, 1970, *31*, 930A.

Leighton, A. H. and D. C. Leighton. "Elements of Psychotherapy in Navaho Religion." *Psychiatry*, 1941, *4*, 515–23.

Levy, J. E., and S. J. Kunitz. *Indian Drinking: Problems of Data Collection and Interpretation*. Proceedings of the First Annual Alcoholism Conference of NIAAA. Washington, D.C.: U.S. Government Printing Office, DHEW Publication No. (NIH) 74-676, June 25–26, 1971.

Liberman, D., and J. Frank. "Individuals' Perceptions of Stressful Life Events: A Comparison of Native American, Rural, and Urban Samples Using the Social Readjustment Rating Scale." *White Cloud Journal*, 1980, *1*; 15–19.

Locke, P. "Indian Gifts of Culture and Diversity." *Cultural Diverse Exceptional Children Conference Presentations*, August 1973. The Council for Exceptional Children, 1920 Association Drive, Reston, Vir. 22091. (Cassette tape)

McKinley, K. *Oklahoma Indian Education Needs Assessment*, vols. 1–4. Stillwater: College of Education, Oklahoma State University, March, 1976.

Martig, R., and R. DeBlassie. "Self-Concept Comparisons of Anglo and Indian Children." *Journal of American Indian Education*, 1973, *12*, 9–16.

Meyer, G. G. "On Helping the Casualties of Rapid Change." *Psychiatric Annals*, 1974, *4*, 44–45; 48.

Montagu, A. *Man's Most Dangerous Myth*, 5th ed. New York: Oxford University Press, 1974.

Ortiz, A. *The Tewa World*. Chicago: University of Chicago Press, 1969.

Ortiz, A. "American Indian Philosophy and Its Relation to the Modern World." In *Indian Voices: The First Convocation of American Scholars*. San Francisco, Calif.: Indian Historian Press, 1970, 9–47.

Pepper, F. C. "A Conflict of Values: Teaching Indian Children." *Culturally Diverse Exceptional Children Conference Presentations*, August, 1973. Council for Exceptional Children, 1920 Association Drive, Reston, Va. 22091. (Cassette tape)

Schoenfeld, L. S., and S. L. Miller. "The Navajo Indian: A Descriptive Study of the Psychiatric Population." *International Journal of Social Psychiatry*, 1973, *19*, 31–37.

Shore, J. H. "Psychiatric Epidemiology among American Indians." *Psychiatric Annals,* 1974, *4,* 56–57, 61–63, 66.

Shore, J. H., and B. Von Fumetti. "Three Alcohol Problems for American Indians." *American Journal of Psychiatry,* 1972, *128,* 1450–54.

Spang, A. "Counseling the Indian." *Journal of American Indian Education,* 1965, *5,* 10–15.

Steiner, S. *The New Indians.* New York: Harper and Row, 1968.

Stillwell, M. P., and R. U. Allen. "Two Reports from Head Start." *Teachers College Record,* 1966, *47,* 443–47.

Trimble, J. E. " 'In Sacred Manner They Are Sending Voices': Partial Results of a Survey of the Self-Image of the American Indian." In J. W. Berry and W. J. Lonner (eds.), *Applied Cross-Cultural Psychology.* Amsterdam: Swets and Zeilinger, 1975, 148–53.

U.S. Bureau of the Census. 1970 Census of Population, U.S. Summary, PC (1) CI and PC (1) DI, Detailed Characteristics; American Indians, PC (2) LF. Washington, D.C.: U.S. Government Printing Office, 1970.

U.S. Bureau of the Census. *Race of the Population by States: 1980.* Washington, D.C.: U.S. Government Printing Office, 1981.

U.S. Department of the Interior. *Federal Indian Law.* U.S. Government Printing Office, 1958, 4–12.

U.S. Department of Labor, Manpower Administration. *Evaluation of the Role of Manpower Programs in Assisting American Indians in the Southwest.* Washington, D.C.: Department of Labor, 1977.

U.S. Department of Labor. *An Evaluation of the Public Employment Program for Reservation Indians.* Washington, D.C.: Manpower Administration, Office of Policy, Evaluation and Research, 1973.

Voyat, G., and S. Silk. "Cross-Cultural Study of Cognitive Development on the Pine Ridge Reservation." *Pine Ridge Research Bulletin,* 1970, *2,* 50–73.

Wallace, A. F. *The Death and Rebirth of the Seneca.* New York: Alfred A. Knopf, 1970.

Wax, M. L. *Indian Americans—Unity and Diversity*. Englewood Cliffs, N.J.: Prentice-Hall, 1971.

Westerman, J. "The Urban Indian." *Current History*, 1974, 67, 259–62; 275.

Westermeyer, J. "The Drunken Indian: Myths and Realities." *Psychiatric Annals*, 1974, 4, 29–31; 35–36.

White, R. A. "The Lower-Class 'Culture of Excitement' among the Contemporary Sioux." In E. Nurge (ed.), *The Modern Sioux: Social Systems and Reservation Culture*. Lincoln: University of Nebraska Press, 1970.

Youngman, G., and M. Sandongei. "Counseling the American Indian Child." *Elementary School Guidance and Counseling*, 1974, 8, 273–77.

Zintz, M. V. *Education across Cultures*, 2d ed. Dubuque, Iowa: Kendall and Hunt, 1969.

3

Puerto Rican Americans

FREQUENTLY, MIDDLE-CLASS COUNSELORS are blind to or unaware of the strengths and difficulties faced by Puerto Ricans. Counselors' unawareness of such experiences often leads to barriers in communication within the counseling setting. Additionally, many counselors are not cognizant of the cultural beliefs that restrict many Puerto Ricans from seeking professional counseling or therapeutic assistance. The discussion in this chapter offers some practical suggestions that may prove useful when counseling Puerto Rican clients. The reader should note that the focus of discussion will be mostly on those Puerto Ricans living on the Mainland United States rather than those on the island of Puerto Rico.

SOCIAL AND PSYCHOLOGICAL CHARACTERISTICS

Who Are Puerto Ricans?

Puerto Ricans are American citizens as proclaimed by the Jones Act of 1917; Puerto Rico is a U.S. territory. Christensen (1975) states that the Puerto Rican population is a mixture of Taino Indian, African, and Spanish. He states that Spanish influence is of a biological nature only, since the Spaniards nearly decimated the Puerto Ricans; the heaviest cultural influence is Indian.

Puerto Ricans' skin colorations "range from as white as any Scandinavian to as black as the darkest African, with all shades and mixtures in between." (Christensen, 1975, p. 350).

Puerto Ricans are referred to as Spanish-speaking Hispanics, Latinos, Spanish-Surnames, and Neo-Ricans. This indicates, according to Jaffe and Carleton (1974), that the concept of who a Puerto Rican is is not a clear-cut one in most Anglos' minds. A Puerto Rican can be defined as anyone born on the island of Puerto Rico, or anyone who had at least one parent born there. Jaffe and Carleton describe four subgroups of this population who live in the United States: (1) Those who were born on the Mainland and live in New York City, about one in four of all Puerto Ricans; (2) those born on the Mainland who live elsewhere in the United States, about one in seven; (3) those born on the island of Puerto Rico who live in New York City, about one in three; and (4) those born on the island who live outside New York City, about one in five (p. 7). Puerto Ricans are a highly diverse group of American citizens. For purposes of discussion, we will refer to this group interchangeably as Puerto Rican Americans or Puerto Ricans.

Where Are They?

Puerto Rico is an island in the Caribbean approximately 1,650 miles from New York and 1,050 miles from Miami. The Puerto Rican migration to the Mainland United States occurred because Puerto Rico was overpopulated and lacked sufficient employment opportunities and sufficient natural resources. This migration peaked during the 1950s and 1960s. New York City was initially the major area of concentration (Murrillo-Rohde, 1976). Since then, Puerto Ricans have settled in other cities such as Buffalo and Rochester, New York; Boston and Springfield, Massachusetts; Philadelphia, Pennsylvania; Hartford, Connecticut; Chicago, Illinois; Newark, New Jersey; and Miami, Florida. Puerto Ricans live in Ohio, Illinois, and California. Few states are without Puerto Rican residents, but Puerto Ricans live in very concentrated numbers where they have settled.

The Puerto Rican population on the Mainland was estimated in 1970 to be 1.5 million; 2.7 million lived on the island. Between 1940 and 1974, it was estimated that there was a net migration of nearly three quarters of a million islanders to the Mainland (Jaffe and Carleton, 1974). In March, 1977, the United States Bureau of Census reported that there were about 1.7 million Puerto Ricans in this country (U.S. Bureau of Census, 1978). In 1980, the Puerto Rican population in the United States totalled 2,013,945, with almost one million living in New York (U.S. Bureau of Census, 1982).

The number of Puerto Ricans who continue to migrate fluctuates greatly. In years when jobs are unavailable on the Mainland, more Puerto Ricans return to the Island than leave it. The peak period of movement to the Mainland occurred in the first half of the 1950s when there was a net outflow of more than one-quarter million persons (Jaffe and Carleton, 1974). Since 1970, there has been a return movement to the Island of only a few thousand Puerto Ricans. A significant result from these mass movements is that in 1970, one in three of all Puerto-Rican Americans lived on the Mainland (Jaffe and Carleton, 1974).

In 1980, there were only about five in ten Puerto Ricans residing in the state of New York (nearly all of them lived in New York City in 1970). One in ten Puerto Ricans lived in New Jersey; and Massachusetts, Connecticut, Pennsylvania, California, Illinois, and Florida accounted for three in ten Puerto Ricans. Slightly more than one in ten resided in the remaining forty-two states and in the District of Columbia. We may conclude that the Puerto Rican population is vastly more concentrated than the general population (U.S. Bureau of Census, 1982).

Puerto Ricans living on the Mainland face political, social, and economic factors that influence all aspects of their behavior. Because Puerto Ricans comprise a diverse group of citizens, however, we will be reminded that the impact of these factors varies among individuals, families, and communities. Yet there are some basic commonalities inherent in the Puerto Rican culture. These influences, brought from the Island, consist of cultural pride, shared values, family ties, and language.

Cultural Values

Certain attitudes, beliefs, or cultural values have been instrumental in shaping and directing individual behavior. Some of the more generally agreed upon cultural values associated with Puerto Ricans are *fatalism, dignity, respect, machismo* (Wagenheim, 1970; Fitzpatrick, 1971; Christensen, 1975) and *personalism* or *individualism* (Fitzpatrick, 1971).

Fitzpatrick (1971) explains *personalism* as a kind of individualism that deals with the ideal the Puerto Rican holds for himself. Such an ideal points up the value of goodness one assigns to himself that signifies uniqueness as an individual in accordance with one's socioeconomic status; that is, the adult male demonstrates and maintains those appropriate behaviors that make him good or respected and that are consistent with his socioeconomic status. This behavior provides him with an inner sense of dignity *(dignidad)* and, he, in turn, may expect other persons to respect *(respeto)* his dignity. Personalism is not synonymous with individualism in the Anglo culture, where it is defined as an ability to compete and achieve upward socioeconomic mobility.

Christensen (1975) states that the terms *dignidad* and *respeto* overlap. There is respect for authority, family, and culture. An individual may confront another, but stripping him of personal respect and dignity before other people is unacceptable.

Closely linked to personalism is *machismo*, which refers to masculinity or male superiority (Fitzpatrick, 1971; Christensen, 1975). Machismo may be a personal behavior style of daring wherein the male encounters challenge, risk, and threat with coolness and self-composure. There is also a value of personal attraction, where others are positively influenced and are likely to follow someone as a leader. Fitzpatrick (1971) states that this quality is associated "with sexual prowess, influence, and power over women reflected in a vigorous romanticism and a jealous guarding of sweetheart or wife, or in premarital and extramarital relationships" (p. 91). Washabaugh (1971) concludes from his observational study of young male Puerto Ricans in a New England area that machismo suggests "manly qualities such as exercise of sexual potential, lack of fear of others, and aggressiveness in defense of one's reputation" (p. 3).

These values are most typical of first-generation Mainland Puerto Ricans. Fitzpatrick (1971) and Christensen (1975) suggest that these behaviors are exhibited to some extent by most Puerto Ricans, but exist to a lesser degree among second-generation Mainland Puerto Ricans. Ruiz (1978) argues that some facets of *machismo*, such as the domination of females by males and male sex-role superiority, are myths held by many outsiders (p. 76). The value structure of Puerto Rican culture on the Mainland ranges from tradition to modern, including a mixture of both. Counselors must realize the diversity among individuals of this group and perceive them in relationship to how they act on such values. There is further discussion on values under the section on family characteristics.

Socioeconomic Characteristics

As stated earlier, the most important motivation for Island Puerto Ricans to migrate to the Mainland is socioeconomic improvement. For some, this goal of improvement does indeed become a reality, while others must continue to suffer the economic plight of the Island environment.

Several factors have an impact on Mainland Puerto Ricans' socioeconomic development. The high rate of unemployment is a major factor in socioeconomic development. Jaffe and Carleton's (1974) analysis shows that in 1970 there were fewer Puerto Rican men employed than men in the general population. Unemployment for the former was slightly lower in New York than in other states. However, the rate of unemployed Puerto Rican men was significantly higher (about 50 percent) than for men of the general population of the United States. Jaffe and Carleton state that these employment patterns in 1970 were also present during the 1960s. In March 1977, the labor force participation for men of Puerto Rican origin was 72 percent, compared with 30 percent for women of the same group (U.S. Bureau of Census, 1978).

Overall variabilities, in 1970, among Puerto Rican women varied from that of Puerto Rican men; and there were high variabilities among the four groups of Puerto Rican women, unlike Puerto Rican men, who were uniformly unemployed. Proportions of Puerto Rican women born on the Mainland who were in the work force were similar to proportions of women in the general United States population, e.g., four in ten. Less than three in ten of the Island-born women were in the work force. A slightly higher percentage of both Island and Mainland Puerto Rican women who live outside New York are in the work force. There seemed to be two important differences between first- and second-generation Mainland women. Jaffe and Carleton (1974) cite two factors that might account for these variations: (1) Mainland-born women were better educated and more of them were likely to be in the work force; and (2) Mainland-born women had fewer children, and thus had a greater opportunity to participate in the labor market. There was a higher rate of unemployment among Mainland Puerto Rican women than among women of the general population of the United States.

A brief description of the vocational composition among Puerto Ricans gives us a clear picture of their socioeconomic condition. Most Puerto Ricans seem to hold undesirable jobs. The men were generally classed as operatives (persons who work with a machine), laborers, service workers, or craftsmen, while women were operatives, service workers, and clerical workers.

Jaffe (1971) states that age is an important consideration when viewing the characteristics of Puerto Rican workers because a young person may begin a work career with a less desirable job but gradually move toward some higher level. Dillard and Perrin (1980) investigated the career aspirations, expectations, and maturity of Black, Anglo, and Mainland-born Puerto Rican adolescents of Buffalo, New York. One important research finding suggests that the Puerto Ricans had a significantly greater desire to attain higher level careers than did the Black and Anglo adolescents. In a similar investigation, Dillard and Campbell (1982) report that the adult Mainland Puerto Rican women more strongly valued taking active interest in their co-workers and their company's functions than Anglo women, and wished more to contribute to career-related decisions than Black women did. According to Jaffe and

Carleton (1974), many Mainland-born Puerto Ricans hold better jobs than Island-born Puerto Ricans because they are better educated and have better command of the English language. Four in ten of Mainland-born men held white-collar jobs in 1970 compared to two in ten Island-born men. Nearly two in ten of each of the above groups were craftsmen or foremen. Jaffe and Carleton (1974) state that Mainland-born men ages thirty-five to forty-four compared somewhat favorably with men of the general population of the United States. Yet, the former group continued to lag behind men of the general population.

Mainland-born women also held better jobs than did Island-born women. In 1970, nearly two in three Mainland-born women, ages twenty-five to thirty-four, held white-collar jobs compared to one in three Island-born women. There were little differences between the two groups in terms of craft positions held; however, nearly half of the Island-born women were operatives, while only one in six Mainland-born women functioned in that capacity. Generally, according to Jaffe and Carleton (1974), Mainland-born women approached the occupational structure of women in the general population of the United States. There were fewer of the former group in such positions as upper level, white-collar jobs, professional, and managerial positions. The same small proportions of Mainland-born Puerto Ricans as the general population were in manual and service jobs.

The average annual income for men of the general population in the United States in 1969 was reported to be about $7,500, while Mainland Puerto Rican men earned about $5,200. In 1970, 3.9 percent of the men of the general population were unemployed; 6.2 percent of Puerto Rican men were unemployed. Unemployment among women of the general population was 5.2 percent compared to 8.3 percent among Puerto Rican women. Approximately three of ten Puerto Ricans lived in families with incomes below the poverty level compared to slightly less than one in ten in the general population (Jaffe and Carleton, 1974). In 1976, the median income of families of Puerto Rican origin was $7,700, a figure that was significantly lower than the median income of families of either Mexican or Cuban origin, whose median incomes were $10,300 and $11,800, respectively (U.S. Bureau of Census, 1978). In March 1977, Puerto Rican men had a median income of $8,100 compared to a median of $4,200 for Puerto Rican women. The median income for both Puerto Rican men and women was $5,536. Approximately 16 percent of all Spanish-origin families had incomes below $5,000 (U.S. Bureau of Census, 1979).

The socioeconomic conditions of Mainland Puerto Ricans are diverse with several within-group variations. These economic conditions have placed them at various positions along the social-class continuum, ranging from below the poverty level to middle class. Although social and economic conditions are slowly improving among Puerto Ricans, great strides must still be made.

Religious Background

Cultural values often are supported by or interrelated with an ethnic group's religious and ceremonial practices. Yet social, economical, and political favors may also influence religious affiliations and practices. Much of the religious practices among Mainland Puerto Ricans come from the Island. Traditional beliefs and/or practices are related to Catholicism, Protestantism, and spiritualism.

It is estimated that the Catholic church has effective contact with nearly 20 percent (if there is a reliable figure) of the Mainland Puerto Rican community (Fitzpatrick, 1971). This small percentage does not mean that many Puerto Ricans do not regard themselves as Catholics. Several factors have worked to weaken many Puerto Ricans' affiliation with the Catholic church as it operated on the Island. Other factors that contributed were the use of Latin rather than Spanish in Catholic rituals; the shortage of Catholic churches in rural settlements; the expense of ceremonials; and the difficulty in living up to the basic principles of Catholicism (Brameld, 1972; Soy and Sanchez, 1975, p. 14). For example, men who were seen too often in church were considered unmasculine. According to Fitzpatrick (1971), the religious efforts of the church have been further handicapped on the Mainland because some Catholic schools emphasize English and charge tuition; many religious-school personnel do not adequately communicate in Spanish nor fully understand the Puerto Rican culture.

It was estimated in 1970 that about 20 percent of Island Puerto Ricans were Protestant, and a majority of these persons were members of the Pentecostal sects (Fitzpatrick, 1971). Early findings (Poblete, 1972) suggest that most Puerto Ricans in New York were in contact with Pentecostal sects. The Pentecostal groups are mainly self-starting, self-sustaining, evangelical, and missionary-minded (Poblete, 1972, p. 23). The ministers are generally lay persons from the community with cultural experiences similar to those of their congregation. The Pentecostal sects demand a genuine austerity concerning attitudes and living patterns, which includes nonsmoking, refraining from alcoholic consumption, and nonuse of cosmetics for women. A person may secure membership in this religion only by following a probation period of six months to a year and making a public confession of his religious experience.

Another popular Puerto Rican folk religion, more common on the Island than on the Mainland, is spiritualism—"belief that the visible world is surrounded by an invisible world populated by spirits" (Rogler and Hollingshead, 1972, p. 50). These spirits may be either "good" or "bad," and they are thought capable of entering the visible world and binding themselves to human beings. According to Soy and Sanchez (1975), the beliefs and practices of spiritualism are distributed throughout Puerto Rican society, but are more pronounced for members of lower classes. Fitzpatrick (1971) states that the practice of spiritualism functions on various levels and includes attempts to effect the "good" or "bad" spirits that may be influencing one, sessions where sincere persons provide assistance to those in need, and sessions that involve scientific and experimental character of beliefs. In spiritualism, a person who asserts that he is capable of communicating with the spirit world is called a medium. The focus of attention within spiritual activities is usually on the medium (Ralph, 1977).

The spiritual medium (sometimes referred to as a *curandero* or *curandera*) is knowledgeable about folk medicine (Fitzpatrick, 1971, p. 122). This person prescribes various treatments such as herbs or potions and uses cooling and heating processes to heal individuals suffering from a variety of ailments. Individuals who receive personal treatment from the *curandero* believe they have undergone an important experience. Some elements of spiritualism are related to mental illness. The medium functions as a folk psychiatrist; this will be discussed in a later section of this chapter.

Family Characteristics

Christensen (1975) states that many Puerto Ricans have raised their families on the Mainland; thus, members of second and third generations are different in several ways from Puerto Ricans raised on the Island. The language of Puerto Ricans raised on the Mainland tends to be English-dominant. Although this group may have adapted to Mainland surroundings, there is still a strong attachment to the Puerto Rican culture.

Puerto Ricans have a strong feeling of love for their children. Christensen (1975) contends that "Perhaps because of the love for children, illegitimacy is not frowned on or punished among Puerto Ricans. It is not unusual for families to add to their broods with nephews, nieces, godchildren, and even the children of husbands' alliances with mistresses" (Christensen, 1975, p. 351). Murillo-Rohde (1976) explains that one element of life that conflicts with the general Mainland culture is the tendency of many Island Puerto Rican families to have as many children "as the Lord sends them" (p. 175). According to Jaffe and Carleton (1974), Puerto Rican women who were born on the Mainland and are better educated have fewer children than Island-born women.

Murillo-Rohde (1976) says that in Puerto Rican families headed by the father, sex roles are well-defined, and there is strict control. (Many Puerto Rican families, however, are female-headed.) Family values among Mainland Puerto Ricans are in slow transition, particularly with regard to male dominance and well-defined sex roles. The most notable shift is in the roles of husband and wife and has occurred, in part, because it is easier for Puerto Rican women than for Puerto Rican men to secure employment (Fitzpatrick, 1972). This phenomenon provides these women an economic advantage over their husbands, who are unable to find work. Furthermore, Mainland Puerto Rican women are far more involved in community, social, and political activities than are Puerto Rican women on the Island .

Faced with these changing values, Mainland Puerto Rican children behave differently from Island Puerto Rican children. Many Puerto Rican parents view the current patterns of behavior among young males as disrespectful, because traditionally, Puerto Rican children are expected to manifest submissive behavior. Non-Puerto Rican children are reared to be self-reliant, self-assertive, competitive, and questioning; these two patterns are conflicting and often confusing to traditional parents who have not fully adapted to Mainland values. A Mainland Puerto Rican child of traditional parents will be acutely aware of her family values, but her socialization with her non-Puerto Rican peers may result in the display of newly adopted behaviors that weaken her family ties (Fitzpatrick, 1971).

The traditional Puerto Rican family insists on the chaperoning of the daughter on outings away from the home. Parents insist that their daughters have a chaperone; while they say they can trust their daughters, they cannot always trust young men. On the Island, it would be a moral dilemma and a negative reflection on his character for the father to allow his daughters to go unprotected; such an act would lower his prestige in the community. Therefore, conflict sometimes occurs between parents and the daughters who insist that they not be chaperoned. Among middle- and lower-class families, the chaperone has traditionally been a mother, sister, brother, relative, or friend. According to Murillo-Rohde (1976), however, many Mainland Puerto Rican parents have altered this practice by permitting their daughters to attend activities or go on dates in groups. She noted that there are still some Mainland parents who insist that their daughters be chaperoned.

Christensen (1977) contends that the strengths of the Puerto Rican culture seem to hinge on two important factors: the family system as a whole and the unique and influential function of the mother. Among traditional Puerto Ricans, strength is only partially gained through the immediate or nuclear family. The extended family also provides security and is a reservoir of pride (Murillo-Rohde, 1976). The extended family "is a network of nuclear families, a network by marriage, responsibility as a godparent [*compadre*] or even through close friendships" (Christensen, 1977, p. 413). The relationship between the child and the *compadre* is an especially sacred one that ensures assistance in situations involving adversity and misfortune. This relationship is often a valuable social mechanism at times when the family is unstable. The *compadre* relationship takes on an added dimension as Puerto Ricans move into communities where family relationships are not as close as theirs.

Fitzpatrick (1972) suggests that the process of migration to the Mainland from the Island perhaps weakens the family ties that once served as a support system by which members could sustain themselves. Fitzpatrick states that urban lifestyles of Mainland living further erode Puerto Rican family values. Among many Mainland Puerto Ricans, for example, personalist values are being replaced by those of the dominant culture. There is a gradual replacement of impersonal relationship patterns of the general population on the Mainland as opposed to the personal relationships of the Island. Such an adaptation seems almost necessary in order to strive for a job on the basis of excellence or competence. Adaptation, however, is often difficult for those Puerto Ricans who continue to view society as an extended pattern of personal relationships (Fitzpatrick, 1972).

Many Mainland Puerto Rican families consist of intermarriages or marriages to non-Puerto Ricans. This phenomenon is especially common among second-generation Puerto Ricans (Fitzpatrick, 1972).

There are several differences between Mainland and Island Puerto Rican families. Family values are slowly changing as Puerto Ricans associate with non-Puerto Ricans on the Mainland, yet most Mainland Puerto Ricans remain attached to their traditional family patterns, which are influential factors in their lives.

Educational Characteristics

Since 1960, the attendance rates for Puerto Ricans in schools have increased. This increase was most apparent for those aged 14 to 24. Jaffe and Carleton (1974) state that Puerto Ricans receive less education than the general United States population. The average twenty-five-year-old has completed elementary school; only one-quarter complete high school. For the general United States population, slightly half have completed high school.

Jaffe and Carleton (1974) provide a secondary analysis of data on the education of Mainland Puerto Ricans as reported by the 1970 United States census. According to these investigators, a somewhat smaller proportion of Puerto Rican children were enrolled in school in 1970 than youth of the general United States population. Nearly all children at the elementary level attended school; the large majority from fourteen to seventeen were in attendance; but comparatively few were in attendance between the ages of eighteen and twenty-four. According to Jaffe and Carleton (1974), Puerto Rican youth born on the Mainland have school attendance rates that approximate those of the general population. Of the children who do not attend school, a high proportion of children were born on the Island. The Island-born Puerto Ricans, in fact, seem to have comparatively less education than their Mainland peers. Jaffe and Carleton (1974) note: "In the future, we expect the Mainland-born to far outnumber the Island-born, in which case the Puerto Rican population as a totality will have had much more schooling than was the situation in 1970" (p. 27).

A closer look at the educational future of Puerto Ricans may be obtained by examining Mainland-born persons aged twenty to twenty-four in 1970. Of this age group, slightly more than six in ten had completed high school, compared with slightly fewer than eight in ten in the overall United States population. However, fewer than four in ten of the Island-born population completed high school. Although Mainland-born Puerto Ricans have improved their educational position, they remain behind the national population in educational achievement (Jaffe and Carleton, 1974).

Jaffe and Carleton (1974) maintain that failure to finish high school, particularly in New York City, is related to the large number of high school dropouts in the 1960s. Nearly seven of twenty of all Mainland-born Puerto Rican youth who entered high school in that period failed to finish. The males had significantly higher drop-out rates than did the females.

A similar pattern was observed for entry into college. Approximately three in ten Mainland-born Puerto Ricans aged twenty to twenty-four who completed high school went on to college. About five in ten of the general United States population entered college.

Although some improvements in education have occurred among Mainland-born Puerto Ricans in recent years, considerably more are required before the educational level parallels that of the general population. In addition, limited awareness of the Puerto Rican culture on the Mainland may be one of the factors that restricts educational achievement.

Language

The native language of Mainland and Island-born Puerto Ricans is Spanish. English is a second language, although for some, it is the most frequently used language. There are at least ten million Spanish-speaking people in the United States; a substantial part of this group are of school age. According to Hoffman (1971):

> The more one functions within the Puerto Rican values system, the more he would be compelled to speak the language variant required by that system. As a person moves further away from an exclusively Puerto Rican value orientation, his freedom of language choice is increased, subject only to the constraints imposed by new value orientations. [P. 41]

Wolfram (1971) concluded from his research findings in New York City that English and Spanish were used among Puerto Ricans in Harlem and other Puerto Rican communities in the city, at least among first and second generation speakers. There is no completely monolingual Spanish enclave. The one setting that approaches a Spanish enclave is the home, particularly if the adults speak little English because they are relatively new arrivals to the Mainland or because there is frequent association with new arrivals from the Island.

Children of preschool age learn English from the older siblings and companions on the street rather than from their parents. Many youngsters are fluent in English yet speak Spanish with their parents and other relatives. Both English and Spanish are used in the neighborhood, depending on the age of the speakers and their orientation. Wolfram (1971) states that integrated neighborhoods discourage Spanish monolingualism, therefore, forcing Puerto Ricans to become bilingual.

Language is an expression of cultural identity. Pastoria San Juan Cafferty (1975) maintains that

> the phenomenon of the retention of Spanish among Puerto Ricans on the Mainland, the increase of use of English in Puerto Rico, and the growth of "Spanglish" or the "language of the *barrio*" among Puerto Ricans both on the Island and on the Mainland is new to American society. [P. 54]

Self-Concepts

Research data are sparse dealing specifically with the self-concepts of Mainland Puerto Ricans as a separate group among Spanish-speaking peoples. Many research studies remain vague in terms of who is included in "Spanish-speaking group." The studies that do exist focus on Puerto Ricans of a low socioeconomic level. (Examples of such studies are those by Moses, Zirkel, and Green, 1973.)

Studies have been done dealing with self-concepts of Puerto Ricans as they are related to academic success, school dropout rates, culture, and language. Zirkel and Moses (1971) investigated self-concepts of Puerto Rican, Black, and Anglo fifth and sixth graders to determine if differences were present. The results indicated that the self-concepts of the Puerto Rican children were significantly lower than those of the Blacks and Anglos.

Moses, Zirkel, and Green (1973) compared the findings from two self-report tests (McDaniel's Inferred Self-Concept Scale and the Coopersmith Self-Esteem Inventory) in an assessment of ethnic group memberships and mixture relationships to self-concepts of disadvantaged children. One hundred twenty Black, Anglo, and Puerto Rican fifth and sixth graders were tested. The results were contradictory. The self-concept of the Puerto Ricans (as measured by the CSEI) was significantly lower than those of Blacks and Anglos. Conversely, the scores from the MISCS suggested that neither ethnic group membership nor mixture was significantly related to self-concepts of the disadvantaged children. In another study, Greene and Zirkel (1971) found that Puerto Rican students' self-concepts were significantly related to their scholastic achievement in English and Spanish, as well as to teacher ratings of aural ability in both languages. These investigators concluded that the self-concept of Puerto Rican students seemed to be higher, albeit not significantly higher, when they were in a majority rather than a minority in a school setting.

In an earlier experimental study, Evans (1968) reported that teaching science bilingually (Spanish and English) resulted in improved self-concepts among Puerto Rican junior high school students. Similar research results on the self-concept of Puerto Ricans were reported by Cohen and Promisel (1970). These researchers reported evidence of a significantly enhanced self-concept for Puerto Rican elementary school children in bilingual education programs.

Isidro Lucas' (1971) investigation of Puerto Rican dropouts in Chicago revealed that these youth tended to have low self-images. He concluded that their low self-images were related to the schools' unwillingness to promote improved self-concepts among many Puerto Rican youth.

ENCOUNTERS WITH ASSIMILATION AND ACCULTURATION: SITUATIONAL ADJUSTMENT CONFLICTS

Torres-Matrullo (1976) maintains that problems for Puerto Ricans—poverty, identity crises, rural background, emigration, unemployment, education, and cultural change—are viewed basically as arising from language difficulties. Some problems are embedded in conflicts between two cultures; Puerto Ricans who encounter them are often divided between their indigenous culture and the general American culture. Being forced to cope with or adjust to two different cultures frequently generates a high degree of stress. The education system as an assimilative device has failed most Mainland Puerto Ricans; this failure, however, is not unique to Puerto Ricans.

Many Puerto Ricans acculturate well, adopting the cultural elements of American society, and have few problems adjusting to the Mainland. However, other Puerto Ricans either balance the elements of both cultures or refuse to adopt the culture of American society. Torres-Matrullo (1976) demonstrated that the better Puerto Ricans can acculturate, the lower the stress and anxiety factors experienced. The following areas of discussion attempt to clarify as well as identify some of the factors that cause Puerto Ricans to seek counseling.

Ethnic Identity and Discrimination

For European immigrants to the United States, assimilation or integration into American society has been far easier than for groups whose skin color sets them apart, such as Blacks, American Indians, Puerto Ricans, and Orientals. According to Fitzpatrick (1971), Puerto Ricans who migrate to the Mainland often face negative attitudes because of their color, coupled with a type of discrimination perhaps not encountered on the Island. Rodriguiz (1975) maintains that many Puerto Ricans are perceived as non-Anglo. A higher percentage of Puerto Ricans identify themselves as black, brown, or "colored" than are identified in the census reports (Fitzpatrick, 1971, pp. 106–107). Acceptance into American communities is not always easy for Puerto Ricans identified within these categories.

It was concluded from a medical investigation of eighty Puerto Rican families that stress and anxiety concerning ethnicity and skin color were associated with difficulties in health. Of twenty young addicts, each was the darkest member in his family (Berle, 1959). Many light-skinned Puerto Ricans may assimilate into the Anglo community, but others, with dark skins, are unable or unwilling to assimilate into the Black communities. Many remain within the Puerto Rican community. An illustrative account of personal distress over ethnicity and skin coloration is Piri Thomas' description of his experiences in the autobiography, *Down These Mean Streets*. Thomas frequently questioned whether he was Black or Puerto Rican while growing up in New York.

Rodriguez (1975) investigated first-generation Puerto Rican parents, Puerto Rican students and workers, and recognized Puerto Rican community leaders in New York to determine their views on assimilation. The results indicated that they perceive the American society as ethnically stratified and believe it should continue to be. They also feel that their anticipated gains in assimilating are not as beneficial as "melting pot" rhetoric have led them to expect. Additionally, many Puerto Ricans place themselves on the lowest rung of the ladder. They believe institutions treat them unfairly. The possibility of succeeding socially and economically is seen as limited. There seem to be two alternatives to assimilating: (1) returning to the Island and (2) biculturation. Across the generational and leadership groups, there was a strong adherence to retaining their ethnic identity.

Social mobility is, in fact, difficult for Puerto Ricans because of ethnic origin and language barriers and the resulting social discrimination. This discrimination influences the basic elements of the family life and social condition (Murillo-Rohde, 1976). According to Murillo-Rohde (1976), even experienced and skilled Puerto Ricans such as carpenters, plumbers, and electricians are directed to the lowest paid and least desirable jobs. Membership in professional unions is restricted, thus limiting opportunities to move into skilled professions. According to Alers (1978), minority workers like Puerto Ricans have been restricted from craft positions (among others)—a practice which continues as tradition. Approximately 84 percent of craftsmen are Anglo. Puerto Ricans are frequently required to work for shop proprietors who profit from the workers' labors and skills while the families endure the consequences of the workers' low pay. A high proportion of Puerto Ricans are underemployed, unemployed, or on welfare rolls. Murillo-Rohde (1976) concludes that serious economic insecurity is common among Puerto Rican families. Elam (1969) concludes from her research that the many difficulties involved in the acculturation of a Puerto Rican family locked in poverty allow only a minimal transition to Mainland ways. Although adjustment and acculturation may occur for some, it is slow and fraught with strain, tension, and insecurity.

Acculturation and Personal Adjustment

Torres-Matrullo (1976) notes that the association of mental illness and migration is well known as a significant phenomenon of psychopathology among Puerto Ricans. The occurrence of mental disorders in this population is a result of stress accompanied with loss of identity. The uprooting from familiar to unfamiliar settings has been designated as a basic element in the mental problems of Puerto Ricans (Minuchin et al., 1967; Fitzpatrick, 1971; Torres-Matrullo, 1976). The degree of stress also may be a function of conflict with acculturation.

Observations by Malzberg (1963) suggested a high proportion of schizophrenia among Puerto Ricans in New York state. Torres-Matrullo's (1976) research does not support Malzberg's finding: she found high rates of depression among this group. Malzberg's observations appear to be what Fitzpatrick (1971) hypothesized as misdirected diagnosis rather than an accurate picture of behavior. That is, Malzberg's observations of Puerto Ricans were based on those types of behaviors that are typically found in a middle-class Anglo society. It is likely that the results would have been different had their behavior been diagnosed in a Puerto Rican sociocultural context.

Haberman (1976) surveyed psychiatric symptoms among Puerto Rican residents of Puerto Rico and Puerto Rican residents of the Washington Heights Health District and in the five boroughs of New York City; he found that the symptom scores for Puerto Ricans living in Puerto Rico were higher than for those in New York City, and that, generally, in almost every population subgroup, the scores changed inversely with length of time in the city.

One kind of hysterical behavior widely described in psychopathologic literature as being common among Puerto Ricans is an affective disorder characterized by violent fits of laughing and crying, imaginary illnesses, as well as physical symptoms that are psychogenic in nature, and general lack of self-control. Yet, what is viewed as pathological in one culture may not be in another, and hysterical behavior is commonly accepted as normal within the Puerto Rican culture. Torres-Matrullo (1976) describes this behavior:

> Puerto Rican Syndrome or *ataque* [is] a pseudoepileptic fit characterized by mutism, self-mutilation, and bizarreness, as well as fright, agitation, and personal violence. Other terms that have been used to refer to this phenomenon are *mal de pelea* and hyperkinetic seizures. [P. 712]

Torres-Matrullo (1976) noted that when Puerto Ricans discuss feelings of nervousness, they are often reflecting feelings of anger. She contends that there seems to be a great deal of guilt stemming from "feelings of anger, suppression, and of assertiveness and aggressiveness, and the need to preserve calm at the expense of psychological needs" (p. 712). The manifestation of assertive behavior in the presence of other persons is not accepted in a Puerto Rican culture. Repression of assertiveness is considered maladaptive in the American society, which places a high premium on assertiveness and socioeconomic gains. Thus, sociocultural change may engender special problems for Puerto Rican women.

According to Torres-Matrullo (1976), several psychosomatic symptoms have been reported in Puerto Ricans. These symptoms may be associated with an early inhibition of aggression and autonomy that is part of their socialization process (Wolf, 1952). Torres-Matrullo further states that somatic symptoms such as headaches and fainting spells might be viewed as aggression turned against the self, and a mechanism of social control. She also suspects that high rates of depression among Puerto Ricans may be related to turning anger and aggression against the self (p. 721).

Torres-Matrullo (1976) investigated the changes experienced by Puerto Rican women with increased exposure to American society as related to their personality adjustment or maladjustment. The investigation included seventy-two Puerto Rican women in the state of New Jersey who were either born in Puerto Rico or were of Puerto Rican parentage. Their ages ranged from 18 to 55, and they were from a broad range of vocational, educational, and socioeconomic backgrounds. The data was gathered with the Wittenborn Psychiatric Rating Scales. The results indicated that those Puerto Rican women who were low in acculturation were likely to show symptoms of psychopathology; women low in acculturation exhibited signs of depression, withdrawal, and compulsive obsession. The results

> support the idea that, as recent arrivals to an urbanized and culturally different setting, low-acculturated women were likely to show such symptoms of psychopathology as aggression, hostility, isolation, loss of self-esteem, and a sense of personal inadequacy. [Torres-Matrullo, 1976, p. 716]

Torres-Matrullo had hypothesized that Puerto Rican family and sex-role related attitudes undergo change with acculturation, but her data suggest that these attitudes remained essentially the same. The education of the women was a significant factor that influenced variations in attitude change, personality adjustment, and psychopathology.

It is apparent that the serious problems that arise when Puerto Ricans attempt to adapt to the American culture create a situation that demands attention in order to improve the cultural conflicts that bring on psychological ills.

Drug Abuse and Cultural Conflict

Often, sources of stress emanate from outside the person rather than inside and are beyond the individual's control. Some of these extrapsychic, or external sources, are prejudice, discrimination, unemployment, and deteriorating communities. One method of coping with such environmental or situational conditions on the Mainland has become the use of drugs. Inability or unwillingness to assimilate also might be associated with the drug abuse among Puerto Ricans.

Alers' (1978) research indicates that among the health problems encountered in New York City, drug abuse was rated by Puerto Rican respondents as the most important concern. Among Puerto Rican adolescents, drug abuse is a serious problem—it occurs more than six times as often than for Blacks or Anglos. Drug addiction is believed to be the most urgent health issue in the Puerto Rican community, even when compared with other health issues such as alcoholism, venereal disease, and birth control.

Puerto Ricans were reported using an average of 3.2 percent of drugs other than heroin; Blacks reported using 2.7 percent additional drugs; and Anglos an additional 4.6 percent drugs. Additionally, Puerto Ricans were less likely to use amphetamines, barbiturates, and LSD than Anglos (Langrod, 1973). Kaestner, Rosen, and Appel (1977) found similar results in their research among thirty Puerto Rican, thirty Black, and thirty Anglo male narcotic drug abusers. These researchers concluded that differences categorized by ethnic background were possibly due to the different availability of various types of drugs in different neighborhoods. Langrod's (1973) research study affirms that ethnicity is related to the number and type of drugs used in a population of urban heroin addicts. For instance, high quality heroin may be more readily available in Puerto Rican and Black urban neighborhoods, while pills and psychedelic drugs may be more readily accessible to Anglos. Ethnicity also appeared to be more closely related to drug-use patterns than were motivational variables such as sensation-seeking and anxiety.

Hence, drug abuse should be an essential consideration in counseling Puerto Rican clients. Counselors need to be knowledgeable about various drugs, as well as the factors linked to the causes of their use.

Attitudes toward Health Services

Research indicates that many Puerto Ricans report having difficulties with access, language, and effectiveness of health services (Alers, 1978). Nearly half of the Puerto Rican respondents suggested that they avoided health services because of fear and embarrassment that something medically wrong will be found by the physician.

An important factor contributing to underuse of health services is the paucity of Spanish-speaking service personnel. While only 21 percent of Puerto Rican patients were able to use only Spanish while obtaining health services, 99 percent preferred that it be used.

Alers (1978) cites the East Harlem (New York) study (Johnson, 1972), which examined Puerto Ricans' use of spiritualists versus psychiatrists and home remedies versus pharmacy medicine. Only 6 percent indicated that spiritualists would be better than psychiatrists, while 14 percent responded that they did not know. Seven percent preferred home remedies over prescription drugs, while 2 percent did not know.

The extent of feelings and attitudes of Puerto Rican clients toward health services administered to them is perhaps uncertain. It appears from the data presented that greater concentrated efforts are necessary in public health facilities to ensure adequate health services to this population. Counselors need to be aware of these established attitudes and feelings, which encourage many Puerto Ricans to underuse counseling and other health services.

School Dropout and Cultural Conflict

Since language is an expression of cultural identity, one might question the emphasis on monolingualism in a society that identifies itself as pluralistic. The removal of foreign languages from American schools suggests the removal of foreign cultures. The attainment of English as the chief language by different ethnic groups is the first sign of assimilation and a new American identity. Yet some ethnic groups such as Mainland Puerto Ricans wish to retain their native language.

About 25 percent of the students in public schools of New York City are Puerto Rican. Vazquez (1969) maintains that these students have the lowest record of achievement of any ethnic group attending New York City public schools. Moreover, new programs introduced to help the situation have not resulted in significant differences in scholastic achievement. Margolis (1968) concluded from his study that students in the public schools usually learn less, perhaps feel unassured, and eventually drop out. He estimates the dropout rate at 60 percent. Research conducted by Isidro Lucas (1971) indicated that there were high percentages of dropouts among Chicagoan Puerto Rican students. Their educational problems appeared similar to those of other Spanish-speaking students in the urban situation. The total dropout rate was found to be 71.2 percent for Puerto Rican students who had received a substantial part of their education on the Mainland. The motivation for dropping out included self-identity problems caused by discrimination, difficulty in relating to parents (and lack of high values of education in the home), and a progressive estrangement of the student from the school. Knowledge of English was greater among dropouts than among graduating seniors.

According to Fitzpatrick (1971), the chief reason for the failure of the schools is related to culture differences. That is, the school communicates cultural and preparational styles unfamiliar to Puerto Rican students.

The inability of Puerto Rican students to cope with the cultural patterns in Mainland schools may be related to their high level of dropping out. Counselors in educational settings are likely to encounter Puerto Rican students who have difficulty acculturating to educational environments on the Mainland. They can assist those students by advocating education that includes Puerto Rican culture.

SUGGESTED APPROACHES FOR COUNSELING PUERTO RICANS

Counselors can expect Puerto Rican clients to verbalize concerns about their relations with other family members. Although evidence of such relations may be brief, counselors, on greeting and bidding farewell to clients, should inquire about certain members of the immediate family, other kin, and even those related through *campadrazgo* (uniting families through godparenting or close friendships) (Christensen, 1977, p. 413).

Some Puerto Ricans may be reluctant to work with counselors on a one-to-one basis. Because the family is such a vital support system, counselors may find that they need to work with one or even several family members rather than one to affect any changes. Yet the success of this venture is contingent on a counselor's knowledge of the family and whether or not the client will permit him to speak with the family member who is the closest or most helpful. After a family member has been selected, a sound relationship must be developed between that member and the counselor. According to Christensen (1977), the client is generally accepting of this kind of relationship and may even assist in establishing it. Counselors must adhere to clients' requests in cases where they are unwilling to share their concerns with family members.

If at all possible, the counselor should speak Spanish. In many instances where Puerto Rican clients are not fluent in English, they are less inhibited when communicating in Spanish with counselors who understand the language.

Torres-Matrullo (1976) suggests that since many Puerto Rican women are inhibited by traditional customs within the Puerto Rican culture, it is necessary in clinical settings to educate them regarding the adaptive value of assertiveness. For example, many clients behave in accordance with a belief system that dictates that others' wishes come first, or that it is polite to be submissive. Such self-identity messages frequently are deeply internalized and cause clients to feel guilty when they do show assertive behavior. The counselor might want to help Puerto Rican clients trust themselves enough to establish and then substitute an assertive belief system. A client's ability and even desire to be assertive might be limited because of the presence of interfering emotions, such as inappropriate guilt, debilitating anxiety, and rage. Dysfunctional, internal dialogue often leads to excessive emotions. These problems must be dealt with. Wolfe and Fodor (1978) contend that when feelings are left unattended, they may manifest themselves in aspects of hysterics or aggression. Cognitive restructuring of clients' negative self-evaluations (anxiety) or negative evaluations of other persons (anger) helps to facilitate culturally appropriate assertive behavior. The implementation of this process requires: (1) assisting clients to become aware of their culturally inappropriate beliefs; (2) suggesting methods to test the reality of traditional beliefs in relation to their new environment; and (3) substituting new and better adaptive attitudes, feelings, and behavior for the old systems.

Another situation frequently encountered is counseling chronic drug users. Counselors may want to first recognize that such clients usually blame others for their misfortunes. What they think about themselves is a reflection of how they think others view them. Drug use is a natural inclination for individuals with external personality orientations. They seek outside aids to bring themselves out of a "down" that they believe is externally caused (Dyer and Vriend, 1975, p. 32).

Counselors should avoid focusing on why clients use drugs, and deal instead with what is in the client's world and thoughts that leads to the depression. Clients can be instructed to see that they have labeled other persons or external events as causes for their negative emotional states. Counselors can help clients gain insight into their negative emotions and refrain from going "down" by exercising self-control. Dyer and Vriend (1975) suggest that counseling efforts be directed to the enculturated, externalized, self-defeating thinking that causes drug dependency.

Through individual and group counseling, behavioral goals are mutually agreed upon between the drug user and counselor. Once workable goals are established, concrete observable steps are applied, encouraging clients to take responsibility for and action toward an individually and culturally tailored program. Homework assignments for clients have increasingly proven to be one of the most effective components of drug counseling. For example, the client who was making progress in reducing intake finds himself with more time on his hands than he can handle. As a result, he slips back into spending a great deal of his time with friends who are less willing to shake their drug use. Thus, the client chooses as his objective to make more efficient use of time. He also selects the homework assignment that requires his choosing meaningful nondrug activities that he will be involved in daily, maintaining a detailed record of these activities, and reporting the weekly activities and their outcomes in subsequent counseling interviews. Clients are encouraged to select from a list of general assignments. Additionally, clients should be requested near the close of the session to give themselves a homework assignment that will lead to attainment of their established goals. In group sessions, other clients or the counselor may suggest assignments when a client is unwilling or unable to suggest an assignment. Clients are asked to maintain a log of weekly assignments and their performed behavior along with the journal concerning their feelings about the assignments and dialogue of their negative emotions and statements. The journal for each homework assignment is dealt with in the following session.

SUMMARY

Mental health services to Puerto Rican clients must take into account their language, culture, religion, and the difficulties inherent in transcultural adjustment. Counselors need to recognize the intragroup differences among Puerto Ricans on the Mainland as well as their differences from other ethnic groups. Effective counseling with this population requires counselors to be bicultural as well as bilingual.

EXERCISES

The following exercises are designed to help students attain a conceptualization of the information discussed in this chapter pertaining to Puerto Ricans.

A. Read the following description of Puerto Rican persons described in the two examples:

1. Maria is a twenty-two-year-old woman, the daughter of parents who live on the island of Puerto Rico. Her father is a farmer in an isolated rural area. Both parents adhere strongly to traditional Puerto Rican values and do not have formal education. Yet Maria has managed to secure a scholarship to attend a college on the Mainland in New York City. Despite her parents' value orientation, she was able to go to New York City and live with one of her brothers and his family while attending college. After finishing her undergraduate degree, she was faced with returning to Puerto Rico and, possibly, living with her parents. Maria has become extremely disturbed regarding this return, because she has begun to favor the life patterns of New York City, and because she has become seriously involved with a male friend.
2. Juan is a nineteen-year-old male who has completed only the tenth grade. Juan lives with his mother and five other younger siblings in an urban high-rise building. The family lives on social welfare subsistence issued by the state of New York. Juan's mother is unable to secure employment because of poor health and young children

who need constant parental assistance. Their apartment has limited bedroom space and one bathroom.

Because he has a limited education, Juan has been unable to secure employment. He would like to help his mother, brothers, and sisters, but finds it extremely difficult to obtain any type of employment. With nothing but time on his hands, Juan has become involved with one of the community gangs who frequently engage in petty theft, smoking marijuana, drinking liquor, and gang fights. Juan, along with other gang members, has been arrested by the police and placed on probation. Yet, he continues to engage in the activities of the gang.

Write a brief description of the situation as you perceive it. Compare your description with other students' descriptions to determine if class members of different ethnic and/or cultural groups have perceived the picture selectively or differently.

B. Use the two examples delineated in A for role-playing. Students should be divided into groups of threes to assume the roles of client (Maria or Juan), counselor, and observer. Role-play so the counselor attempts to assist the client in a one-to-one counseling relationship, while the observer evaluates the counselor's performance. Continue until each group member has taken a turn assuming each of the three roles. Discuss the results.

C. Divide students into groups of four or five to discuss nontraditional approaches that a counselor can apply in assisting Maria and Juan. Each group should devise a list of nontraditional approaches and display these approaches on poster board so that all can view them. Each group should present its approaches and state its rationale for them to the other groups. Finally, a comparison and contrast of these approaches should be made by the instructor.

D. Divide the students into small interethnic discussion groups (five or six students). With frankness, the instructor should help all group members describe to each other the ways in which Puerto Ricans do or do not conform to the ethnic group stereotypes attributed to them.

References

Alers, J. O. *Puerto Ricans and Health: Findings from New York City.* Bronx, N.Y.: Hispanic Research Center, Fordham University, 1978.

Berle, B. R. *Eighty Puerto Rican Families in New York City.* New York: Columbia University Press, 1959. Pp. 45–49.

Brameld, T. "Explicit and Implicit Culture in Puerto Rican Culture: A Case Study in Educational Anthropology." In F. Cordasco and E. Bucchioni, (eds.), *The Puerto Rican Community and Its Children on the Mainland.* Metuchen, N.J.: Scarecrow Press, 1972. Pp. 19–35.

Cafferty, P. S. J. "Puerto Rican Return Migration: Its Implications for Bilingual Education." *Ethnicity,* 1975, *2,* 52–65.

Callan, J. P. "Meeting Mental Health Needs of Puerto Rican Families." *Hospital and Community Psychiatry,* 1973, *24,* 330–33.

Christensen, E. W. "When Counseling Puerto Ricans." *Personnel and Guidance Journal,* 1977, 55, 349–56.

Christensen, E. W. "Counseling Puerto Ricans: Some Cultural Considerations." *Personnel and Guidance Journal,* 1975, 53, 349–56.

Cohen, B., and D. M. Promisel. *Final Evaluation Report (1969–1970): New Haven Bilingual Education Program.* Darien, Conn.: Dunlap and Ass., 1970. (Mimeo)

Dillard, J. M., and N. J. Campbell. "Career Values and Aspirations of Adult Female and Male Puerto Ricans, Blacks, and Anglos." *Journal of Employment Counseling,* 1982, 19, 163–70.

Dillard, J. M., and D. W. Perrin. "Puerto Rican, Black, and Anglo Adolescents' Career Aspirations, Expectations, and Maturity." *Vocational Guidance Quarterly,* 1980, *28,* 313–21.

Dyer, W. W., and J. Vriend. "Understanding and Counseling the Chronic Drug User." *Journal of Drug Education,* 1975, 5, 23–35.

Elam, S. "Poverty and Acculturation in a Migrant Puerto Rican Family." *Teachers College Record,* 1969, *70,* 617–26.

Evans, O. "Now the Bilingual Course." *New York Times,* March 17, 1968, Section E, p. 9.

Fitzpatrick, J. P. *Puerto Rican Americans: The Meaning of*

Migration to the Mainland. Englewood Cliffs, N.J.: Prentice-Hall, 1971.

Fitzpatrick, J. P. "Transition to the Mainland." In F. Cordasco and E. Bucchioni, (eds.), *The Puerto Rican Community and Its Children on the Mainland: A Source Book for Teachers, Social Workers and Other Professionals.* Metuchen, N.J.: Scarecrow Press, 1972. Pp. 114–120.

Greene, J. F., and P. A. Zirkel. *Academic Factors Relating to the Self-Concept of Puerto Rican Pupils.* Paper presented at the 79th Annual Convention of the American Psychological Association, Washington, D.C., 1971 (ED 054 284).

Haberman, P. W. "Psychiatric Symptoms among Puerto Ricans in Puerto Rico and New York City." *Ethnicity,* 1976, *3,* 133–44.

Hoffman, G. "Puerto Ricans in New York: A Language-Related Ethnographic Summary." In J. A. Fishman, A. L. Cooper, and R. Ma (eds.), *Bilingualism in the Barrio.* Bloomington, Ind.: Indiana University, 1971. Pp. 13–42.

Jaffe, A. J. "The Middle Years: Neither Too Young Nor Too Old." *Industrial Gerontology,* September, 1971 (special issue).

Jaffe, A. J., and Z. Carleton. *Some Demographic and Economic Characteristics of the Puerto Rican Population Living on the Mainland, U.S.A.* Bureau of Applied Social Research, Columbia University, November 1974 (ED 114 440).

Johnson, L. A. *East Harlem Community Health Study.* New York: Mt. Sinai School of Medicine, 1972.

Kaestner, E., L. Rosen and P. Appel. Patterns of Drug Abuse: Relationships with Ethnicity, Sensation Seeking, and Anxiety. *Journal of Consulting and Clinical Psychology,* 1977, 45, 462–68.

Langrod, J. "Multiple Drug Use among Heroin Users." In L. Brile and E. Harms (eds.), *The Yearbook of Drug Abuse.* New York: Behavioral Pubns., 1973.

Leighton, A., *et al. Psychiatric Disorders among the Yoruba.* Ithaca, N.Y.: Cornell University Press, 1963.

Lucas, I. *Puerto Rican Dropouts in Chicago: Numbers and Motivation.* Council on Urban Education. Chicago, Ill.: March 1971 (ED 053 235).

Malzberg, B. "Migration and Mental Disease among the Popu-

lation of New York State, 1949–1951." *Human Biology*, 1963, *34*, 89–98.
Margolis, R. J. *The Losers: A Report on Puerto Ricans and Public Schools*. New York: Aspira, 1968.
Minuchin, S., et al. *Families of the Slums: An Exploration of Their Structure and Treatment*. New York: Basic Books, 1967.
Moses, E. G., P. A. Zirkel and J. F. Greene. "Measuring the Self-Concept of Minority Group Pupils." *Journal of Negro Education*, 1973, *42*, 93–98.
Murillo-Rohde, I. "Family Life among Mainland Puerto Ricans in New York City Slums." *Perspectives in Psychiatric Care*, 1976, *14*, 174–79.
Poblete, R. "Anomie and the Quest for Community: The Formation of Sects among Puerto Ricans in New York." In F. Cordasco and E. Bucchioni (eds.), *The Puerto Rican Community and Its Children on the Mainland: A Source Book for Teachers, Social Workers, and Other Professionals*. Metuchen, N.J.: Scarecrow Press, 1972. Pp. 158–73.
Ralph, J. R. "Voodoo, Spirtualism and Psychiatry." In E. R. Padilla, and A. M. Padilla (eds.), *Transcultural Psychiatry: An Hispanic Perspective*. Los Angeles, Calif.: Spanish Speaking Mental Health Research Center, 1977. Pp. 97–98.
Rodriguez, C. "A Cost-Benefit Analysis of Subjective Factors Affecting Assimilation: Puerto Ricans." *Ethnicity*, 1975, *2*, 66–80.
Rogler, L. H. and A. B. Hollingshead. "Puerto Rican Spiritualist as a Psychiatrist." In F. Cordasco and E. Bucchioni (eds.), *The Puerto Rican Community and Its Children on the Mainland: A Source Book for Teachers, Social Workers, and Other Professionals*. Metuchen, N.J.: Scarecrow Press, 1972. Pp. 49–55.
Ruiz, R. A. *La Familia: Myths and Realities*. Paper presented at the Seminar on Ethnic Life Styles and Mental Health: Section on Hispanic Americans, Department of Psychology, Oklahoma State University, Stillwater, Okla., April 12–13, 1978.
Ruiz, R. A., and A. M. Padilla. "Counseling Latinos." *Personnel and Guidance Journal*, 1977, *55*, 401–8.
Soy, R. H. and I. Sanchez. *The American Pressure Cooker . . .*

The Puerto Rican on the Mainland. Kean College, N.J.: 1975 (ED 120 310).

Torres-Matrullo, C. "Acculturation and Psychopathology among Puerto Rican Women in Mainland United States." *American Journal of Orthopsychiatry* 1976, *46*, 710–19.

U.S. Bureau of the Census. *Persons of Spanish Origin by State: 1980*. Washington, D.C.: U.S. Goverment Printing Office, 1982.

U.S. Bureau of the Census, Current Population Reports, Series P-20, No. 329, *Persons of Spanish Origin in the United States: March 1977*. Washington, D.C.: U.S. Government Printing Office, 1978.

U.S. Bureau of the Census, Current Population Reports, Series P-20, No. 339, *Persons of Spanish Origin in the United States: March 1978. Washington, D.C.: U.S. Government Printing Office, 1979.*

Vazquez, H. I. "Puerto Rican Americans." *Journal of Negro Education*, 1969, *38*, 247–56.

Wagenheim, K. *Puerto Rico: A Profile*. New York: Praeger, 1970.

Washabaugh, B. *Correlates of Attitude Variability of Young Puerto Rican Men in Milltown, New England*. Detroit, Mich.: Wayne State University, 1971. (ED 072 138).

Wolf, K. "Growing Up and Its Price in Three Puerto Rican Subcultures." *Psychiatry*, 1952, *15*, 401–33.

Wolfe, J. L., and I. G. Fodor. "A Cognitive/Behavioral Approach to Modifying Assertive Behavior in Women." In J. M. Whiteley and J. V. Flowers (eds.), *Approaches to Assertion Training*. Monterey, Calif.: Brooks/Cole Pub. Co., 1978. Pp. 141–58.

Wolfram, W., et al. *Overlapping Influence in the English of Second Generation Puerto Rican Teachers in Harlem—Final Report*. Washington, D.C.: Center for Applied Linguistics, 1971. (ED 060 159).

Zirkel, P. A., and E. G. Moses. "Self-Concept and Ethnic Group Membership among Public School Students." *American Educational Research Journal*, 1971, *8*, 253–65.

4

Mexican Americans

LIKE MAINLAND PUERTO RICANS, Mexican Americans are struggling to rise above their plight to find their rightful place in American society. It would be erroneous, however, if not unjust, for counselors to generalize the problems or cultural strengths of Puerto Ricans to Mexican Americans based on interethnic similarities. It is also essential for counselors to become cognizant of the intraethnic differences and similarities among various Mexican Americans. Some Mexican Americans, for example, encounter fewer sociocultural problems than others. On the other hand, cultural elements indigenous to Mexican Americans frequently conflict with those of an Anglo society (Martinez, 1977).

Most counselors and other mental health professionals are Anglos who lack understanding of and sensitivity to Mexican American clients' cultural and individual needs (Martinez, 1977). Mexican Americans' awareness of counselors' bicultural ignorance of counseling strategies leads to ineffectiveness and underuse of counseling services. Hence, the intent of this chapter is to: (1) discuss some of the social and psychological elements of the Mexican American culture; (2) identify problems for counseling; and (3) make practical suggestions to assist counselors in helping to alleviate such problems through counseling.

SOME SOCIAL AND PSYCHOLOGICAL CHARACTERISTICS

Identifying the People

As with other ethnic groups, Mexican Americans can be identified in several ways, although attempts at identification by non-Mexican Americans have resulted in stereotypes and generalizations. Casaventes (1970) offers some general traits that appear to identify Mexican Americans. The descendants of Mexican Americans came from Mexico (or from Spain, where the Hispano of northern New Mexico and southern Colorado originate). Mexican Americans speak Spanish as their native language. The majority are Roman Catholics. Many of them have dark skin and hair (Casaventes, 1970, pp. 22–23).

Several single terms are used by Mexican Americans to identify themselves. DeBlassie (1976) suggests such terms defining this population as Mexican American (with or without a hyphen), Latin American, Latino, Spanish American, La Raza (the ethnic group), and Chicano. He maintains that these terms are preferred by members of this population. Webster (1971) contends that members of this group do not identify themselves as Mexican American but prefer such terms as Spanish-speaking, Spanish, Latin, Mexican, or Chicano. The latter term is most popular among many of the young and militant members of this ethnic group along the West coast such as California. Stoddard (1973) warns counselors:

> The most preferred name changes according to where in the Southwest it is used and also by social class and in what historical era. Some names are appropriate to English (i.e., Spanish surname Americans), while others are more meaningful in Spanish (i.e., La Raza, La Gente). Some ethnic labels are polite terms suitable to the argot of the barrio. [P. 58]

In spite of the various terms for ethnic identification, DeBlassie (1976) notes that there is lack of an intraethnic consensus concerning an identity label. Mexican Americans form such a diverse and heterogeneous group that no single term or label is applicable to this ethnic group. In subsequent discussions, the author will refer to members of this population in terms of Mexican Americans or Chicanos.

Geographical Place of Residence

According to the 1979 United States Census, in March 1978, there were approximately 12 million persons of Spanish origin in this country. Slightly over seven million, or about 60 percent, are located in five Southwestern states: New Mexico, Arizona, Colorado, Texas, and California. They are also heavily concentrated in the states of Illinois and Michigan (U.S. Bureau of Census, 1982). Mexican Americans reside in urban and rural areas. The Mexican American population is continually on the increase. For instance, the 1980 census reported that there were 8,740,439 Mexican Americans living in the United States (U.S. Bureau of Census, 1982).

Value Orientations

Castaneda (1977) wrote that "analysis suggests that the character of both interethnic and intraethnic variability may be strongly influenced by the unique pattern of confluence of traditional and modern [or dominant American cultural] beliefs in the history of any ethnic group" (p. 356). The majority of ethnic groups' traditional values prevail, yet these beliefs come in conflict where multiethnic societies attempt to practice traditional and modern beliefs in daily living. It is unclear whether or not two belief systems are psychologically incompatible.

Fabrega and Wallace (1968) conducted an investigation to better define group differences in value identification among patients and nonpatients Mexican Americans. The results indicated that there were no significant differences between the groups in their degree of traditional emphasis. Members of each group were distributed across a value continuum between traditional (Mexican) and nontraditional (Anglo) value preferences. The comparison did demonstrate that the nonpatients group consisted of a significantly larger proportion of individuals who preferred either end of the continuum as compared to the patients.

Castaneda (1976) states that most Mexican Americans live in one of the three basic types of communities: (1) traditional; (2) dualistic; or (3) atraditional. The community determines the value orientation of most of the families and individuals residing in it. While Mexican American families and individuals may practice all three orientations, a community usually exhibits the one value orientation, which generally characterizes the majority of its members. These value orientations also are in a constant state of change. Traditional Mexican American communities exhibit values that most closely related to Mexican orientations (Castaneda, 1976). Communities that have a dualistic value orientation show *some* acceptance of modern or dominant American cultural values and also many of the traditional Mexican values. Atraditional communities exhibit Mexican American values integrated with those of modern or dominant American society.

According to Castaneda (1976), value orientations of Mexican Americans fall into four clusters: (1) identification with family, community, and ethnic group; (2) personalization of interpersonal relationships; (3) status and role definition in family and community; and (4) Mexican-Catholic ideology (p. 185). The first cluster instills in persons a keen sense of identity within and loyalty to their community, family, and ethnic group as a whole. Individual identity is highly associated with the family, and a sense of achievement is instilled in individuals' early development. The focus is on cooperation of family, community, and ethnic unity rather than individual success as found within the dominant American culture (Castaneda, 1976; 1977).

The second value cluster evolves around personalizing interpersonal relationships. Traditional values among Mexican Americans within this orientation emphasize a humanistic approach to personal-interpersonal interactions, which emerges through the cooperative achievement and historical kinship exhibited in traditional Mexican American communities. While individuals are obligated to assist each other, there is an extended sensitivity to each others' feelings as well as needs. This sensitivity functions in nonverbal and verbal interpersonal associations. This mode of behavior allows Mexican Americans to interpret and understand the feelings of others without pressuring them into a state of self-conscious distress by begging for assistance. Individuals who are able to give help to others can assume that they will receive help and respect from others in return.

In status and role in the family and community, the third value cluster, the relative status and role of each person in relation to other members within the family matrix is requisite. Each person must be aware of his responsibilities to other members, aware of what is expected of himself, and what he may expect from others.

The fourth value cluster hinges on identification with Mexican-Catholic ideology. This value cluster plays a significant role in socialization by reinforcing many of the beliefs previously discussed, especially identification with the family, community, and ethnic group (Castaneda, 1976). According to Castaneda (1977), Chicanos' traditional belief in the creation of the universe rests on a sacred account of the presence of a supernatural force, a belief that is contrary to the American cultural belief stressing scientific explanations for universal phenomenon.

These value orientations should serve as a reminder that no single value orientation describes the attitudes of Mexican Americans. The four value orientations outlined here function within each Mexican American community, and one may eventually surface as being more dominant than the others. Castaneda (1977) believes that Mexican Americans can best function by using traditional Mexican and modern or dominant American beliefs.

Socioeconomic Conditions

According to the United States Census, about five million persons of Spanish origin (Mexican, Puerto Rican, Cuban, Central or South American, or other Spanish) were in the civilian labor force (U.S. Bureau of Census, 1979). The unemployment rate of these persons, 10 percent, was substantially higher than the unemployment rate (7 percent) of the civilian labor force in the entire United States. The unemployment rate for Spanish men, 9 percent, was high when compared to all men in the United States, 6 percent. Unemployed women of Spanish origin were more numerous compared to the rate for all women. The employment picture of Mexican Americans is

FIG. 4.1.
BROAD OCCUPATIONAL GROUP OF
MEXICAN ORIGIN 16-YEARS OLD AND OVER, BY
SEX FOR THE UNITED STATES, MARCH 1978.

Sex and Broad Occupational Group	Mexican Origin (in thousands)
Male	
Total, employed persons	1,619
Percent	100.0
White-collar workers	18.5
Blue-collar workers	63.1
Service workers	11.5
Farm workers	6.9
Female	
Total, employed persons	938
Percent	100.0
White-collar workers	44.8
Blue-collar workers	29.1
Service workers	24.5
Farm workers	1.6

Source: Adapted from a table with a similar title in: U.S. Bureau of the Census, Current Population Reports, Series P-20, No. 339, *Persons of Spanish Origin in the United States: March, 1978* (Washington D.C.: U.S. Government Printing Office, 1979).

summarized in figure 4.1. While almost half of employed females were in white-collar positions, there were fewer males in white-collar positions compared to those employed as blue-collar workers. Females were almost evenly distributed between blue-collar and service work. A higher proportion of males than females were employed as farm workers. Overall, only about 5 percent of Mexican American workers were employed as farm laborers, which contradicts the image of Mexican Americans held by many non-Mexican Americans.

Thirty-one percent of Mexican American men had incomes below $5,000, and 66 percent of Mexican American women had incomes at that level. The median income for Mexican American men in 1977 was $7,700; the median income for Mexican American women was $3,400. The median income for Mexican American women and men combined was slightly more than $5,500; the combined income for 46 percent of them was less than $5,000. These data suggest that the economic conditions warrant immediate attention, and that employment conditions and earning power for most Mexican Americans are less than desirable. Still, counselors should recognize "that there are [Mexican American] families that are poor and a few that are wealthy" (Murillo, 1976, p. 16). Recognizing these conditions means that counselors will be able to provide appropriate assistance to meet the needs of members of this ethnic group.

Religious Characteristics

Mexican Catholicism is an important dimension and socializing agent for Mexican Americans. The impact of this ideology varies across the three kinds of communities discussed (Castaneda, 1976). Mexican Catholicism encourages respect for convention within the traditional community; disrespect and rebelliousness against the teachings of the family, community, and ethnic group are considered sinful. Consequently, individuals may experience a sense of guilt should they not fulfill their responsibilities and obligations or if they manifest disrespectful behavior. Dualistic communities show an adherence to the basic ideology of Mexican Catholicism, but there are some signs of accepting Protestantism and Anglo-dominant beliefs. The impact of dualistic and atraditional belief systems has encouraged some younger Mexican Americans to question the ideology of the Catholic church. Atraditional communities are an amalgamation of Mexican Catholicism, Protestantism, and other ideologies. Ramirez and Castaneda (1974) suggest that Mexican Catholic ideology has little influence as a socializing agent among Mexican Americans, especially with the young within the atraditional community.

Rutter (1972) notes that Protestantism has been an influencing factor among Mexican Americans in the state of Kansas, and that some early Mexican immigrants converted to Protestantism out of gratitude for assistance from Protestant organizations. Mexican Protestants were outnumbered ten to one by Mexican Catholics. According to McNamara (1973), the assimilationist doctrine of the Catholic Archdiocese of Los Angeles has generated a negative picture, suggesting that many Chicanos do not accept assimilation as a goal. Conversely, Grebler et al. (1970) contend that many Mexican Americans in the Southwest are slowly moving toward increased participation in the Roman Catholic church. This indicates an improved social situation and greater faith in the church. As economic status increases among some members of this ethnic group, attendance at Catholic mass decreases (Stoddard, 1973).

The religious characteristics of Mexican Americans or Chicanos appear to be of a diverse nature. Because of vast social changes and the impact of Protestantism and Anglo dominant values, counselors should deal with Chicanos as individuals rather than as a homogenous group.

Some Family Characteristics

There is no single type of Mexican American family; families differ in such dimensions as history, socioeconomics, politics, geographic location, and degree of assimilation and acculturation (Sierra, 1973; Murillo, 1976). Yet within this diverse ethnic group, there are some common traditional family patterns of behavior, as well as modern ones.

According to Murillo (1976), the family is likely to be the single most important social unit to Mexican Americans. Personal identification is usually secondary to identification with the family.

The Mexican American family as a basic unit provides a source of psychological-emotional material support to the individual. An individual obtains emotional and material security through members of the family. To seek support outside the family dishonors the family's pride and dignity. There is sharing of material goods among family members and relatives even when materials are limited (Murillo, 1976).

Mindel (cited in Ruiz, 1978, p. 8) concluded that in Chicano families, there is considerable closeness between parents and children. While there is a degree of dependence, there is little assistance and support from kinship outside the nuclear family. The nuclear family may be surrounded by and have more contact with kinship on the mother's side.

Both Sierra (1973) and Murillo (1976) state that problems involving the family have the highest priority; individual needs may become secondary when other family members require assistance. For instance, a Chicano client might forego her appointment with a counselor to assist her mother across town and act as interpreter between her Spanish-speaking mother and a non-Spanish-speaking staff at the local medical facility. Non-Chicano counselors might misinterpret this client's behavior as irresponsible, but it is in keeping with the Chicano's value system.

The Chicano or Mexican American family exhibits a humanistic value orientation that is best exemplified through the concept of the extended family. According to Murillo (1976) and Castaneda (1976), the parents and godparents of a child are known as *compadres*—godfather or godmother, protector, friend, or benefactor. The process of developing a relationship with one's *compadre* is a fundamental way of forming links with other extended families, particularly with those members of other extended families who have high social community status or with persons who are considered good friends of the family. Godparents *(padrinos)* are expected to carry out economic and spiritual responsibilities to a godchild *(ahijado)* should something happen to the real parents. *Padrinos* assist in rearing and socializing the child, thus extending and reinforcing the teachings of the parents.

Socialization practices in the traditional sense have a hierarchical structure within the family (Castaneda, 1976), that is, increased status and responsibility are extended to older sisters and brothers over younger ones. The hierarchy also radiates downward from grandparents to parents to children (Castaneda, 1976). Castaneda suggests that this hierarchical system of status and role function among traditional Mexican Americans is contrary to the modern or dominant American cultural belief system that values equality for each individual regardless of family status (Castaneda, 1977).

According to Castaneda (1976), sexual roles are also clearly defined among traditional Mexican Americans. Males are masculine dominant in their behavior, while females tend to exhibit passive, submissive behavior to their spouses, provide nurturance for their young, and maintain a largely domestic role. This notion has been supported by some earlier researchers (Ramirez, 1959; Gonzalez, 1976; Aramoni, 1961; and Madsen, 1969); however, some later Mexican American or Chicano writers, such as Cotera (1976) and Ruiz (1978) have taken issue with such findings. Ruiz (1978) cites research findings that do not support previous research pointing toward masculine dominance and feminine passivity and submissiveness among Chicanos. Chicano couples did not equally endorse male dominance in decision making any more than did Anglo and Black couples. Chicano couples also did not differ significantly from Black and Anglo couples in responding to a pattern of endorsing traditional marriages, that is, ones in which the wife's place should be in the home.

Another important aspect of the Chicano family relates to patterns of behavior between males and females. Murillo (1976) states that males are usually given more latitude to participate in social activities outside the home than are females. Women are expected to remain close to the family for protection while men are expected to provide protection for their sisters when they are outside the presence of the immediate family.

Traditionally, family members are encouraged to exhibit positive behavior outside as well as inside the home (Murillo, 1976). Manifestations of negative behavior by individual members outside the home bring shame or dishonor to the family. Murillo (1976) states that a Chicano who brings shame to his family runs the risk of the family's terminating its relationship with him.

Despite these patterns, Mexican American families are heterogeneous rather than homogeneous. Their behavior patterns are diverse and in a constant state of change. Therefore, members of this ethnic group are best assisted by counselors who view each client as an individual, as well as a member of a Chicano family.

Educational Characteristics

Male Mexican Americans have higher educational attainment levels than females of this ethnic group. The United States Census (1979) indicates that 36.6 percent of Mexican American men have completed four years of high school or more compared to 32.1 percent of women of the same group. Fewer males have completed less than five years of school (21.9 percent) than females (24.4 percent).

The educational attainment level for Chicanos appears to be less than desirable. Sierra (1973) notes that Chicanos have completed an average of 9.6 years of school, compared to 12.1 years that is the national average (U.S. Commission on Civil Rights, 1971). Almost 50 percent of the Chicano students in Texas physically withdrew from school prior to completing the twelfth grade. Less than two of every three Chicano students in California failed to finish the twelfth grade. Sierra contends that many Chicano children did not make it to the first grade. For those who did reach the first grade, however, four out of five of them lagged behind Anglo students by two grade levels by the time they entered the fifth grade.

Ramirez (1973) and Castaneda (1976) suggest that Chicanos' low academic achievement may be related to public schools' refusal to implement the concept of bicognitive development. According to Ramirez, public education favors a teaching style that places Chicano students at odds with their Anglo counterparts. Ramirez and Castaneda determined that, as a result of Mexican American culture, particularly home socialization, Chicano students tend to have what they label as a field-sensitive cognitive style (as contrasted to field-independent cognitive style), that is, Chicanos tend to have preferred modes of communication, human-relational, and incentive-motivational learning styles. Most school curricula, classroom materials, and teacher-education programs emphasize the field-independent approach (abstract thinking, independent achievement); hence, educational institutions do not effectively respond to the field-sensitive cognitive style prevalent among Chicano students.

Another cultural factor that hampers Chicanos' academic

attainment in educational institutions is language. For instance, a young Chicano typically comes to school with a language—Spanish—that has served him quite well for his first five years; he may possibly have some knowledge of English. The lack of Spanish bilingual-bicultural programs limits the Chicano student's opportunities. Although most Chicanos of the Southwest are bilingual, Spanish is their native language, and English is often a second language (Nava, 1976).

The damaging impact of public schools' insensitivity and the scarcity of Chicanos in institutions of higher education means that few Chicanos enter the critical professions needed to maintain effective participation in the American society.

Chicanos in the Southwest are grossly underrepresented in the decision-making process within the educational structure, and until changes occur, the educational attainment of Chicanos will probably not rise above the levels of previous conditions. Better teaching methods that include bicultural and bicognitive development of Chicanos should be seriously considered.

Language

The 1969 United States Census data indicate that more than 68.9 percent of Spanish-speaking persons maintain a degree of fluency in Spanish. And 28.8 percent of them claim English as a first language. Cortes states that ". . . because the subjective [personal and emotional] is more commonly used in Spanish than in English, some Chicanos from bilingual or Spanish-speaking homes may tend to overuse the subjective mood in speaking and writing English" (1978, p. 31).

There are variations in the proficiency of English spoken among Mexican Americans. When helping clients for whom English is not a first language, counselors should seriously consider the need to be skilled in Spanish and English. A refusal to recognize Mexican Americans linguistically as well as culturally may be viewed as gratuitous or a denial or misinterpretation of their culture.

Self-Image, Ethnic Pride, and Identity

Recently, several reports have indicated an image of increasing ethnic pride and identity among Chicanos. Much of this pride and identity can be seen in community festivals, intriguing mural paintings on walls within the community, and a rise in community and political activism. Several studies document Chicanos' ethnic pride and identity (Larkin, 1972; Rice, Ruiz, and Padilla, 1974; Gecas, 1973).

An investigation conducted by Larkin (1972) revealed significant differences between racial and ethnic groups on self-esteem among fourth-, fifth-, and sixth-grade Black, Anglo, Mexican American, and Oriental children. Orientals had the highest self-esteem, followed by Blacks, Anglos, and Mexican Americans, respectively. Larkin concluded that variations in self-esteem appeared greater among lower-middle class than among lower- and upper-middle class youth. Although the Mexican Americans' self-esteem appeared lowest of the four groups, race or ethnic group and lowered-class status were not related to lower self-esteem.

Rice, Ruiz, and Padilla (1974) examined the ethnic and racial awareness, self-identification, and ethnic group preference in Anglo, Black, and Chicano preschool and third-grade children. When the children were presented color photographs of males of the ethnic groups represented in the study, the resultant data suggested that all children could discriminate between the Black and Anglo males, but the preschool children were unable to differentiate between Anglo and Chicano males. Neither the Black nor the Chicano preschool children expressed a significant preference for Anglo males, compared to the Anglo preschool children, who expressed a significant preference for Anglo pictures. At the third-grade level, however, the Chicano children expressed a strong preference for their own ethnic group. Could these data mean that Chicanos' ethnic consciousness and identification are related to advanced socialization? The socialization of the Mexican American and family members may have an increasingly significant impact on the ethnic identity of young Chicanos as they mature.

Cultural socialization also might signify variations of self-concepts and ethnic identity between migrant and settled Mexican Americans. Viktor Gecas (1973) studied the self-concepts of poor, rural migrant, and settled Mexican American adults and children. He concluded that the migrants seemed to be more firmly entrenched in the structural sources of ethnic identity with regard to family, religion, and work than were settled Mexican Americans. Relative to statements pertaining to their sense of moral worth, competence, self-determination, and altruism, migrants were more positive and generally had a more favorable image of themselves than did settled Mexican Americans. Settled children endorsed gender as a higher identity variable, whereas the migrant children felt that religion, family, and name have greater significance to them. The most similar factor among migrant and settled groups was their attachment to the family. Other investigations of self-evaluations by Chicanos appear inconclusive. For instance, results in data of Coleman's (1966) and Hishiki's (1969) studies suggested that Chicanos' self-evaluations were lower than Anglos, but DeBlassie and Healy (1970) and Carter (1968) found no significant differences in the self-evaluations between the two ethnic groups.

The Mexican American value system plays a significant role in ethnic pride and identity among most Chicanos, yet identity with the Mexican American culture is likely to become weakened as increased socialization occurs with value systems outside of this culture, which could be a mental health problem area. It is also well-known that a spirit of Chicano dignity and consciousness movements is on the increase, which may be a source of strength with regard to mental health. In spite of research attempting to delineate cultural pride, identity, and self-concepts, Chicanos are still best assessed on an individual basis, rather than collectively as members of the Mexican American culture or by interethnic comparisons among Spanish-speaking groups.

THE ENIGMA OF MEXICAN-AMERICAN CULTURE IN COUNSELING

The preceding discussion in this chapter was focused on variables crucial to the behavior of most Mexican Americans. Yet the reader was cautioned to consider differential effects of these variables on individuals of this ethnic group, since social, educational, and economic variables do not equally influence behaviors of Mexican Americans. Values and family orientations were seen as strong support systems which significantly affect behavioral patterns. While Mexican Americans generally aspire to upward mobility, attainment of this goal is limited by such extrapsychic (factors outside of the person) barriers as discrimination and prejudice. Most Mexican Americans, as well as other ethnic minorities, have little, if any, economic or political power to remove or reduce these external barriers. Aside from having visible physical features that often prevent many of them from being assimilated into the dominant society, most of them do not desire being stripped of their ethnic identity. Their tenacious sense of cultural pride permits them to function satisfactorily in a middle-class ethnocentric society. But while some individuals attempt to function in both the Mexican American and the dominant American cultures simultaneously, others succumb to an identity that is primarily "Mexican" or "Anglo" in nature. These two socialization patterns represent cultural behaviors and personal perceptions at both ends of the continuum: traditional and modern. Variations of value orientations on this continuum may have serious counseling implications; counselors must examine the degree to which a Chicano identifies with Mexican or middle-class American values.

Acculturation and Mexican Americans

Persons of an ethnic minority group frequently find it imperative to assume the standard behavior patterns supported by the dominant Anglo society (Marden and Meyer, 1968). The steps by which ethnic minorities ascertain world views and cultural or social values of the dominant group and adopt their cultural patterns is referred to as psychological acculturation (Graves, 1967; Marden and Meyer, 1968). The degree of an individual's or a group's acculturation has been measured on the basis of such variables as educational stratum, quality of living, type and size of home, customs, values, and attitudes (Cardenas, 1970).

Some investigators such as Cabrera (1963) argue that many Chicanos are caught between two conflicting societies, a situation that is comparable to having a cultural split personality. Kiev (1972) asserts that, as changes occur, there are conflicts in cultural roles. He further states that conflict between norms of the traditional culture and those of the dominant Anglo society is an important source of mental health problems.

The struggle to function effectively in a bicultural environment often requires a detachment of one's original identity that may result in an identity crisis (Go, 1975; Murillo, 1976). Many Chicanos who experience acculturation endure this kind of stress. To illustrate, a Chicano may aspire to attain economic access to the resources and rewards of the dominant Anglo society but also realize that the value of religion should transcend material success. Straddling both traditional Mexican American and dominant Anglo societies may induce a desire for individualism and less reliance on the family as a support system, (Go, 1975). Some research concerning Mexican American acculturation indicates that those persons who do not identify with their traditional values are more susceptible than others to mental stress and disturbance (Ramirez, 1971; Gecas, 1973).

Go's (1975) investigation failed to establish a significant relationship between acculturation and anxiety, although she maintains that this finding does not necessarily rule out the conclusion that acculturation is stressful or anxiety producing. For instance, the Chicano females demonstrated significantly higher levels of anxiety than the males, and highly acculturated females also had higher anxiety than did males of that group. These findings suggest that acculturative experiences varied between the two sexes.

While many Mexican Americans are marginally acculturated, the extent to which each client has been acculturated and has accepted middle-class American values must be seriously considered in counseling. Recognition of acculturational levels will result in culturally relevant counseling approaches that are consistent with the values of the Mexican American client involved.

Views of Mental Health and Mental Illness

The degree of acculturation among Mexican Americans is related to their perceptions of mental illness, mental health, and use of counseling services. Research (Karno and Edgerton, 1969) has demonstrated that there are few significant differences in perceptions and definitions of mental illness between urbanized Chicanos and Anglos. Both social and cultural factors, however, accounted for the underrepresentation of Chicanos in psychiatric treatment facilities. Furthermore, there were important within-group variations for Chicanos. For example, less acculturated persons believed that psychological problems were initiated during childhood, and it was expected that persons with psychological problems would remain in the home until relieved of their problems. Most Chicanos sought assistance for nervousness and emotional illness from their physicians rather than from counseling professionals.

Go (1975) investigated the extent to which high school and university Chicano students' attitudes favored counseling and psychotherapy. The results indicated a significant, positive relationship between acculturation and favorability toward counseling and psychotherapy. The more acculturated Chicanos evidenced favorable attitudes toward counseling and psychotherapy than those Chicanos who were less acculturated. These findings were in part corroborated in a similar investigation by Acosta and Sheenan (1976).

Several explanations have been offered to the issue of Chicanos' underuse of professional counseling services. Ruiz and Padilla (1977) suggest that Chicanos refer themselves to counseling facilities less often because certain cultural factors are considered to lower incidents of negative effects of stress; counteracting factors include turning to one's extended family or religious values, and the use of *curanderos*, Mexican American folk psychiatrists or faith healers who practice traditional folk medicine and medical beliefs with ritualistic acts claimed to have positive influences on health (Gonzales, 1976; Kiev, 1972). However, research results on East Los Angeles Chicanos by Edgerton, Karno, and Fernandez (1970) suggest that although *curanderismo* is practiced in the community, most Chicanos would seek treatment for mental health problems from their family physicians rather than *curanderos*. Yet highly acculturated and urbanized persons as well as unacculturated persons practice folk beliefs or folk remedies or seek out *curanderos* when acute stress continues to persist, especially after modern interventions or professional counseling and psychotherapy have been unsuccessful (Castro, 1977).

These observations tend to suggest that Chicanos' perceptions toward counseling are influenced by the degree of their acculturation and definition of mental illness. More frequent self-referrals to the family physician than to mental health professionals may be related to Chicanos' knowledge of the physician's practices and an ignorance of the methods of other professionals. Although folk psychiatry appears to have less influence in large, urban areas, it continues to be practiced, particularly in traditional communities.

Attitudes toward Counselors

Client attitudes toward counselors are important factors in attaining positive counseling outcomes. Ruiz and Padilla (1977) found that counselor characteristics often hinder Chicano employment of counseling facilities. They maintain that Chicanos frequently have rejected traditional counseling services, which tend to hinge on lingiustic problems, class, and cultural variations, because they restrict intercultural communication. For example, Mexican American clients express concern over professionals' impersonalization and detachment when delineating their experiences with mental health professionals (Kline, 1969). Other research indicates that non-Anglo psychiatric patients, including Chicanos, disliked their therapists; and more than 10 percent of the therapists (Anglos) disliked these ethnic minority clients (Yamamoto, James, and Palley, 1968). The significance of the language barrier between Chicano clients and counselors or therapists was demonstrated in a study by Torrey (1972) and supported by Edgerton and Karno (1971).

In a recent study, Acosta and Sheehan (1976) investigated preferences and attitudes among Mexican Americans toward Mexican and Anglo therapists. The study included ninety-four Mexican American and ninety-three Anglo American college students. The college students saw the Anglo American professional and Mexican American nonprofessional as more understanding, trustworthy, attractive, and skillful than the

Anglo nonprofessional and the Mexican American professional. The Mexican American nonprofessional was endorsed by both the Mexican American and Anglo American students as being more favorable than the Mexican American professional. The Anglo American students were generally less favorable toward the usefulness of psychotherapy than were the Mexican American students.

A preference for a counselor or therapist will depend upon the Mexican American clients' willingness to disclose personal concerns to the counselor. Recent research (Acosta and Sheehan, 1978) indicates that Mexican American college students showed substantial willingness to disclose personal matters to therapists without regard for whether the therapist was professional (trained) or nonprofessional (untrained) or Anglo American or Mexican American. However, Mexican Americans' willingness to disclose personal information is slightly less than that of Anglo Americans.

The finding that the ethnic background did not matter is contrary to findings by Torrey (1972) and Padilla and Ruiz (1977), which suggest that bilingual and/or bicultural professionals are likely to be more productive than others in counseling Mexican Americans. The research was done on college students; it is possible that many Mexican Americans who are less acculturated than those investigated by Acosta and Sheehan (1976, 1978) might disclose fewer personal concerns to non-Mexican American counselors as suggested in the literature. Therefore, degree of acculturation of the client, language used, and awareness of and sensitivity to the client's culture are crucial factors determining the client's attitudes and preference toward the counselor.

Communication in Counseling Services

The language used with Mexican American clients in the therapeutic setting will influence the diagnostic impressions of counselors. This outcome is particularly evident when English is the Mexican American's second language, or when he is fluent in Spanish and English. For example, an investigation of ten schizophrenic patients whose native language was Spanish revealed more psychopathology when the patients were interviewed in English than when interviews were conducted in Spanish (Marcos et al., 1973). This suggests that clinically significant variations in the patients were influenced by difficulties experienced with English as a second language. In addition, what appears applicable to native English-speaking clients may not be directly applied to the assessment of clients of other cultures (Marcos et al., 1973). Even those patients who had a larger vocabulary of English than Spanish revealed more pathology when interviewed in English than when interviewed in Spanish.

The results of an investigation by Marcos et al. (1973) are contrary to the results of a similar study by Del Castillo (1970). On the other hand, Del Castillo's results are questionable because of his study's methodological shortcomings. Edgerton and Karno (1971) believe that Spanish is a powerful source of culture among most Mexican Americans, who maintain family cohesiveness and identity through it. To require a change during counseling from the more familiar and intimate language to a less personal and unfamiliar one such as English could damage the overall process involved and thus circumscribe the client's desired outcome(s). When counseling Mexican American clients, conducting the counseling session in Spanish seems to improve the delivery of counseling services.

Drug and Alcohol Abuse: Coping with Culture

In spite of the dissemination of drug information, drug and alcohol abuse is nearing epidemic proportions in some Chicano barrios. Research by Padilla et al. (1977) suggested that Chicano adolescents are well-informed of the dangers of drug abuse and tend to participate regardless of the consequences. Research by Padilla et al. (1977) on 457 Chicano youths from age 9 to 17 who lived in housing projects of East Los Angeles suggested that inhalant abuse was fourteen times higher among Chicanos than among all drug users. The prevailing rate of marijuana use or abuse was twice the national average; however, the alcohol rate was comparable to the rest of the population. The Los Angeles Chicano youth community are frequent users of Phencyclindine (PCP). According to Padilla et al., background variables such as age, sex, family size, family intactness, drug familiarity, number of peer inhalers tended to predict the youths' use of marijuana (36 percent), alcohol (22 percent), and inhalants (18 percent). The youths' familiarity with drugs, however, was the highest predictor of their drug use among the background variables.

Observations of these Mexican American youth and their drug-use habits support theories about drug use and drug abuse in general. Singer (1972) maintains that drugs are rarely the abuser's real difficulty; they are, rather, symptomatic of a more deeply seated problem. Drugs are believed to provide a means of escape and rebellion against the mores of the older generation, and to satisfy youngsters' curiosity. Heilbrunn (1967) attributed drug abuse to sociological factors such as economic changes, political instability, and an atmosphere of liberation. These conditions lead to a sense of insecurity and skepticism in youth, which, in turn, leads them to use drugs. Halleck (1967) attributes drug abuse to youths' feelings of alienation. He views drug abuse as an attempt to change a world that is seen as sterile and unchangeable. Drug users also often feel they are unable to change the external world, so they attempt to create a new inner reality through the use of drugs.

Chicano Students and Schools

It is well-documented that many Chicano students have been subject to ethnically inequitable and educationally discriminatory classroom experiences (U.S. Commission of Civil Rights, 1973), which are believed to have had deleterious effects on their academic achievement and scholastic self-esteem (Cortes, 1978). Compared to Anglos, Chicano students received significantly less praise, encouragement, acceptance or use of their ideas, positive response, noncriticizing talk, and fewer questions from their teachers.

Many educational systems have failed to incorporate the Chicano culture into the curriculum in order to enhance students' identity development and academic achievements. Some authors such as Anderson and Johnson (1971) suggest that the underlying causes of low academic achievement for many Mexican American students are associated with the unpleasant experiences Spanish-speaking students face in their early years in English-speaking schools. To avoid a student's sense of alienation and psychological and physical withdrawal from school, bilingual and bicultural programs are needed. Fisher (1974) researched the changes of self-concept among Chicano children who participated in a bilingual-bicultural program with results that indicated that Chicano females' self-concept had significantly improved, but that Chicano males' self-concepts did not change during the experimental period of seven months when compared to the control group. Many Chicano students are likely to continue being handicapped where school personnel deny them a bilingual-bicultural curriculum that lends itself to bicognitive development.

SOME PRACTICAL APPROACHES TO WORKING WITH MEXICAN AMERICANS

Obviously, counselors and other mental health professionals can obtain the best results through a bilingual-bicultural approach to counseling. To achieve this, counselors need fluency in Spanish as well as English and thorough familiarity with Mexican American culture. Counselors who attain these qualities, however, may still be unable to assist Chicanos in obtaining positive client outcomes (Morales, 1976), if the counselor continues to employ only middle-class Anglo treatment interventions with Chicano clients (cf., Lorion, 1974).

Bilingualism in counseling is particularly significant even where the Chicano client speaks fluent English because this type of client often uses Spanish and English. In matters outside the personal and family realm, the client will tend to use English, while personal or emotional factors pertaining to one's self or family are likely to be communicated in Spanish. This is sometimes referred to as code switching (Padilla, 1976). The counselor must bear with such behavior as well as be able to understand both languages.

Whether Spanish or English should be used while assisting the client depends on the degree to which the client has acculturated. Consistent with research discussed earlier, Chicano clients who identify strongly with Mexican American culture may indeed require communication in Spanish in addition to nontraditional counseling interventions. Chicanos who identify strongly with Anglo dominant culture are likely to communicate in English, and with them, therapeutic interventions from middle-class traditional counseling theories may be used with satisfactory results. Clients who tenaciously adhere to both Mexican American and Anglo cultures will communicate mostly in English and will require traditional therapeutic interventions. Finally, clients in transition who are seeking identity as members of dominant Anglo culture could require English with an Anglo-cultural approach (Ruiz, Casas, and Padilla, 1977).

Levels of acculturation are the determining factors for employing bilingual-bicultural or monolingual-monocultural counseling interventions with Chicanos. The effectiveness of implementing either of the two approaches with Chicano clients requires counselors to be culturally competent in Anglo and Mexican American cultures. Counselors also should be knowledgeable about the client's manner of communication, cultural background, and personality.

The serious problems centered around drug abuse should be major concerns for counselors who work with Chicano adolescents. Programs can be developed in elementary schools to disseminate information through movies, filmstrips, literature, former Chicano adolescent drug and alcohol abusers, and school curriculum. Family members might be trained as paraprofessionals to work in orienting or informing young Chicanos about drug abuse. Counseling and mental health facilities should be established within the neighborhoods so they are accessible and viewed as part of the Mexican American community. Research findings cited earlier indicated that Chicano adolescent non-users were less informed of the dangers regarding drugs and alcohol than those Chicano adolescent users and abusers. It may be necessary to help Chicano adolescent drug users (and non-users) to enhance their positive feelings as useful contributors to American society. Counselors can help them obtain employment for weekdays after school and weekends. Adults as well as adolescents could be involved in such career/vocational activities ranging from learning appropriate interviewing skills or learning to fill out employment applications to learning about career and educational opportunities and requirements, scholarships, and financial assistance for entry into higher education. These activities are only a few that may help adolescent Chicanos and adults plan and use their time and energy in a more positive and constructive manner rather than engage in drug related activities.

Since the Chicano family is a basic source of identity, its members might be encouraged to participate in group counseling with the client, where appropriate, to provide a vital sense of emotional support. The inclusion of family members may increase the client's self-expression and encourage him to take greater responsibility for setting therapeutic goals mutually agreed upon by family, client, and counselor, and to determine the best therapeutic interventions to attain the goals. Counselors must provide structure and actively direct the group to clarify the problem, establish and evaluate alternative approaches, and test the chosen alternative to be applied. Structure and organization need not imply coldness; on the contrary, the group process should emphasize personal warmth. Some strategies that may facilitate the group process are role playing; modeling; role reversal; and family sculpting, which involves using various poses as a basis to discuss effects of the client upon the rest of the family and allowing fantasizing of their frustrations.

Counselors in school settings can provide ongoing inservice programs that represent the cultural orientations of the Mexican American family. Mexican American children are generally encouraged to identify with and to achieve for the family. A highly personalized style of instructions to Chicano children is especially effective in enhancing their academic sense of self-worth as well as their academic achievement. Methods to retool instructional skills or develop new skills that reflect culturally relevant learning styles of Chicano children such as field sensitive and field independent cognitive learning styles should be developed.

Another area of concern is individual appraisal. Counselors and psychologists are encouraged to assess personal, social, and intellectual dimensions of Chicano children in accord with their (Chicano children's) cultural experiences. The System of

Multicultural Pluralistic Assessment (Mercer and Lewis, 1978) appears to be a promising assessment tool that considers the Chicano student's cultural background in evaluating his learning potential. The SOMPA consists of a series of assessments that measure the current level of functioning and potential of children from Anglo, Chicano/Latino, and Black cultural backgrounds. The SOMPA is used in conjunction with the Wechsler Intelligence Scale for Children-Revised (WIS-R), the Binder-Gestalt, and other measurement tools to establish medical, social system, and pluralistic profiles of students which can be used for program planning. This device (SOMPA) has been standardized only on children in California, and the comparative results of students in other locations are being eagerly awaited.

SUMMARY

Counselors and other mental health professionals who work with Mexican Americans are strongly urged to recognize that many psychological and social factors within their culture influence the course of counseling. The impact of these factors varies for individual persons. Mexican Americans are a diverse ethnic group whose within-group socialization processes result in continuous change as well as in differences in world views. These world views seem to influence Mexican Americans' perceptions toward mental health professionals and services.

Research suggests that levels of acculturation among Mexican Americans must determine counseling intervention strategies. The success of either traditional or nontraditional counseling intervention is contingent upon the individual's overall experiences. While counselors should have bilingual-bicultural training in counseling, culturally relevant intervention strategies also should be an essential part of such training.

EXERCISES

The exercises below are designed to help sensitize students to Chicanos' diverse needs and cultural situations. Students are given the opportunity to apply culturally relevant facts to hypothetical counseling situations.

A. Study the example below and answer the questions following it during group discussion.

A Mexican-American mother who has an ill young son has a doctor's appointment. Because the mother speaks only Spanish, Luis, another son, is expected to accompany her to the doctor and act as translator between the two adults. However, Luis must miss school that day to accompany his mother. Maria, a daughter, now must remain home and miss school, too, because her brother Luis will not be in school to protect her. School personnel have become extremely concerned about the children's frequent absences.

1. What are the issues involved in this situation?
2. As a counselor, what approaches would you apply to improve the children's school situation?
3. To what extent should bilingual/bicultural counseling be applied to this situation?

B. In small groups, study the example below and answer the questions following it during group discussion.

Gloria, an unmarried, twenty-three-year-old woman, is experiencing difficulty adjusting to two cultural worlds: traditional Mexican customs and middle-class, Anglo American society. She is employed as a secretary, and most of her co-workers are middle-class Anglos. Many of her co-workers (both women and men) invite Gloria to participate in activities such as dinner and parties after working hours. Although she would like to go out and enjoy herself with them, Gloria usually declines their invitations. She has noticed recently that her co-workers are no longer asking her to join them.

1. What are the major difficulties that Gloria has encountered?
2. What possible sociocultural factors influence Gloria not to engage in after-work activities with her co-workers?
3. How would you intervene as a counselor to help Gloria allay her problem?

C. Study the example below and discuss possible answers to the questions that follow the example.

> Gogelio, a nineteen-year-old, completed high school a year ago. Before he finished school, he was interested in becoming an electronic engineer. However, Gogelio has been unable to secure any kind of employment to support himself in college or to help support his mother, father, and three younger brothers and sisters as he would be expected to even if he attended college. He has gradually become involved in smoking marijuana and, more recently, he has begun taking PCP (Phencyclidine). Gogelio has often complained that there is little good in getting a high-school diploma when middle-class Anglo society refuses Chicanos an opportunity to advance themselves. He no longer has any ambition to do anything to improve his life situation.

1. What appear to be the major issues in this example?
2. Which one of Gogelio's problems seems most immediate? Why?
3. What are some possible intervention strategies that might lend themselves to eventual solutions to the problems?
4. Are some of these strategies more feasible than others? Tell why.

D. Have students form small groups to work on the following task. Each group is to make a list of suggested nontraditional counseling approaches that could be applied in a counseling center located in the barrio of a Mexican-American community. Be sure to consider the needs of clients who are monolingual and bilingual (only Spanish, only English, and both Spanish and English speaking), as well as the various socioeconomic and educational levels. Develop a rationale for each approach, along with an example of a Mexican-American client's problem that might benefit from the approach. After the groups have developed their suggested approaches, each group should share its approaches with the other groups. After each presentation, discuss the advantages and disadvantages of the suggested approaches.

REFERENCES

Acosta, F. X., and J. G. Sheehan. "Preferences Toward Mexican Americans and American Psychotherapists." *Journal of Consulting and Clinical Psychotherapy*, 1976, *44*, 272–79.

Acosta, F. X., and J. G. Sheehan. "Self-Disclosure in Relation to Psychotherapist Expertise and Ethnicity." *American Journal of Community Psychology*, 1978, *6*, 545–53.

Anderson, J. G., and W. H. Johnson. "Stability and Change among Three Generations of Mexican-Americans: Factors Affecting Achievement." *American Educational Research Journal*, 1971, *8*, 285–309.

Aramoni, A. *Psiconalsis de la dinamica de un pueblo*. Mexico, D.F.: Universidad Nacional Autonoma de Mexico, 1961.

Cabrera, Y. A. "A Study of American and Mexican-American Culture Values and Their Significance in Education." Unpublished doctoral dissertation, University of Colorado, Boulder, Colo., 1963.

Cardenas, R. "Three Critical Factors That Inhibit Acculturation of Mexican Americans." Unpublished doctoral dissertation, University of California, Berkeley, 1970.

Carter, T. "Negative Self-Concept of Mexican-American Students." *School and Society*, 1968, *96*, 217–19.

Casavantes, E. "Pride and Prejudice: A Mexican American Dilemma." *Civil Rights Digest*, 1970, *3*, 22–27.

Castaneda, A. "Cultural Democracy and the Educational Needs of Mexican American Children." In R. L. Jones, ed., *Mainstreaming and the Minority Child*. Reston, Vir.: Council for Exceptional Children, 1976, 181–94.

Castaneda, A. "Traditionalism, Modernism, and Ethnicity." In J. L. Martinez, Jr., ed., *Chicano Psychology*. New York: Academic Press, 1977. Pp. 335–60.

Castro, F. G. *Level of Acculturation and Related Considerations in Psychotherapy with Spanish Speaking/Surnamed Clients*. Los Angeles: Spanish Speaking Mental Health Research Center, 1977.

Coleman, J. S. *Equality of Educational Opportunity*. Washington, D.C.: U.S. Government Printing Office, 1966.

Cortes, C. E. "Chicano Culture, Experience, and Learning." In L. Morris, G. Sather, and S. Scull (eds.), *Extracting Learning Styles from Social/Culture Minorities*. Norman, Okla.: Southwest Teacher Corp. Network, 1978, 29–39.

Cotera, M. *Profile on the Mexican American Woman*. Austin, Tex.: National Educational Laboratory, 1976.

DeBlassie, R. R. *Counseling with Mexican American Youth*. Austin, Tex.: Learning Concepts, 1976.

DeBlassie, R. R., and G. W. Healey. *Self-Concept: A Comparison of Spanish-American, Negro, and Anglo Adolescents across Ethnic, Sex, and Socioeconomic Variables*. Las Cruces: New Mexico State University, 1970.

Del Castillo, J. C. "The Influence of Language upon Symptomatology in Foreign-Born Patients." *American Journal of Psychiatry*, 1970, *127*, 242–44.

Edgerton, R. B., and M. Karno. Mexican-American Bilingualism and the Perception of Mental Illness. *Archives of General Psychiatry*, 1971, *24*, 286–90.

Edgerton, R. B., M. Karno and I. Fernandez. "Curanderismo in the Metropolis: The Diminished Role of Folk Psychiatry among Los Angeles Mexican-Americans." *American Journal of Psychotherapy*, 1970, *24*, 124–234.

Fabrega, H., Jr., and C. A. Wallace. "Value Identification and Psychiatric Disability: An Analysis Involving Americans of Mexican Descent." *Behavioral Science*, 1968, *13*, 362–71.

Fisher, F. I. "A Study of Non-Intellectual Attributes of Children in First Grade Bilingual-Bicultural Programs." *Journal of Educational Research*, 1974, *67*, 323–28.

Gecas, V. "Self-Conceptions of Migrant and Settled Mexican Americans." *Social Science Quarterly*, 1973, *54*, 579–95.

Go, O. "Mexican American Acculturation: Its Relation to Self-Report Anxiety and Attitudes Towards Counseling and Psychotherapy." Unpublished masters thesis, San Bernardino, Calif.: California State College, 1975.

Gonzales, E. "The Role of Chicano Folk Beliefs and Practices in Mental Health." In C. A. Hernandez, Haug, M. J., and N. N. Wagner (eds.), *Chicanos: Social and Psychological Perspectives*. St. Louis: C. V. Mosby, 1976, 263–81.

Graves, T. D. "Psychological Acculturation in a Tri-Ethnic Community." *Southwestern Journal of Anthropology*, 1967, *23*, 337–50.

Grebler, L., J. Q. Moore and R. C. Guzman. *The Mexican American People*. New York: Free Press, 1970.

Halleck, S. "Psychiatric Treatment of the Alienated College Student." *American Journal of Psychiatry*, 1967, *124*, 642–50.

Heilbrunn, G. "Comments of Adolescent Drug Users." *Northwest Medicine*, 1967, *66*, 457–60.

Hishiki, P. C. "Self-Concepts of Sixth-Grade Girls of Mexican Descent." *California Journal of Educational Research*, 1969, *20*, 56–62.

Karno, M., and R. B. Edgerton. "Perception of Mental Illness in a Mexican-American Community." *Archives of General Psychiatry*, 1969, *20*, 233–38.

Kiev, A. *Transcultural Psychiatry*. New York: Free Press, 1972.

Kline, L. Y. "Some Factors in the Psychiatric Treatment of Spanish Americans." *American Journal of Psychiatry*, 1969, *125*, 1674–81.

Larkin, R. W. "Class, Race, Sex, and Preadolescent Attitude." *California Journal of Educational Research*, 1972, *23*, 213–27.

Lorion, R. P. "Patient and Therapist Variables in the Treatment of Low-Income Patients." *Psychological Bulletin*, 1974, *81*, 344–54.

Madsen, W. "Mexican-Americans and Anglo-Americans: A Comparative Study of Mental Health in Texas." In S. C. Plog and R. B. Edgerton, eds., *Changing Perspectives in Mental Health*. New York: Holt, Rinehart and Winston, 1969.

Marcos, L. R., M. Alpert, L. Urcuyo, and M. Kesselman. "The Effect of Interview Language on the Evaluation of Psychopathology in Spanish-American Schizophrenic Patients." *American Journal of Psychiatry*, 1973, *130*, 549–53.

Marden, C. F., and G. Meyer. *Minorities in American Society*. New York: American Book Co., 1968.

Martinez, J. L., Jr. *Chicano Psychology*. New York: Academic Press, 1977.

McNamara, P. H. "Catholicism, Assimilation, and the Chicano Movement: Los Angeles as a Case Study." In R. O. de la Garza, Z. A. Kruszewski, and T. A. Arciniega (eds.), *Chicanos and Native Americans*. Englewood Cliffs, N.J.: Prentice-Hall, 1973.

Mercer, J. J., and J. F. Lewis. "Using the System of Multicultural, Pluralistic Assessment (SOMPA) to Identify the Gifted Minority Child." In A. Y. Baldwin, G. H. Gear, and L. J. Lucity (eds.), *Educational Planning for the Gifted—Overcoming Cultural, Geographic, and Socioeconomic Barriers*. Reston, Va.: The Council for Exceptional Children, 1978, 7–14.

Mindel, C. H. "Kinship in a Multiethnic Community." Cited in R. A. Ruiz, *La Familia: Myths and Realities*. Paper presented at the Seminar on Ethnic Life-Styles and Mental Health: Section on Hispanic Americans, Oklahoma State University, Stillwater, Okla.: April 12–13, 1978.

Morales, A. "The Impact of Class Discrimination and White Racism on the Mental Health of Mexican-Americans." In C. A. Hernandez, M. J. Haug, and N. N. Wagner (eds.), *Chicanos: Social and Psychological Perspectives*. St. Louis: C. V. Mosby Co., 1976. Pp. 211–16.

Murillo, N. "The Mexican American Family." In C. A. Hernandez, M. J. Haug, and N. N. Wagner (eds.), *Chicanos: Social and Psychological Perspectives*. St. Louis, Miss.: C. V. Mosby Co., 1976. Pp. 15–25.

Nava, J. Educational Challenges in Elementary and Secondary Schools. In G. Tyler, ed., *Mexican-Americans Tomorrow*. Albuquerque: University of New Mexico Press, 1976. Pp. 107–36.

Padilla, A. M. "Psychological Research and the Mexican American." In C. A. Hernandez, M. J. Haug, and N. N. Wagner (eds.), *Chicanos: Social and Psychological Perspective*. St. Louis: C. V. Mosby Co., 1976. Pp. 152–259.

Padilla, E. R., A. M. Padilla, R. Ramirez, A. Morales and E. L. Olmedo. *Inhalant, Marijuana and Alcohol Abuse among Barrio Children and Adolescents*. Los Angeles, Calif.: Spanish Speaking Mental Health Research Center, 1977.

Ramirez, M., III. "Cognitive Styles and Cultural Democracy in Education." *Social Science Quarterly*, 1973, *53*, 895–904.

Ramirez, M., III. "The Relationship of Acculturation to Educational Achievement and Psychological Adjustment in Chicano Children and Adolescents: A Review of the Literature." *El Grito*, 1971, *4*, 21–28.

Ramirez, M., and A. Castaneda. *Cultural Democracy, Bicognitive Development, and Education*. New York: Academic Press, 1974.

Ramirez, S. *El Mexicano, Psicologia de Sus Mativaciones*. Mexico, D.F.: Editorial Pax-Mexico, S.A., 1959.

Rice, A. S., R. A. Ruiz, and A. M. Padilla. "Person Perception, Self-Identity, and Ethnic Group Preference in Anglo, Black, and Chicano Pre-School and Third-Grade Children." *Journal of Cross-Cultural Psychology*, 1974, *5*, 100–9.

Ruiz, R. A. "The Delivery of Mental Health and Social Change Services for Chicanos: Analysis and Recommendations." In J. L. Martinez, Jr. (ed.), *Chicano Psychology*. New York: Academic Press, 1977. Pp. 233–48.

Ruiz, R. A. "La Familia: Myths and Realities." Paper presented at the Seminar on Ethnic Life-Styles and Mental Health: Section on Hispanic Americans, Oklahoma State University, Stillwater, April 12–13, 1978.

Ruiz, R. A., J. M. Casas, and A. M. Padilla. *Culturally relevant Behavioristic Counseling*. Los Angeles, Calif.: Spanish Speaking Mental Health Research Center, 1977.

Ruiz, R. A., and A. M. Padilla. "Counseling Latinos." *Personnel and Guidance Journal*, 1977, *55*, 401–8.

Rutter, L. G. "Mexican American in Kansas: A Survey and Social Mobility Study, 1900–1970." Unpublished masters thesis, Kansas State University, Manhattan, 1972.

Sierra, V. "Learning Style of the Mexican American." In L. A. Bransford, L. Baca, and K. Lane, eds., *Cultural Diversity and the Exceptional Child*. Reston, Va.: The Council for Exceptional Children, 1973. Pp. 42–49.

Singer, H. "The School Counselor and the Drug Problem." *School Counselor*, 1972, *19*, 284–88.

Stoddard, E. *Mexican Americans*. New York: Random House, 1973.

Torrey, E. F. *The Mind Game: Witch Doctors and Psychiatrists*. New York: Emerson Hall, 1972.

United States Bureau of the Census. Persons of Spanish Origin in the United States: March, 1978. *Current Population Reports*. Series P-20, No. 339. Washington, D.C.: U.S. Government Printing Office, 1979.

United States Bureau of the Census. *Persons of Spanish Origin by States: 1980*. Washington, D.C.: U.S. Government Printing Office, 1982.

United States Commission on Civil Rights. Report 11: The Unfinished Education. Mexican American Educational Series. Washington, D.C.: U.S. Government Printing Office, 1971.

United States Commission on Civil Rights. Report V: Difference in Teacher Interaction with Mexican American and Anglo Students. *Mexican American Education Study*. Washington, D.C.: U.S. Government Printing Office, 1973.

Webster, S. W. *Knowing and Understanding the Socially Disadvantaged: Ethnic Minority Groups*. Scranton, Pa.: Intext Educational Pub., 1971.

Yamamoto, J., Q. C. James, and N. Palley. "Cultural Problems in Psychiatric Therapy." *Archives of General Psychiatry*, 1968, *19*, 45–49.

5

Black Americans

FOR COUNSELORS TO FULLY understand and effectively serve Black American clients, a firm knowledge of their sociocultural background should be established. The paucity of literature focusing on the strengths of Blacks, particularly the Black family, presently contributes to irrelevant counseling approaches and inadequate outcomes. Black Americans do not represent a homogeneous population but rather, they are a highly diverse ethnic group. Knowledge of the cultural diversity among members of this group may serve to facilitate communication between practitioners and Black clients. In spite of recent social, educational, and economic gains, most members of this ethnic group continue to strive to improve their social conditions. Their psychological problems are related to their social status. As yet, Blacks have limited political power and this contributes to psychological problems. They also suffer the effects of limited education, deteriorated housing, low income, and poor consumer skills.

Only recently have counselors begun to perceive the relationship between their clients' personalities and their social environment. Blacks are upwardly mobile. Kincaid (1969) suggests that counselors also must be cognizant of the new

Coleman, J. S. *Equality of Educational Opportunity*. Washington, D.C.: U.S. Government Printing Office, 1966.

Columbia Broadcasting System. "CBS News Special: Four Portraits in Black." New York: CBS Television Network, April 26, 1974. (Mimeographed transcript.)

Deutsch, M. "Minority Groups and Class Status as Related to Social and Personality Factors in Scholastic Achievement." In M. Deutsch and Ass. (eds.), *The Disadvantaged Child*. New York: Basic Books, 1967. Pp. 90–131.

Dillard, J. L. *Black English: Its History and Usage in the United States*. New York: Random House, 1972.

Dillard, J. M. "Relationship Between Career Maturity and Self-Concepts of Suburban and Urban Middle- and Urban Lower-Class Preadolescent Black Males." *Journal of Vocational Behavior*, 1976, *9*, 311–20.

Dillard, J. M. "Some Unique Career Behavior Characteristics of Blacks: Career Theories, Counseling Practices, and Research." *Journal of Employment Counseling*, 1980, *17*, 288–98.

Dillard, J. M. and N. J. Campbell. "Career Values and Aspirations of Adult Female and Male Puerto Ricans, Blacks, and Anglos." *Journal of Employment Counseling* (1982).

Dillard, J. M. and N. J. Campbell. "Influences of Puerto Rican, Black, and Anglo Parents' Career Behavior on their Adolescent Children's Career Development," *Vocational Guidance Quarterly*, 1981, *30*, 139–48.

Dillard, J. M. and D. W. Perrin. "Puerto Rican, Black and Anglo Adolescents' Career Aspirations, Expectations, and Maturity." *Vocational Guidance Quarterly*, 1980, *28*, 313–21.

Dillard, J. M., R. L. Kinnison, and B. Peel. "Multicultural Approach to Mainstreaming: A Challenge to Counselors, Teachers, Psychologists, and Administrators." *Peabody Journal of Education*, 1980, *57*, *276–90*.

Epstein, C. F. "Positive Effects of the Multiple Negative: Explaining the Success of Black Professional Women." *American Journal of Sociology*, 1973, *78*, 913–35.

Etzkowitz, H., and G. M. Schaflander. *Ghetto Crisis: Riots of Reconciliation?* Boston: Little, Brown, and Co., 1969.

Locating Black Americans

According to the United States Census, *Current Population Reports* (1979), in 1978, 25.4 million Black Americans resided in the United States, an increase of one million over 1975. In 1980, there were 26,488,218 Black Americans living in the United States (U.S. Bureau of Census, 1981). The 1978 and 1980 Black population figures represented about 12 percent of the total national population.

Patterns of resident distribution among Blacks throughout this country are interesting. A slight migration toward the North began during World War I and increased following the war. Significant migration of Blacks from the South to the North occurred during the 1920s; the rate slowed during the 1930s. From 1940 to 1970, approximately 1.5 million Blacks left the South. A different migration trend occurred during the 1970s when fewer Blacks left the South and many Blacks moved there. Fifty-three percent of the Black population resided in the South in 1970; this figure had not changed in 1975. The migration of Blacks into and out of the South leveled off after 1975 (U.S. Bureau of Census, *Current Population Reports*, 1979).

In 1978, the regional population distribution of Black Americans was 9 percent in the West, 18 percent in the Northeast, 20 percent in the North Central section, and 53 percent in the South. Metropolitan and nonmetropolitan residence figures of 1978 indicate that 20 percent of the Black American population lived in suburbs, 25 percent in nonmetropolitan areas, and 55 percent in central cities (U.S. Bureau of Census, *Current Population Reports*, 1979).

Social Values

Any attempt to identify common experiences among Black American values is risky; Blacks are not a homogeneous population. Yet literature suggests that Black Americans generally share a past of ethnocentric oppression, discrimination, and prejudice. Within these shared experiences, a commonality of variables emerge to unify cultural experiences; for example,

Blacks share a strong sense of collective consciousness regarding their ethnic identity, kinship, or collective unity.

The Black movement that flowered in the 1960s grew out of a Black community that sought to preserve the self-definition of the Black Americans' identity. This reaffirmation of an ethnic unity was necessary to enable Blacks to rise above social and economic obstacles. Thus, for most Blacks, individual identity and achievement orientations are transcended by identifying with and achieving for their reference group—Black Americans.

Few data have been presented to describe the strengths of Black families. Hill (1972), using statistical data obtained from the United States Census Bureau; the Department of Labor; and the Department of Human Services, documents five fundamental strengths that have enabled Black families to survive in a dominant Anglo society: (1) strong kinship bonds, (2) adaptability of family roles, (3) high achievement orientation, (4) strong work orientation, and (5) religious orientation.

Strong Black American ties have helped to bond family members into basic social units. Kinship often extends beyond the nuclear family to include other individuals such as grandparents, uncles, and aunts. Elderly parents often share their children's homes rather than going into nursing homes. Psychological, social, and economic deprivation fostered this close-knit, protective family sharing.

Historically, as well as presently, the adaptability of family roles among Black Americans has been a significant factor in maintaining stability. For example, in the absence of two parents in the home, many older Black children are left with the responsibility of caring for their younger siblings. There are many female-headed households. Because both parents often work, the reversal of spouse roles may occur; for example, the mother may wash the car or repair a minor household appliance, and the father may clean the house or prepare meals.

Several writers, such as Goodwin (1971), Sochen (1972), Johnson (1974), and Columbia Broadcasting System (CBS) (1974), maintain that Blacks espouse the American work ethic in the manner of lower and middle-class Anglos. Goodwin's (1971) and CBS's (1974) studies of attitudes toward work indicated that more than half of the Black and Anglo respondents indicated that they would work whether they had to or not. In their study of career values, Dillard and Campbell (1982) found that Black women strongly prefer to stay active and busy in a work setting.

Many investigations suggest that Blacks have high career and educational aspirations (Willie, 1974; Smith, 1976; Dillard and Perrin, 1980; Dillard and Campbell, 1981). Results of within-group research on aspirations among lower and middle-socioeconomic status Blacks further suggest that the two groups have similar aspirations (Willie, 1974; Smith, 1976).

Religion is another dominant value. Although there are diversified religious orientations among Black Americans, a strong adherence to religion continues to be an important dimension of Blacks' lives (Frazier, 1964; Richardson, 1966; Pinkney, 1969). According to Frazier (1964), Christianity played a major role in developing solidarity among Blacks when they otherwise lacked social cohesion and a structured social life. It also organized the Blacks' existence and provided a rationale for life. As late as 1965, according to Richardson's study (1966), 80 percent of approximately 19 million Black Americans participated in a religion. Even after taking into account the decline in attendance among the young in recent years, religion continues to provide an important link between the church and the Black American family.

In short, these orientations—kinship bonds, adaptable family roles, high achievement and strong work incentives, and strong religious ties—are essential ingredients in the lives of most Black Americans. Yet counselors should remember that individual differences are important. Acceptance and practice of these values will vary according to an individual's socialization and identification with Black and Anglo value systems. Identification may be stronger with some values and weaker with others.

Family Characteristics

Analyses of Black families have focused mostly on the weakness of the family structure: the high incidence of broken homes, female-headed homes, and separation of children (Frazier, 1939; Moynihan, 1965; Etzhowitz and Schaflander, 1969). In past decades, many authors and researchers ignored two-parent Black families and those Blacks who had obtained middle-socioeconomic status.

The Black family household may consist of only a husband and wife; it may be a nuclear family—including children and a husband and a wife; or it may be an attenuated family—children and only one parent. Such families also might be subdivided into the extended family that includes one or more kin and the nuclear family; a subfamily that includes kin of one family who joins another nuclear family; and the augmented family that comprises individuals who have no blood or kin ties (e.g., boarders and roomers).

Only recently have conscientious efforts been focused on the positive functions (Hill, 1972) rather than the mere structures of the Black family. Recent research results reveal that the traditional Black family is not structurally determined from Anglo family patterns. Rather, the Black family represents, to a large extent, a unique culture model with its own inherent resources. The extended family might be considered one of these resources. Several individual households coexist within this kind of family structure. According to Bims (1974), this family structure represents a multi-household. A multi-household has advantages. Usually, at least one member is present to provide emotional and economic support, and family members often perform necessary social duties for one another, even teaching the young and positively assisting in the family's internal conflicts. Also, family members often assist other members in searching for a job or home and in caring for the children and the ill. While some characteristics may be determined by social and economic conditions, the underlying basis of the Black extended family is similar to that in some western African colonies where such families prevail (Nobles, 1972).

Usually, concern is shown to all family members. Status is observed, but not emphasized; a family member who is educationally, vocationally, or financially superior to other members is respected and accepted. Additionally, there is mutual respect for "blood" kin that discourages interpersonal conflicts. The family interrelationship underscores cooperation and sharing .

Also included in the extended family are the illegitimate children born into a Black family. These children are not viewed as socially embarrassing or stigmatizing (Staples, 1971; Blackwell, 1975). Although Black families are concerned with illegitimacy, children are not stigmatized by the conditions of their birth. Staples (1971) contends that Black children possess a significant value separate from their birth. Essentially, the notion of "illegitimate Black children" in the Black community is nonexistent. Staples (1971) further states, "All (Black) children are legitimate and have a value to their families and their community" (p. 135).

Another characteristic of the Black family is its ability to maintain integrity while adapting to different economic and social conditions; for example, while migrating from the rural South to industrial settings in the North. Many Black households have been reestablished from a rural to an urban area. Bims (1974) reports that few changes in the structure of the family occur even though life-style, residence, and income are altered.

Analysis of 1970 United States Census Data (Blackwell, 1975), indicates that approximately 70 percent of all Black family units represent a "two-parent, nuclear family" (p. 40). This is the dominant pattern among Black families in this country. Spaights (1973) states that "most Black families are stable and are headed by men . . . most still married to their first wives" (p. 128). According to the U.S. Bureau of Census, 1979, the number of two-spouse Black families went down from 77 percent in 1940 to 61 percent in 1975 to 56 percent in 1978. The general population is also experiencing a similar downward trend in two-spouse families.

Herzog and Lewis (1970) maintain that an urban Black family headed by a woman (and generally mislabeled as matriarchal) is not the norm among lower-class Blacks. The norm is a stable marriage where the male is the major breadwinner. TenHouten (1970) found that "lower-class Black husbands are highest on male dominance ideology, about the same as

[Anglos] on conjugal decision power, and similar to middle-class Blacks and [Anglos] on family type" (p. 164).

Although literature and research findings are scanty concerning middle-class Blacks, some attention has been given to their life-styles and values. For instance, according to Jackson ("The Black Middle Class Defined," 1973), most middle-class Black families value achievement and talent, education, property, and love for their children (as do most lower-class Black families). She further maintains that there is egalitarianism in spouse relationships. Willie (1974) investigated values and life-styles in two hundred case studies of middle, working, and lower-class Black families. His research findings indicated that there is equal sharing between middle-class Black parents in household responsibilities. Further, his study revealed that middle-class Black families place a high degree of emphasis on educational achievement. Most parents of such families strive to provide their children with opportunities that were lacking in their own experiences: music lessons, recreational activities, and social opportunities. Parents have a strong attitude toward work and success. Work is a time-consuming experience that provides little time for recreation and community involvement, except for regular participation in church activities. Finally, Willie found that middle-class Black parents attempt to instill in "their children positive attitudes toward work and thrift" (p. 54). For example, each child is expected to perform some kind of work within the home to earn his allowance.

In conclusion, the Black family adapts to society in various ways, depending upon its socioeconomic standing. The unique adaptation by the Black family is further differentiated by variations in family life-style reflecting degrees of identity with certain values. Yet, the basis for understanding the Black family is through its interactional processes.

Socioeconomic Characteristics

Regional income data reported by the United States Bureau of Census, *Current Population Reports* (1979), indicated that in the South, North, and West, Black families have experienced growth in real income; the rise was higher in the South than in other regions. From 1963 to 1974, the median income for

Black families doubled in the South, going from $3,350 to $6,730. In the North and West, income rose from $6,450 in 1953 to $9,360 in 1974. Approximately 30 percent of 5.8 million Black families in 1977 had incomes of $15,000 or more, compared to 57 percent of all Anglo families.

Wattenberg and Scammon (1973) maintain that 52 percent of Blacks have obtained middle-class status. In a special issue of *Ebony* (1973) on the Black middle-class, however, several prominent Blacks refuted Wattenberg and Scammon's claim. These Blacks argued that more than 50 percent of Black people in America are below the middle-socioeconomic level. A national survey conducted by CBS (1974) found that the earning of both Black husbands and wives often are essential to obtain and maintain middle-class standards. Thus, the wife's income is a significant contribution to the Black family's financial status. The earnings of Black women increased sevenfold from 1947 to 1974, compared to a fourfold increase for Anglo women. The income gains for Black men during that period were significantly less. There was no improvement in median income for Black families from 1974 to 1977. During this time the number of poor Black families increased significantly; the increase in poverty for Anglos was negligible.

Black unemployment statistics are also significant socioeconomic indicators. The unemployment rate for Blacks decreased somewhat from 1975 to 1977 from 14.7 to 13.9 percent; during this same period, however, the unemployment rate for Anglos decreased substantially from 7.8 to 6.2 percent.

Unemployment conditions for Black teenagers did not improve during the 1975 to 1977 period. It remained at 40 percent compared to 36.9 percent for the national teenage unemployment rate (U.S. Bureau of Census, *Current Population Report*, 1979, p. 188).

In 1977, 23 percent of all Black men and 44 percent of all Black women were employed in white-collar positions. Fifty-eight percent of Black men were employed in blue-collar positions, while one-third (37 percent) of the Black women were employed in service work. Black women made up approximately 11 percent of all women employed, and they held 7 percent of the white-collar occupations.

Despite the recent socioeconomic gains, most Blacks have not yet attained middle-class status. There are inter- and intra-regional variations among Blacks' socioeconomic conditions. Socioeconomic conditions affect the Black's behavior in the counseling setting.

Educational Characteristics

The United States Bureau of Census, *Current Population Reports* (1979), indicates an increase in school enrollment of Blacks across most age groups during the 1890–1975 period. Substantial growth in school attendance among Blacks enrolled in school above the compulsory attendance age of 16 reflects a rise in the number of Blacks enrolled in higher education institutions. While there was only a slight increase of Black men and women enrolled in college during the 1950s, college enrollment surged in the 1960–1970 period and continued into the early 1970s. A 21 percent college enrollment rate was reported in 1975 for Black men and women who were 18 to 24 years old, compared to only 5 percent in 1950. Seven in ten Blacks between the ages of 25 to 34 completed high school in 1975, compared to three in ten in 1960 and one in ten during 1940. This educational gain was still 13 percentage points lower than that of Anglos in the same age bracket, and twice as many Anglos as Blacks graduated from college. While fewer Blacks age 25 to 34 graduated from high school in the South than in the North and West during 1975, the percentage of Black college graduates in the South was generally the same as that in the North and West.

A surge in the literacy rate among Blacks occurred between the nineteenth and twentieth centuries. For instance, only about 39 percent of Blacks aged 15 and over were literate in 1890, compared to about 96 percent of Blacks aged 14 and over in 1969. The literacy rate for Blacks is higher in the North and West than in the South, and higher for younger age groups than for individuals aged 45 and over.

In spite of these educational gains, many young Blacks continue to be plagued with less than desirable educational achievement. For instance, as recently as 1950, substantial numbers of Black students functioned below their grade level in school. Although there has been a decrease in grade retardation (functioning below grade level) since 1950, nearly one-fifth of the Black students between the ages of fourteen to seventeen were overage for their grade in 1970.

Black people can be found at every educational level. Many young Blacks who graduate from high school elect immediate entry into the employment market, while others who do not want a college education choose vocational or technical education. Many young Blacks are now pursuing positions in such fields as medicine, engineering, business, psychology, and law.

The educational levels of Blacks vary from individual to individual as well as from region to region. Although educational gains have been made, greater improvements are still warranted in certain areas; for example, in decreasing the student dropout rate and increasing scholastic achievement.

Language Characteristics

The language spoken by Black Americans in the United States is English, which is not to say that there are not varieties of Black speech. Many Blacks communicate eloquently, using standard American English, while others speak one of several Black dialects.

Some researchers (Labov, 1966, 1972; Dillard, 1972; Taylor, 1978) have noted that Black persons exhibit a variety of English dialects. Blacks' use of the English language straddles both Mainstream American English and what some researchers, such as Dillard (1972), label as "Black English," "Black dialect," or "nonstandard" speech. According to Wright and Isenstein (1975), one expert, Dr. Robert Williams, has chosen the term *Ebonics*, "Ebony or black plus phonics or speech sounds" (p. 13), to counterbalance the derogatory connotations attached to such terms as "Black English," "Black dialect," or "nonstandard" speech. An example of Ebonics and its meaning in Mainstream American English (MAE) is: "I don't know what page you are on" meaning "I don't understand what you are saying" (Wright and Isenstein, 1975, p. 13). Another example is what Jones (1979) considers as "phonological distinctions between Ebonics and MAE, such as the use of /d/ for /th/ in the initial position (the=d or they=day) or the use of /f/ for /th/ in the terminal position (e.g., mouth=mouf or Ruth=ruf)." (pp. 424–425). Tolliver-Weddington (1979) states that "Ebonics is more inclusive than Black English, Black language, or Black dialect, because it refers to both linguistic as well as paralinguistic features of the language" (p. 165). Wofford (1979) maintains that "Ebonics is an oral communication system used consistently by 80 percent of the Americans of African ancestry; 19 percent of the Black Ebonics speakers' language is indistinguishable from Mainstream American English (or standard English) speakers except for slight differences in pronunciations and vocal quality; and 1 percent being non-Ebonics speakers" (p. 368). She states that Ebonics "consists of phonology, syntax, morphology, semantics, lexicon, rate, rhythm, stress, and nonverbal communication" (p. 368).

Language is a result of an individual's socialization. Ethnic and cultural experiences, as well as interaction with other groups, help to determine how a person uses language. Counselors, therefore, should note that many Black persons use only Mainstream American English, while others may communicate with Ebonics. Many Blacks are proficient at both Mainstream American English and Ebonics, but they selectively apply them, depending upon the situation.

Religious Characteristics

As stated earlier, religion is one of the fundamental strengths of American Blacks. Religion plays a significant role in the lives of most Black people, with the church functioning as the central meeting place in the community—the place to attain the emotional inspiration needed for adaptation to social and economic conditions. About 90 percent of Black people are Protestant.

Religious beliefs range from the sects and cults of lower-class congregations, wherein emotionalism is a central factor, to services in upper-class Protestant churches such as Presbyterian, Episcopal, and Congregational, where emotionalism is unimportant (Pinkney, 1969, p. 112). Black Americans' religious affiliations run the gamut from Baptist, Methodist, Episcopal, Roman Catholic, Seventh-Day Adventist, Congregational, Holiness, Black Muslim, to Judaism. Rabbi Abel Respes, a Black Jew, is the founder of a Black Jewish community in New Jersey. Many of the new cult services are conducted in languages other than English, most commonly, Arabic and Hebrew.

These are but a few features that delineate the religious orientations of Black Americans. The Black church (where the congregation is predominantly Black) has also played an important role in the civil rights protest actions.

Self-Concepts and the Black Image

Early research literature on Blacks' self-concepts reflected a mostly negative image compared to those of their Anglo counterparts. Several researchers, such as Deutsch (1967), Ausubel and Ausubel (1967), and Goldberg (1967) suggested that Black persons viewed themselves as inferior, with self-hatred, negative self-esteem, and self-deprecatory attitudes. Such reports reflect a dismal picture of Blacks' self-image, but in some cases, the research was faulty. For example, inappropriate theoretical models and insensitive instrumentations were used in some research. Because of this, Poussaint (1974) maintains that the negative self-concepts of Black youth should be valued only in relative terms. He advocates that a self-concept is best assessed in the context of the independent values of Black people and should not be measured against that of Anglo society. Poussaint noted that the self-concept of a middle-class Black youth residing in an integrated community differs from that of the low-income Black youth residing in a central city and attending a segregated school. He further states that some older Black persons whose social experiences differ from those of youth of the new generation may have self-images of submission and passivity. Such self-images are no longer acceptable to Black youth reared in a society that has undergone important changes in ethnic and cultural policy, which have resulted in an increasingly positive self-image for Blacks.

An investigation conducted by Dillard (1976) among 252 suburban and urban middle-class and urban, lower-class, sixth-grade Black males from forty-two different school settings in Monroe, Erie, and Westchester Counties of New York state revealed that there were no significant differences in these males' self-images. Levine (1976), who investigated the ethnic esteem among Anglo, Black, and Chicano second and fifth graders, reported that the Black students generally indicated a higher preference for their own ethnic group than did the Anglo and Chicano students. Some research literature maintains that the Black children's self-concepts are comparable to those of their Anglo counterparts (Coleman, 1966; Gibby and Gabler, 1967) while other research indicates that Black children's self-concepts are more positive than those of Anglos (Soares and Soares, 1969, 1970; Trowbridge, 1972; Larkin, 1972).

Most of the early research contained data to support the postulate that a Black person's self-concept was lower or negative when compared with that of Anglos; this was especially true of lower-class Blacks. In recent years, however, a growing body of research findings has uncovered a more positive view of the Black self-concept.

IMPERATIVES FOR DIFFERENTIAL COUNSELING WITH BLACK AMERICANS

Despite Blacks' positive orientations in work, adaptability of roles, religion, and educational achievement, most Black people continue to be plagued by many ethnocentric biases in employment hiring practices, low pay, monocultural education modes, poor housing facilities in central cities, and inadequate state and federal social services. Few Black persons have been fully absorbed into the predominantly Anglo society. These and other biases are predictors of significant amounts of psychological stress, frustration, and depression. The central source of extrapsychic stress for many Black people, particularly those at the lower end of the educational and economic spectrum, is their inability to adjust to an alienating and discriminating middle-class, Anglo society.

Some Black persons do not experience the full impact of prejudice; they identify more with the cultural patterns or value orientations of the dominant Anglo culture as well as with their Black Afro-American culture. Other Blacks identify solely with value orientations in the Black culture while still others emulate only those of middle-class Anglos. Therefore, to provide appropriate treatments and attain positive desired outcomes, it must be remembered that Blacks have a broad spectrum of value orientations or cultural behaviors that must be considered in counseling.

Acculturation and Black Americans

The early historical experiences of Black people indicate that they were stripped of much of their African culture during slavery; however, there still remain traces of Africanism among many Blacks, e.g., the pattern of family socialization. Furthermore, some Black individuals and organizations, e.g., National Improvement Association, Black Muslims, and the United States Nationalist groups, have attempted to regain or preserve the Black Afro-American culture. Nonetheless, unlike most European immigrants to the United States, Black Americans have not been assimilated into the American society as full, participating citizens. Ethnocentric attitudes and practices have limited most Blacks' progress in such areas as employment. A recent survey (Williams, Buckley, and Lord, 1979) indicated that Black respondents felt discrimination continued to be strong in 1978. Also, these Blacks felt that alienation of Black people was on the increase in 1978 more so than they did in 1970.

Despite the continued discrimination and alienation practices against Black Americans, Black people have acculturated or adopted many of the cultural patterns and value orientations of the dominant Anglo society. Gordon (1964) maintains that Blacks' acculturation varies with their social class. For example, Gordon argues that most middle- and upper-class Blacks have approximated the standard behavior patterns sanctioned by the dominant Anglo society rather than those of other Black social-class groups. However, it should be noted that a vast majority of Black people are in the lower socioeconomic group.

Black people are still faced with the challenge of assimilation. A great many Blacks are encapsulated in their own ghettos and have limited power to participate in the dominant culture of the United States. Such conditions often adversely affect mental health. Thomas and Lindenthal (1975) report that there is mounting evidence highly associated with physical and emotional illness and inequities inherent in dominant social systems.

The psychological consequences of being a Black person may vary according to the degree of acculturation experienced by that person. For example, at one end of the continuum, Blacks identify strongly with their Afro-American culture but are locked into low economic conditons and unable to penetrate the system to eradicate these economic conditions; this is a stressful experience. Increased acculturation for Black people, particularly for Black women, may be an extremely expensive experience that far exceeds ethnocentric practices encountered by many members of other ethnic and cultural groups. Wright (1978) states: "A predominantly Anglo university setting is more stressful for Black students because of the complicating factors of racial and cultural variations between the Anglo students and the Blacks" (p. 3). For example, Wright's research results showed that 33 percent of the Black women who attended a predominantly Anglo university experienced difficulty in finding activities on campus that were relevant to the Black culture. The Black male may also experience a lack of culturally relevant activities, but to a lesser degree; since most have greater access and mobility to activities off-campus than most Black women at predominantly Anglo institutions. Wright further reported that 38 percent of the Black women reported having problems with their health, such as "migraine or tension headaches, depression, and exhaustion" (Wright, 1978, p. 6) as a result of their inability to adjust to a stressful environment. Thirty-nine percent of the Black women disclosed that they had problems in developing good heterosexual relationships because there were too few Black men on campus.

Many Black women who strive to acculturate Anglo cultural patterns endure frustration and stress from fear of succeeding as professionals in the career marketplace. Such professionals may feel that certain career levels are indeed counterproductive to maintaining and/or developing sound relationships with Black men who might view their success as threatening. Mosely's research finding (cited in Smith et al. 1978) tends to support this notion. For instance, more than half of the Black women administrators in the study were single (in addition to divorced, widowed, or separated). Similarly, about a third of the Black professional women surveyed by Epstein (1973) were single .

Some Black women expect that success in achievement-related situations will be followed by negative consequences; this arouses fear of success in achievement-motivated women, which then inhibits their performance and levels of aspiration. For example, Turner and McCaffrey (1974) reported that Black women's career choices were made on the basis of preferences and expectations from their families and others rather than their own. These Black women did not expect to achieve their preferred career goal despite the level of career expectation.

These are only a few examples that suggest that adopting Black as well as dominant Anglo value orientations can be anxiety producing for many Black persons. The difference in strength of identification with Black or Anglo value orientations may also promote conflict, particularly where the individual's cultural and personal needs are not met. How Black persons identify with cultural patterns or value orientations determines how they perceive themselves and affects the counseling relationship. The extent to which Black clients have acculturated dictates counseling strategies. How Black people view counseling and use counseling facilities appears to be associated with their level of acculturation.

Black Americans' Attitudes toward Mental Health and Mental Illness

Blacks' attitudes toward mental health may be affected by the kinds of cultural experiences they have encountered. Tinling (1967) reported that some rural Southern Blacks and Anglos practice mental health and mental illness as a form of "root work," a derivative of voodoo. Tinling found that the Northern migration of Blacks has brought this practice to most industrial cities in the north. Persons who practice root work believe that illness or death can occur to an individual who has been hexed, affected by an evil spirit. Root workers or root doctors assist in putting a hex on someone. A hex is generally done by placing powders in a person's food or drink. Other forms of hexing are touching the victim with your hand that has been "dressed" by the root worker, acting on the victim's personal belongings such as hair, clothing, or an image of the victim (outside the victim's presence), or giving the victim the evil eye by looking him or her directly into the eye. The root worker's treatments to remove the hex are vague. Tinling suggests that a root worker's "treatment includes listening to the patient's complaints, certain incantations, use of powers of liquids to counter the spell, and specific advice for future behavior" (p. 484).

Attitudes and perceptions of mental health and mental illness are important considerations for counselors when working with Black clients. Black acculturation levels are associated with differing levels of reception to and usage of counseling services. Social class may likewise be linked to Blacks' attitudes toward mental health and mental illness.

Ring and Schein (1970) investigated attitudes of lower-middle-class Blacks of 388 households in a Philadelphia community. They found that 85 percent of the Black respondents knew that there were various types of mental illnesses. Approximately 70 percent of these respondents believed that certain types of emotional disturbances can be treated in the home. More than 75 percent of those respondents felt that emotional illness could be positively affected through treatment. Ring and Schein also found an overall pattern suggesting acceptance of mental illness. Forty-eight percent of the respondents would seek treatment from physicians and 19 percent from psychiatrists for psychological-emotional problems. Three percent of the Blacks indicated they would seek treatment from the clergy; fewer than 2 percent, from psychologists and social workers; and fewer than 2 percent, from their family members or friends. Slightly less than 85 percent had sought help from physicians for psychological problems. Eleven percent of the respondents had received treatment from nonmedical personnel. Only 4 percent of the respondents used nonmedical professionals such as social workers, clergymen, and teachers for treatment. Ring and Schein also reported that mental health practices and attitudes toward mental illness within the Black group studied indicated that Blacks tended to be less inclined to use mental health professionals compared to using physicians. Many Blacks said they would not attempt to seek treatment for mental illness from professional counselors. While the degree of acculturation may be related to Blacks' attitudes toward mental health and mental illness, such attitudes may also be associated with their attitudes toward counseling professionals.

Attitudes toward Counselors

The outcomes of the counseling relationship with Black clients are tied closely to their perceptions of and experiences with middle-class counselors. Several experts feel that counseling by middle-class counselors does not reflect the needs of Black clients, and that individual as well as cultural factors of such clients are frequently ignored. Smith (1977) contends that much of this occurs because Black clients are viewed from stereotypical notions that generalize them as a group without regard for their diversity.

Russell (1970) maintains that frequently the Black student perceives counseling services "as an instrument of repression, controlled by counselors who constitute a roadblock he must somehow manage to get around if he has ambitions that do not coincide with those his counselors consider appropriate for him" (p. 722). Such students believe that their counselors have ethnocentric biases that preclude treating them as individuals who have potentials, aspirations, and emotions similar to those of Anglos. Ayers (1970) argues that counselors' attitudes are the variable that has the most impact on the counseling process. Other variables that have an impact on the counseling process, although to a lesser degree, are the counselors' awareness of the clients' values, attitudes, communication patterns, and life-styles.

Can Anglo counselors effectively provide counseling services to Black clients? Arguments have been made on both sides of this issue. Some professionals claim that the counselor's ethnicity does not necessarily limit his effectiveness (Vontress, 1969; Walker, 1970; Backner, 1970; Lewis, Lych, and Munger, 1978), while others assert that clients should have counselors with ethnic and cultural backgrounds and experiences similar to their own (Ayers, 1970; Williams and Kirkland, 1971; Gunnings, 1971; Johnson, 1974).

Recent investigative studies on the counselor preferences of Blacks suggest that counselors of similar backgrounds and socioeconomic positions do carry more weight. For example, Gilsdorf (1978) found that counselor ethnicity was perceived by male college students as an important factor in choosing a counselor. The Black students revealed a significantly higher preference for a Black counselor than did Mexican American or Anglo students, and Anglo students indicated a higher preference for an Anglo counselor than did Black and Mexican American students. Results from a study on Black, Puerto Rican, Chinese, Spanish-American, and Anglo college students conducted by Gordon and Grantham (1979) revealed a slight preference, particularly by the ethnic minority students, for counselors of the same sex, age, and ethnicity as their own. In addition, these students indicated a high preference for counselors of the same social class. Gordon and Grantham's finding on social class preference appears to have a direct relationship to conflict between Black clients and Black therapists who hold dissimilar social class positions. Calnek (1969) contends that Black therapists' levels of acculturation may negatively influence their behavior in the therapeutic setting with lower-class Black clients. Calnek suggests: "Too many [therapists], in order to attract the continued approval of white co-workers or in a general pursuit of white middle-class values, have ignored their unique knowledge of their ethnic background and have aped traditional white-oriented perceptions of the behavior of Blacks" (p. 40).

Clearly, preferences for counselors of the same ethnicity and social class position should be essential considerations in providing effective services to Black clients. Such attitudes and preferences toward counselors may be related to the degree that Black clients have acculturated middle-class values, and the effectiveness of the communication between Black clients and counselors is also linked to the clients' attitudes toward the counseling interaction.

Communication in Counseling

Communicative interactions between the client and the counselor are important considerations, particularly when the client is Black. Effective communication between the two participants is contingent upon linguistic compatability. Many of the goals communicated in counseling are aimed at the counseling process, e.g., empathy and genuineness, rather than at the needs of Black clients. Consequently, many counselors operate under the assumption that most clients are "middle-class neurotics" (Ayers, 1970, p. 197). Too frequently, according to Walker (1968), counselors communicate in vague abstract terms such as "personal adjustment" and "motivation."

According to Schumacher, Banikiotes, and Banikiotes (1972), counselors who effectively communicate with and relate to Black clients are able to meet at least some of their clients' needs, but their research revealed linguistic incompatibility between the two groups. The Black students were significantly more knowledgeable about "Black student words" than were the Anglo students who, in turn, were appreciably more knowledgeable about these words than the Anglo counselors. Another finding indicated that Anglo counselors were significantly more knowledgeable of "counselor words" than were Anglo students, who, in turn, were more knowledgeable about these words than were Black students. These researchers concluded that a constructive counseling relationship between Black students and Anglo counselors is likely to be a difficult task.

Tucker and Gunnings (1974) state that many counselors focus on the individual's responsibility for his dilemma as opposed to examining those factors, within the individual's environment that may cause the problem. For instance, the Black client's counseling needs may be more in the nature of attaining employment than in improving his relations with other individuals or in overcoming his feelings of alienation (Walker, 1968).

The counselor should be aware of within-group variations in language and its use among Black people, which vary to the extent of their acculturation to Anglo patterns. Grantham's study (1973) revealed that Black college students did not use Ebonics (or Black English) in the counseling interviews with Anglo counselors. He surmised that these students received cues that suggested they should use Mainstream American English, and they responded to this. Although the Black counselors in the study provided higher levels of facilitative conditions in the initial interview than did the Anglo counselors, the Black college students explored themselves at greater depth with the Anglo counselors than with the Black counselors.

Value and language orientations of middle-class counselors and Black clients may vary. Such variance can impede the process of Black clients, particularly among the lower class, especially if measured solely by middle-class Anglo standards. Because the expectations of Black clients and counselors often are low, the facilitative or therapeutic communication necessary to develop a sound relationship within the counseling process may not take place.

Drug, Alcohol, and Black-on-Black Crime

According to Harvey (1972), drug and alcohol use and abuse in the Black community are increasing. The oppressive conditions and ethnocentric biases that prevail in a dominant Anglo society are believed to be significantly related to some Black persons' excessive use of both drugs and alcohol.

The August 1979 special issue of *Ebony* Magazines' "Black-on-Black crime" reported that hard drug users are responsible for much of the criminal activity in the Black community. Black drug users victimize other Black persons in close proximity, such as family members and neighbors.

Kaestner, Rosen, and Appel (1977) researched the patterns of drug use and abuse among Black, Hispanic, and Anglo males. They found that most of the Black males perceived the use of pills as less predictable, more dangerous, and less satisfactory for attaining a "good high" than either opiates and cocaine. The research also indicated that ethnicity plays a significant part in the role of drug-use patterns. The study also suggested that anxiety and sensation seeking contributed to the variations in use of drugs. These researchers concluded that the Black males' drug-use patterns were influenced by their world views, which were attained through contact with their social and physical environments. Perhaps those world views or perceptions were attained as a result of oppressed conditions.

Research by O'Neal, Shackleford, and Smith (1973) revealed that the problem of drug abuse is a severe one in the Black community, particularly in the inner city, and that the drug problem among Black students in public schools is increasing; however, Wheeler (1976) maintains that most drug treatment facilities are aimed at problems in suburban communities.

Beverly (1975) found that alcoholism is a problem for many Black people. He further stated that most current intervention strategies have not been standardized for Blacks and do not encompass the Black experience and its uniqueness.

In summary, drug and alcohol use and abuse have been identified as important concerns with many Black communities, and there is a relationship between young Black drug abusers and crime in the Black communities. Treatment facilities and culturally relevant counseling interventions are inadequate.

Black Students and Schools

Breaking through the monocultural education system in most public schools to attain an adequate education has generally been an uphill struggle for Black students. Granted, many Black students have achieved an education despite ethnocentric biases among middle-class Anglo teachers and limited curricula, but many Black students continue to function below their grade level, and there is an overrepresentation of Blacks in special classes for the educable mentally retarded. Achievement is often affected by teachers' anticipated notions, mind sets, attitudes, or expectations (Dillard, Kinnison, and Peel, 1980).

Few educators have identified Black students' cultural backgrounds as a significant factor in their overall development. To ignore or demean them is to contribute negatively to the self-fulfilling prophecy. Differences between Black students and middle-class Anglo students are often used as motivation for further acculturation rather than to promote Anglos' and Blacks' co-existence by encouraging respect for diversity. Dillard, Kinnison, and Peel (1980) suggest that a multicultural philosophy should permeate the entire educational curriculum.

Unless individual and cultural adaptations are made in the curriculum and modes of instruction, little will occur to enhance the potential of Black students who desperately need confluent instructional approaches (affective and cognitive). Some Black students need only a cognitive instructional approach to achieve in school. Educators need to consider the variations in learning styles of Black students and award each student individual attention based on his needs. Failure to deal with these factors effectively will perpetuate the educational dilemma of Blacks.

SOME PRACTICAL APPROACHES TO COUNSELING WITH BLACK AMERICANS

Counselors and mental health professionals can work more effectively with Black Americans through bicultural-bilingual counseling interventions, to do this, counselors must become skilled in Ebonics and mainstream English, and they must develop familiarity with Black (including social class variations) and middle-class Anglo cultural patterns. Although it may be helpful when appropriate, counselors need not communicate to Black clients in Ebonics. Black counselors should avoid using only middle-class Anglo counseling interventions and should seek innovative counselor preparation programs, which include bicultural and bilingual emphasis of Black and middle-class Anglo cultures (Gunnings, 1970; Bell, 1970).

Bilingual counseling with Black persons becomes especially important when the extent of Blacks' acculturation level or the strength of their identity with the Black culture versus middle-class Anglo culture is examined. While acculturation appears to be a class phenomenon, it may also be a rejection of one's early behavioral pattern. For instance, middle or upper-class Black clients may be fluent in both Ebonics and mainstream English, these clients will shift to Ebonics only when emotionally charged. Based on Hartman's (1971) research of sociolinguistic patterns of Blacks, Labov

(1972) maintains that the linguistic patterns acquired during Black preadolescence appear more systematic than those acquired later, more deeply rooted; thus, they tend to surface when attention is relaxed and less focused on speech. The superimposed speech—mainstream English—acquired during late adolescence tends to appear much less systematic, and the speaker seldom has complete control over when he uses each dialect. Labov (1972) states "Speakers shift unconsciously to vernacular rules when they are in a casual situation with peers, or whenever emotional stress reduces their ability to monitor their own speech. Most speakers are only vaguely aware of this shifting" (p. 636). Since a Black client may employ both languages in the counseling interview, the counselor needs to be able to comprehend and communicate (if necessary) in a similar manner.

The use of either Ebonics or mainstream English is contingent upon the extent that Black clients identify with Black or middle-class Anglo cultures. Smith (1977) contends: "There is a difference between recognizing that [Black] people vary in their language style and trying to lump them all together according to their . . . [ethnic group] and socioeconomic status" (p. 383). For example, Black clients at one end of the spectrum may identify with Anglo dominant culture, communicate in mainstream English, and deal effectively with intrapsychic material derived from counseling interventions couched in middle-class traditional theories. Black clients at the other end of the spectrum may communicate in Ebonics and prefer that their positively desired outcomes be attained through nontraditional counseling intervention. Still other Black clients will identify with both Black and dominant Anglo cultures, communicate in mainstream English, and require traditional counseling interventions. Those Black clients at the middle of the spectrum are most likely to profit from bilingual-bicultural counseling approaches, however, some may require either Ebonics or mainstream English employed through nontraditional or traditional counseling to attain the optimal level of cultural relevance necessary for the client.

As one example of nontraditional counseling, Gunnings and

Simpkins (1972) advocate a systemic approach to counseling Black clients. This approach assumes that most problems that have been categorized as the client's problems are, in fact, problems within the system itself rather than the individual. Therefore, the counselor attempts to treat the system, e.g., instructional personnel in school or management and supervisory personnel in place of employment, for its problems by bringing about changed members. The focus is on "reordering of priorities, emphases, and goals, and is strategic in bringing about long-term effects on behavioral changes and personality development" (p. 5) of persons who contribute to the problems faced by Black clients. The "systemic approach" attempts to correct the causes rather than treat the symptoms. The counselor using the systemic approach functions as a change agent, a client advocate, or a consultant rather than as an individual counselor.

Many of the problems centered around drug and alcohol abuse among Blacks are linked to external frustrations wherein a goal, e.g., employment or education, is not attained for reasons over which such persons have no control. Thus, many Blacks experience external stress. Rather than focus strictly on the symptoms of problems, counselors might turn their attention to practical ways of resolving the problem. A client might be taught interview skills. In some cases, those who lack necessary work skills may require assistance in acquiring these skills.

The psychological conflicts faced by many Black women, as discussed earlier, often go unnoticed by counselors and personnel workers. Innovative methods are needed to counteract the stress of college and university environments for Black women on predominantly Anglo campuses. Wright (1978) suggests that information be made available explaining that other Black women encounter difficulties attaining dates on campuses. Counselors should assist organizations of Black women in creating solutions to these problems. The counselor should also assist these women in solving their academic and economic problems by pointing out the availability of tutorial help, financial assistance, and ways they can learn effective study skills. Wright also advocates counseling strategies to assist Black women in coping with ethnic and sexual discrimination in employment, as well as in realizing their self-worth and potential academically and professionally. Counselors should emphasize the strengths of Black women and encourage them to build on their own assets, abilities, and motivations.

In other situations, it may be necessary for counselors to develop assertiveness-training programs as described by Minor (1978) and Cheek (1976) for Black men and women. Assertiveness skills might be needed in situations involving education, job, housing, and obtaining financial assistance. According to Minor (1978):

> The assertiveness trainee (asserter) is aided in identifying situations in which individuals with whom he or she would like to be more assertive and is coached in the development and use of such [assertiveness] skills as eye contact, posture, gesture, tone of voice, timing, facial expressions, and message content. [P. 63]

Such training may be delivered through various methods such as role reversal, role playing, and observation, and through audiovisual materials.

The school setting is an important area of concern for many Blacks. Too often, though, they are left to fend for themselves without the assistance of counselors who understand their needs and concerns. Black students would benefit from the aid of counselors who function as student advocates "in disciplinary situations and in bridging student-teacher and student-administrator relationships" (Gunnings and Simpkins, 1972, p. 7). Similarly, Black students will benefit from counselors working with teachers to improve their perceptions of individual students' learning styles, developmental and behavioral patterns, attitudes, and relations with their peers. Counselors could provide preservice and inservice workshops for teachers to help them to become more familiar with the sociolinguistic conflict that some Black students have between Ebonics and Mainstream American English. (See McGinnis and Smitherman [1978] for a more detailed discussion of this phenomenon.) Jones (1979) contends that most Ebonics speakers understand mainstream English even if they cannot reproduce it in speech. For example, Seymour and Ralabate (1976) reported from their research results that while 80 to 90 percent of the Black third and fourth graders in the study showed competency in the use of the mainstream English "th" (e.g., mouth) in formal tests, 60 percent used the Ebonics "f" sound substitution (e.g., mouf) in spontaneous speech. This phenomenon is referred to as "style switching" (Labov, 1972). Dissemination of this kind of information pertaining to Black students' different linguistic styles may improve teachers' instructional approaches, which, in turn, will provide students with a more nearly equal access to an appropriate education.

Preservice and inservice workshops should also include new and available measures to tap cultural strengths of Black students and to identify gifted Black students whose potential has been clouded. Two promising assessments are Williams' (1972) *Black Intelligence Test of Cultural Homogeneity (BITCH)* and Mercer and Lewis' (1978) *System of Multicultural Pluralistic Assessment (SOMPA)*. Both the *BITCH* and *SOMPA* have been standardized for Blacks and are useful in identifying the potential of Black students.

SUMMARY

Counselors and other mental health workers should be aware of the cultural and individual diversity that exists among Black Americans. The sociocultural experiences of Black people influence their world views: attitudes, values, perceptions, family relationships, and relations with other persons. In counseling Blacks, nontraditional counseling techniques will be more effective with ethnic Blacks, and traditional techniques will work with those who are more acculturated.

The extent of acculturation for each Black client also needs to be considered when planning counseling goals and interventions. Whether the Black client identifies strongly as an Ebonics speaker, a mainstream English speaker, or uses both may have serious implications for bilingual-bicultural counseling, including, as just noted, the selection of strategies.

EXERCISES

The following exercises will give students some practice in understanding the cultural and ethnic variations of Black

Americans. These exercises will also give students the opportunity to examine certain counseling problems of Black clients and will allow students to develop possible solutions to these problems.

A. Divide students into small groups. They should read the example, and then attempt to identify the problem.

> Belinda, a thirty-five-year-old Black woman, is married and lives with her husband and three children. Her husband has completed high school and works as an automobile mechanic. Belinda had finished one-and-a-half years of college when they married, but she dropped out of college shortly after marriage. Now that the children are older, she would like to return to college to complete her bachelor's degree.
>
> However, Belinda states that whenever she tries to tell her husband about her wish to return to college—something that she really feels deeply about—she feels as though he doesn't want to hear about it. If she perceives the slightest hint that her husband isn't listening, she changes the topic rather than continue. But later, she gets angry at herself for not having said what she really wanted to say.

1. Describe Belinda's problem?
2. Do you see the husband as part of the problem? If so, to what extent?
3. Describe specifically what plans you would implement to improve Belinda's situation. To what extent should the husband be involved?

B. Divide students into small groups. They should read the example and then attempt to identify the problem.

> A twenty-three-year-old Black female college student, Katye, approaches a counselor in the corridor and states that she is scared. She has not performed very well in her courses this semester. Katye is achieving C's. She feels that she is not likely to flunk out of college, but she worries that she will lose her scholarship. Additionally, her father will be very angry, since he expects her to remain in school and maintain her scholarship to keep the tuition cost down.

Katye feels indecisive about what to do next. After listening to Katye in the corridor, the counselor responds by telling Katye to make an appointment with her secretary to see her in the counseling center.

1. What are the issues involved?
2. To what extent was the counselor correct or incorrect in not dealing with Katye's problem on the spot?
3. Would a traditional or nontraditional counseling approach be more effective in meeting Katye's needs? Tell why.
4. Devise a plan to assist Katye with her problem.

C. Ask students to read the example and follow the instructions.

Jean is a twelfth-grade Black female who wants to become a certified public accountant. From all indications (teacher recommendations, grades, test scores), Jean appears unable to handle the academic work of accounting school. She has come to you for assistance and support in finding an institution that will accept her. Jean's parents feel that she should be discouraged from applying to an accounting school.

Each student is to write a brief description of the situation and then suggest possible intervention strategies to the problem as he has perceived it. Compare these descriptions with other students' results to determine if class members of different ethnic and/or cultural groups perceive the problem differently.

D. Divide students into groups of three. Each group should read the example below and discuss the questions that follow.

Mrs. Brown, fifty-year-old Black woman, lives alone on her deceased husband's Social Security benefits. In the third counseling interview, she conveys to a middle-class Black counselor that she really feels that the counselor cannot be trusted. Mrs. Brown further states that every time she leaves, the counselor talks to others about her. She tells the counselor that just the other day, as she was walking through the corridor prior to their appointment, she overheard the counselor and other persons laughing about people who have problems like hers. Mrs. Brown doesn't like that kind of behavior. Thus, she wonders why she should tell the counselor her problems, since the counselor will likely make fun of her.

1. How do you perceive Mrs. Brown's problem?
2. To what extent do you see Mrs. Brown's perception of the counselor to be accurate?
3. If you were the counselor, how would you deal with this situation to prevent Mrs. Brown from dropping out of counseling?

References

Ausubel, D., and P. Ausubel. "Ego Development among Segregated Negro Children." In J. I. Roberts, ed., *School Children in Urban Slums.* New York: Free Press, 1967. Pp. 231–60.

Ayers, G. E. "The Disadvantaged: An Analysis of Factors Affecting the Counseling Relationship." *Rehabilitation Literature,* 1970, *31,* 194–99.

Backner, B. "Counseling Black Students: A Place for Whitey?" *Journal of Higher Education,* 1970, *41,* 630–37.

Bell, A. L., Jr. "The Culturally Deprived Psychologist." *Counseling Psychologist,* 1970, *2,* 104–7.

Beverly, C. C. "Toward a Model for Counseling Black Alcoholics." *Journal of Non-White Concerns in Personnel and Guidance,* 1975, *3,* 169–76.

Bims, H. "The Black Family: A Proud Reappraisal." *Ebony,* 1974, *29,* 118–21,123,125,127.

"The Black Middle-Class Defined." *Ebony,* 1973, *28,* 44–50.

Blackwell, J. E. *The Black Community: Diversity and Unity.* New York: Dodd, Mead and Co., 1975.

Calnek, M. "Racial Factors in the Countertransference: The Black Therapist and the Black Client." *American Journal of Orthopsychiatry,* 1970, *40,* 39–46.

Cheek, D. K. *Assertive Black . . . Puzzled White: A Black Perspective on Assertive Behavior.* San Luis Obispo, Calif.: Impact Pub. Inc., 1976.

Coleman, J. S. *Equality of Educational Opportunity*. Washington, D.C.: U.S. Government Printing Office, 1966.

Columbia Broadcasting System. "CBS News Special: Four Portraits in Black." New York: CBS Television Network, April 26, 1974. (Mimeographed transcript.)

Deutsch, M. "Minority Groups and Class Status as Related to Social and Personality Factors in Scholastic Achievement." In M. Deutsch and Ass. (eds.), *The Disadvantaged Child*. New York: Basic Books, 1967. Pp. 90–131.

Dillard, J. L. *Black English: Its History and Usage in the United States*. New York: Random House, 1972.

Dillard, J. M. "Relationship Between Career Maturity and Self-Concepts of Suburban and Urban Middle- and Urban Lower-Class Preadolescent Black Males." *Journal of Vocational Behavior*, 1976, *9*, 311–20.

Dillard, J. M. "Some Unique Career Behavior Characteristics of Blacks: Career Theories, Counseling Practices, and Research." *Journal of Employment Counseling*, 1980, *17*, 288–98.

Dillard, J. M. and N. J. Campbell. "Career Values and Aspirations of Adult Female and Male Puerto Ricans, Blacks, and Anglos." *Journal of Employment Counseling* (1982).

Dillard, J. M. and N. J. Campbell. "Influences of Puerto Rican, Black, and Anglo Parents' Career Behavior on their Adolescent Children's Career Development," *Vocational Guidance Quarterly*, 1981, *30*, 139–48.

Dillard, J. M. and D. W. Perrin. "Puerto Rican, Black and Anglo Adolescents' Career Aspirations, Expectations, and Maturity." *Vocational Guidance Quarterly*, 1980, *28*, 313–21.

Dillard, J. M., R. L. Kinnison, and B. Peel. "Multicultural Approach to Mainstreaming: A Challenge to Counselors, Teachers, Psychologists, and Administrators." *Peabody Journal of Education*, 1980, *57*, *276–90*.

Epstein, C. F. "Positive Effects of the Multiple Negative: Explaining the Success of Black Professional Women." *American Journal of Sociology*, 1973, *78*, 913–35.

Etzkowitz, H., and G. M. Schaflander. *Ghetto Crisis: Riots of Reconciliation?* Boston: Little, Brown, and Co., 1969.

Frazier, E. F. *The Negro Church in America.* New York: Schocken Books, 1964.

Frazier, E. F. *The Negro Family in the United States.* Chicago: University of Chicago Press, 1939.

Gibby, R. G., and R. Gabler. "The Self-Concept of Negro and White Children." *Journal of Clinical Psychology,* 1967, *23,* 144–48.

Gilsdorf, D. L. "Counselor Preference of Mexican-American, Black and White Community College Students." *Journal of Non-White Concerns in Personnel and Guidance,* 1978, *6,* 162–68.

Goldberg, M. L. "Education for the Disadvantaged." In A. H. Passow, M. Goldberg, and A. J. Fannenbaum (eds.), *Education of the Disadvantaged.* New York: Holt, Rinehart, and Winston, 1967.

Goodwin, L. *A Study of the Work Orientations of Welfare Recipients Participating in the Work-Incentive Program.* Washington, D. C.: Brookings Institution, 1971.

Gordon, M. M. *Assimilation in American Life.* New York: Oxford University Press, 1964.

Gordon, M., and R. J. Grantham. "Helper Preference in Disadvantaged Students." *Journal of Counseling Psychology,* 1979, *26,* 337–43.

Grantham, R. J. "Effects of Counselor Sex, Race, and Language Style on Black Students in Initial Interviews." *Journal of Counseling Psychology,* 1973, *20,* 553–59.

Gunnings, T. "Preparing the New Counselor." *Counseling Psychologist,* 1971, *2,* 100–101.

Gunnings, T. S. and G. Simpkins. "A Systemic Approach to Counseling Disadvantaged Youth." *Journal of Non-White Concerns in Personnel and Guidance,* 1972, *1,* 4–8.

Hartman, J. J. "Psychological Conflict in Negro American Language Behavior: A Case Study." *American Journal Orthopsychiatry,* 1971, *4,* 627–35.

Harvey, W. M. "Drugs in the Black Community." In R. L. Jones, ed., *Black Psychology.* New York: Harper and Row, 1972. Pp. 384–97.

Herzog, E. and H. Lewis. "Children in Poor Families: Myths

and Realities." *American Journal of Orthopsychiatry*, 1970, *40*, 375–89.

Hill, R. C. *The Strengths of Black Families*. New York: Emerson Hall, 1972.

Johnson, R. "What a Difference a Black Counselor Makes." In R. Johnson ed., *Black Agenda for Career Education*. Columbus, Ohio: ECCA Pub. 1974. Pp. 63–72.

Jones, C. D. "Ebonics and Reading." *Journal of Black Studies*, 1979, *9*, 423–48.

Kaestner, E., L. Rosen, and P. Appel. "Patterns of Drug Abuse: Relationships with Ethnicity, Sensation Seeking, and Anxiety." *Journal of Consulting and Clinical Psychology*, 1977, *45*, 462–68.

Kincaid, M. "Identity and Therapy in the Black Community." *Personnel and Guidance Journal*, 1969, *47*, 884–96.

Labov, W. "Hypercorrection by the Lower-Middle Class as a Factor in Linguistic Change." In W. Bright (ed.), *Sociolinguistics*. The Hague: Mouton, 1966.

Labov, W. *Language in the Inner-City: Studies in the Black English Vernacular*. Philadelphia: University of Pennsylvania Press, 1972.

Larkin, R. W. "Class, Race, Sex, and Preadolescent Attitudes." *California Journal of Educational Research*, 1972, *23*, 213–27.

Levine, E. S. *Ethnic-Esteem among Anglo, Black, and Chicano Children*. San Francisco, Calif.: R and E Research Associates, 1976.

Lewis, M. H., M. L. Lynch and P. F. Munger. "The Influence of Ethnicity on the Necessary and Sufficient Conditions of Client-Centered Counseling." *Journal of Non-White Concerns in Personnel and Guidance*, 1978, 5, 134–42.

McGinnis, J., and Smitherman, G. "Sociolinguistic Conflict in the Schools." *Journal of Non-White Concerns in Personnel and Guidance*, 1978, 6, 87–95.

Mercer, J., and J. F. Lewis. *System of Multicultural Pluralistic Assessment: Conceptual and Technical Manual*. Riverside, Calif.: Institute for Pluralistic Assessment Research and Training, 1978.

Minor, B. J. "A Perspective for Assertiveness Training for

Blacks." *Journal of Non-White Concerns in Personnel and Guidance,* 1978, *6,* 63–70.

Moynihan, D. P. "The Negro Family: The Case for National Action." Washington, D. C.: U.S. Department of Labor, Office of Policy Planning and Research, March, 1965.

Nobles, W. W. "African Philosophy: Foundation for Black Psychology." In R. L. Jones, ed., *Black Psychology.* New York: Harper and Row, 1972. Pp. 18–32.

O'Neal, T. R., L. Shackleford, and A. Smith. *Assessment of Adequacy of Drug Abuse Programs in Selected Inner-City Areas.* New York: National Urban League, Research Department, 1973.

Pinkney, A. *Black Americans.* Englewood Cliffs, N. J.: Prentice-Hall, 1969.

Poussaint, A. F. "Building a Strong Self-Image in the Black Child." *Ebony,* 1974, *19,* 136–43.

Richardson, H. V. "The Negro in American Religious Life." In J. P. Davis (ed.), *The American Negro Reference Book.* Englewood Cliffs, N. J.: Prentice-Hall, 1966. P. 402.

Ring, S. I., and L. Schein. "Attitudes Toward Mental Illness and the Use of Caretakers in a Black Community." *American Journal of Orthopsychiatry,* 1970, *40,* 710–16.

Russell, R. D. "Black Perspections of Guidance." *Personnel and Guidance Journal,* 1970, *48,* 721–28.

Schumacher, L. C., P. G. Banikiotes, and F. G. Banikiotes. "Language Compatibility and Minority Group Counseling." *Journal of Counseling Psychology, 1972, 19,* 255–56.

Seymour, H., and P. Ralabate, "The Acquisition of /th/ by Speakers of Black English Vernacular." Paper presented at the ASHA Convention, Houston, Tex., 1976.

Smith, E. J. "Reference Group Perspectives and the Vocational Maturity of Lower Socioeconomic Black Youth." *Journal of Vocational Behavior,* 1976, *8,* 321–63.

Smith, E. J. "Counseling Black Individuals: Some Stereotypes." *Personnel and Guidance Journal,* 1977, *55,* 390–96.

Smith, W. D., A. K. Burlew, M. H. Mosely, and W. M. Whitney. *Minority Issues in Mental Health.* Reading, Mass.: Addison-Wesley Pub. Co., 1978.

Soares, A., and L. M. Soares. "Self-Perception of Culturally

Disadvantaged Children." *American Educational Research Journal*, 1969, *6*, 31–45.

Soares, A., and L. M. Soares. "The Self-Concept of Disadvantaged and Advantaged Students."

of the Black Population in the United States, 1970–1978,'' Washington, D.C. : U.S. Government Printing Office, 1979.

Vontress, C. E. ''Cultural Differences: Implications for Counseling.'' *Journal of Negro Education*, 1969, *48*, 721–28.

Walker, J. M. ''The Effects of Client Race on the Level of Empathy of White Counselor-Trainees.'' Unpublished doctoral dissertation, University of Illinois, 1970.

Walker, R. A. ''The Disadvantaged Enter Rehabilitation—Are They Ready?'' *Rehabilitation Record*, 1968, *9*, 1–4.

Wattenberg, B. J., and R. M. Scammon. ''Black Progress and Liberal Rhetoric.'' *Commentary*, 1973, *55*, 35–44.

Wheeler, W. H. ''Blackness Is My Mental Health: A Mind Set for Black Drug-Abuse Prevention and Treatment Programs.'' *Journal of Non-White Concerns in Personnel and Guidance, 1976, 4*, 64–70.

Williams, D. A., J. Buckley, and M. Lord. ''What Whites Think of Blacks.'' *Newsweek*, February 26, 1979, pp. 48; 53.

Williams, R. L., and J. Kirkland. ''The White Counselor and the Black Client.'' *Counseling Psychologist*, 1971, *4*, 114–17.

Williams, R. L. *The BITCH Test (Black Intelligence Test for Cultural Homogeneity)*. St. Louis, Mo.: Williams and Ass., 6374 Delmar Blvd., 1972.

Willie, C. V. ''The Black Family and Social Class.'' *American Journal of Orthopsychiatry*, 1974, *44*, 50–60.

Wofford, J. ''Ebonics: A Legitimate System of Oral Communication.'' *Journal of Black Studies, 1979, 9*, 367–82.

Wright, B. J., and V. R. Isenstein. *Psychological Tests and Minorities*. Rockville, Md.: National Institute of Mental Health, 1975.

Wright, M. ''Problems of Black Female Students at a Predominantly White University.'' *Journal of Non-White Concerns in Personnel and Guidance*, 1978, *7*, 3–8.

6

Chinese Americans

CHINESE AMERICANS WERE THE first Asians to settle in the United States in large numbers. Their reasons were not unlike those of most ethnic groups who have come to this country. According to Sue (1978), Chinese Americans came to the United States with hopes of improving their economic conditions, life-styles, and social and political life, and providing financial assistance to family members who remained in China.

Chinese Americans have been subjected to much discrimination and many ethnocentric biases. The myths and stereotypes ascribed to this ethnic group have contributed to their neglect by mental health professionals. Few professionals look beyond the myths and stereotypes and deal with the realities of Chinese Americans. It is well-known that many ethnic minority groups, particularly Asians who immigrate to this country, experience varying degrees of psychological and physical stress as they encounter conflict in cultural values. Therefore, it is imperative that counselors improve their understanding of Chinese Americans' cultures and traditions in order to assist individuals of this ethnic group.

SOCIAL AND PSYCHOLOGICAL CHARACTERISTICS

Identifying Chinese Americans

Chinese Americans, as noted, have been labeled with several negative stereotypes, myths, or overgeneralizations regarding their images. In recent years, the stereotypes have broken down, and many of the labels have been replaced with positive views (Sue & Kitano, 1973). Because of the diversity of this ethnic group, the Chinese American's own identity varies from generation to generation and with his sociocultural experiences. Professional literature by Chinese American authors suggests that members of this ethnic group refer to themselves in a number of ways: Asian, Asian American (sometimes hyphenated), Chinese, Chinese American (sometimes hyphenated), Orientals, Red Guard (Chinese youth of Chinatown in San Francisco "who protested against the community's poverty and neglect and criticized its anachronistic and conservative power elite") (Lyman, 1977, p. 177), Yellow Peril, and more moderate action-oriented groups such as Oriental Concern, Yellow Brotherhood, and Wah Chings. Wong (1972) maintains that the term "Asian American" was adopted to attain ethnicity that would contribute to group solidarity and identity in the political arena. According to Lyman (1977), the terms "Asian," "Asian American," and "Oriental" are broad and cut across cultural and geographic boundaries that may include other ethnic groups such as the Japanese, Filipinos, Koreans, and Samoans. Orientals, Asians, Asian Americans, and Chinese Americans are terms which will be used interchangeably throughout this chapter to refer to those Chinese living in the United States.

Where They Are Located

According to the United States Census figures for 1970, there were 431,580 Chinese Americans living in this country. In January 1975, there were 113,894 Chinese from China and Taiwan who had permanent addresses in California, Hawaii, Illinois, and New York (Moulton, 1978). Of the major metropolitan areas of the United States in 1979, Honolulu had the largest Chinese population followed by San Francisco–Oakland, Boston, and Chicago. In 1980, there were 806,027 Chinese Americans residing in the United States (U.S. Bureau of Census, 1981). Although statistics are unavailable, it is estimated that there has been a significant increase in the Chinese American population in the last few years.

Although many Chinese Americans live in Chinatowns, these locations are only a part of the broader Chinese community. Weiss (1973) maintains that members of this ethnic group continue to migrate from the Chinatowns to more favorable locations of suburban and urban areas. The 1970 United States Census indicated that 417,032 Chinese had settled in urban areas, 13,671 in rural nonfarm areas, and 880 in rural farm areas.

In short, Chinese Americans are concentrated in urban areas, but are found in suburban and farm areas. Chinese Americans may be found in all geographic regions and divisions of the United States.

Social Values

As with other ethnic groups, cultural values play a significant role in the lives of Chinese Americans. Values strongly influence behavior, but because of the diversity within this ethnic group, there is no single set of values that influences all Chinese Americans. Differences in cultural and social values should be considered by counselors when dealing with individual Chinese-American clients. For counselors to provide effective assistance to such clients, however, requires at least some knowledge of Chinese Americans' shared cultural values.

Ho (1976) summarizes a set of traditional values that he asserts are applicable across all Asian ethnic groups. First among these is unquestioned loyal devotion, respect for, and deference to authority; usually this is familial and social authority. Pei-Ngor Chen (1970) suggests that this value may be waning, that "the traditional belief of Chinese filial piety no longer holds true in the Chinese-American family system" (p. 592). Traditionally, nuclear and extended family systems provided assistance to the elderly; currently, both the elderly and the younger generation Chinese Americans often prefer to live apart. Many elderly Chinese prefer to live in Chinatowns rather than with their children in suburban communities. In Chinese American families, children are expected to respect their parents. Communication flows in one direction, from parents to children, and the latter are to listen and obey.

Self-control, or internal restraint, is viewed by the family unit as a highly important behavior (Sue, 1978b). A family member is expected to enhance the family name through educational and vocational achievement (Sue and Sue, 1972,; Ho, 1976); personal needs are secondary to the needs of the family. All individual behavior, negative or positive, reflects on the family; thus, the inability to inhibit strong feelings and dysfunctional behaviors such as mental illness disrupt the family's harmony.

Also, shame and guilt are used to discourage individualism, which encompasses aggressive competition with others (Ho, 1976). Individualism is seen as leading to family tension and disruption. A person behaving independently of the teachings and commands of family elders experiences a sense of guilt and shame that affects his behavior in the family as well as in society. Sue and Sue (1971) state that in an attempt to shape a family member's behavior, "parents use guilt-arousing techniques such as threatening to disown a person, verbally censuring the person, or having the person engage in activities that accentuate his feelings of guilt and shame" (p. 36). There is a strong sensitivity and interest in the social bond among members of the family unit. Individuals define their feelings, thoughts, and actions in relation to their perceptions of how peers react to their behavior. Therefore, individuals are able to maintain an awareness of their social milieu within the confines of the established social norms.

Early Chinese immigrants were often faced with threats, harassment, and deportation, especially those who were illegal aliens. Thus, inconspicuous behavior came to be valued. Persons were taught to remain silent and inconspicuous and not to attract attention to themselves (Ho, 1976). In China, too, many Chinese Americans suffered through a political upheaval that caused them to lose control of their destinies. Many dealt with such situations with feelings of resignation and by viewing life pragmatically. Chinese Americans still make an effort to accept most conditions without attempting to understand or control their environment or to determine their own destiny.

Among Chinese Americans, traditional values frequently conflict with those of the dominant Anglo culture. For example, while the Anglo culture prizes individualism, along with assertive behavior, traditional Chinese culture views these behaviors as crude and culturally inappropriate.

Heterogeneity of values exists among Chinese Americans. Many persons are what Sue and Sue (1971) refer to as "marginal individuals." Such individuals acculturate or adopt the values of the Anglo dominant culture and attempt to be absorbed into Anglo culture. Other Chinese persons who identify themselves as "Asian Americans" value behavior slightly different from marginal individuals and traditionalists. According to Sue and Sue (1971), Asian Americans also show defiance of traditional values, but this is less a rejection of Chinese customs than an attempt to preserve particular Chinese values in the process of developing a new ethnic identity. For instance, high achievement is perceived as being too materialistic for persons who are attempting to find new self-identity and meaning. Greater emphasis is placed on enhancing group pride and esteem through collective means. Social and political awareness are valued. Further, it is often perceived by traditional parents that Asian Americans should not be assertive, questioning, and active in determining their environment. Such persons may be viewed, in some instances, as militants in their efforts to attain civil rights.

The various sets of values do not necessarily operate in isolation. Any one value may affect one individual more strongly than another. The behavior of each Chinese-American client will be related to the extent that each person identifies with one of the value systems. A counselor should consider these clients first as individuals and then as Chinese Americans (Ho, 1976, p. 291).

Family Characteristics

Cultural values are important factors in Chinese-American family socialization. Attitudes and beliefs, as well as situational events, influence the Chinese American family's socialization processes. Hsu (1971) contends that affective bonds are developed between family members who help to make life meaningful during the process of carrying out defined family roles and rules. These bonds are continually emphasized with the purpose that a person's self-esteem and future become significantly bound up with the family and kin (Hsu, 1971). In comparison, Sue (1977) feels that the individualistic person, socialized in the dominant Anglo culture, is likely to attain meaning through (1) "self-exploration and an existential search for meaning, or (2) finding material goals or social, religious, or political causes in an attempt to satisfy the affective needs" (p. 384). Throughout a person's life, kinship is stressed, with conformity to family and elders. Family members may develop and strongly internalize the expected norms of both kin and family. Individuals may experience a degree of discomfort (or shame) for not achieving well, or guilt for disobeying family norms, since nonachievement and the exhibition of antisocial behavior reflect on the family name. Children are expected to be obedient to their parents.

While traditional Chinese families exist in the United States there are many variations among Chinese-American families. Many Chinese families transmit a mixture of traditional Chinese and dominant Anglo values as a means of family socialization. According to Sue (1978b), this type of family may form a strong alliance with other ethnic minorities, particularly other Asian Americans, on certain issues as ethnocentrism in an attempt to attain full equality. However, Chinese families or persons who adopt the values of other Asian Americans are often perceived by their parents as assertive, disobedient, or less interested in achievement—indicators of disrespect toward the family and traditional beliefs. Sue and Sue (1971) maintain that defiance is not a rejection of Chinese values, but rather, it is an attempt to maintain certain traditional values in developing a new identity.

Other Chinese families identify solely with those values of the dominant Anglo society. There are also marginal families, who define their self-worth in terms of acceptance by the dominant Anglo society, but who preserve some traditional values.

Within each of the three family groups briefly described, there are overlapping differences and similarities. Although many Chinese-American families may be distinctly defined as traditionalist, marginal, or Asian American, counselors should work with caution when dealing with Chinese-American families.

Socioeconomic Characteristics

The 1970 United States Census indicated that 73.3 percent of Chinese males of 16 years old and over were in the labor market, compared to 49.5 percent of Chinese females of similar age. The regional distribution of employed males showed 73.2 percent urban, 71.5 percent rural nonfarm, and 73.4 percent rural farm. The percentage of the labor distribution by residence for females was 49.5 percent urban, 39.9 percent rural nonfarm, and 43.8 percent rural farm. The highest regional number of employed Chinese males and females was in the West, followed by the Northeast, North Central, and South.

Wing-Cheung Ng (1977) stated that approximately 25 percent of the Chinese labor force were professionals. A higher percentage of Chinese were employed as service workers. More Chinese males than females worked in management and craft work. A relatively small number of Chinese females were in service occupations, and nearly double the number of Chinese males as females were service workers.

Within the Chinese male work force, 6.4 percent worked as construction craftsmen, mechanics and repairmen, and foremen in manufacturing industries in comparison to 14.44 percent of Anglo males in similar occupational categories. About 20 percent of Chinese males are employed in food service. About 8 percent of the Chinese males were employed as engineers. Nearly 11 percent held such professional occupations as teachers in higher education (Ng, 1977). Chinese males were also found in occupations such as management and administration.

Ng (1977) found that Chinese females worked in white-collar offices, food service, and teaching. The general occupational structure for Chinese-American females was similar to that of Anglo female counterparts; however, many Chinese females were clustered in sewing and stitching occupations.

According to a 1970 census report, the median income for Chinese males 16 years old and over was $5,223, while the median income for the Chinese females of the same age group was $2,686 in 1969.

Moulton (1978) maintains that unemployment was low in 1970 among Chinese Americans, because many were willing to work at substandard menial jobs rather than be unemployed. This desire to work seems related to the traditional Chinese value that occupational achievement is highly prized.

Peter S. Li (1977) feels that dependence on kinship assistance to succeed in some type of business is common among Chinese immigrants. Such kinship assistance, however, frequently requires reciprocal obligations to the kin who provide the assistance. According to Li: "Such obligations tend to tie some Chinese immigrants to ethnic business for a relatively long period of time, thereby making it difficult for them to move to occupations of higher statuses" (1977, p. 488).

There are various socioeconomic levels among Chinese Americans. Lyman (1974) suggests that middle-class Chinese Americans are on the rise. Chinese Americans cannot be treated as a homogeneous socioeconomic group.

Educational Characteristics

Traditional Chinese Americans place strong emphasis on educational achievement. Educational achievement is perceived as a means of attaining economic and social mobility, as well as a way of improving life conditions. According to Sue and Kirk (1973), many young Chinese Americans pursue careers in nonverbal fields such as science, rather than careers which require proficiency in verbal skills such as the humanities. Daniels and Kitano (1970) found that the proportion of Chinese and Japanese college graduates exceeds that of Anglos.

The 1970 United States Census report indicated that the median level of school years completed for urban, rural nonfarm, and rural farm residence for Chinese Americans was 12.8 years. The total median school years completed for Chinese Americans is slightly above 12 years in states such as California, Hawaii, Illinois, and Massachusetts, with the exception of New York, which had slightly more than 10 years completed. A higher percentage of Chinese males (71.1) eighteen to twenty-four years were enrolled in school than Chinese females (59.0) in the same age group.

Finally, education—as it is certainly for other ethnic minorities—is critically essential as it is the key for someone to obtain entry into the dominant Anglo society. Yet it is false to assume that all Chinese Americans have been educationally successful. While their educational levels appear to be increasing, individual differences are inescapable, and naturally some Chinese Americans are less successful in educational achievement than others.

Language Characteristics

Most of the early Chinese immigrants to the United States spoke Cantonese. Over the years, other immigrant Chinese have brought other dialects into this country. According to Pei-Ngor Chen (1970), there are several Chinese dialects spoken in Los Angeles, alone. The basic dialect spoken by elderly immigrants is Toishanese (derived from Toi Shan, which is a county in the province of Kwong Tung in Communist China). More recent immigrants who enter the United States from the British colony of Hong Kong, speak Cantonese (derived from Canton, which is a municipal county in the province of Kwong Tung). Chinese who were born in the United States speak mostly English. Others may speak Chinese and what Stanford Lyman (1974) refers to as "pidgin English", which is essentially a less developed skill and facility in verbal English expression (p. 134).

Chinese-American language variations must be taken into consideration in the counseling setting. Language acquisition and skills may differ according to the Chinese client's experiences and degree of acculturation. Bilingual and bicultural experiences should be integrated into counseling intervention strategies when working with Chinese-American clients.

Religion

Traditional Chinese Americans are predominantly Buddhist and Taoist. Traditional Chinese home shrines can be found in nearly all homes (Lyman, 1974). Early Chinese immigrants who settled in eastern areas of the United States established shrines in such places as laundries and shops. Later, the Chinese built temples in some eastern American cities, and many of these temples and shrines still exist. Some of the temples have been restored to maintain the Chinese heritage, while others may be used as museums or for other nonreligious purposes. Lyman (1974) maintains that while younger Chinese Americans may not show interest in traditional religions, they do actively participate in some of the religious ceremonies, festivals, and rites that originated from Chinese religions such as Taoism and Buddhism (p. 48).

Lyman (1974) also notes that non-Christian and Christian religions have followers in Chinese-American communities. Many Chinese Americans are affiliated with Roman Catholic or Protestant churches. Moreover, Chinese Americans often, participate in the rites and celebrations of more than a single religion. Lyman contends that Chinese born in the United States often prefer to affiliate with a Christian denomination. Lyman cautions the reader not to assume this. The higher the degree of social contact with the dominant Anglo society, the higher the chance that Western religions may be adopted by Chinese Americans.

Identity, Self-Pride, and Esteem

Like other ethnic minorities, the identity of Chinese Americans is affected by the degree that they have been absorbed into mainstream society and acculturated in the dominant Anglo cultural patterns and values. As noted earlier, Chinese Americans may identify themselves as traditionalist, marginal persons, or mainstream. Each identity is derived from different points of reference—traditionalist from within the family unit, marginal persons from Anglo society, and Asian Americans from reconciliation of past and present values (Sue & Sue, 1971).

In recent years an increasing number of Chinese Americans, particularly students in higher education, have begun to stress "their own heritage, pride, and self-identity" (Sue and Sue, 1972, p. 640). Pei-Ngor Chen (1970) states that Chinese immigrant youth and other Chinese youth who lacked knowledge of Chinese traditions and culture, in an effort to find "a sense of identity and belonging" (p. 594), have established neighborhood gangs. Some Chinese youth who are conscious of the social and political determinants that affected their identity have embraced such militant groups as the Red Guard and Yellow Peril, which advocate social change in the Chinese community. Less militant groups, for example, Yellow Brotherhood, Wah Chings, and Oriental Concern (Pei-Ngor Chen, 1970, p. 594) also strive for social and political improvement for Chinese Americans. Chinese youth who identify as Asian Americans place emphasis on enhancement of group pride and esteem (Sue & Sue, 1972).

Larkin (1972) investigated the self-esteem of fourth-, fifth-, and sixth-grade Oriental, Black, Mexican American, and Anglo children. The results of this investigation suggested that the Oriental children had the highest self-esteem of the four ethnic groups. On the other hand, Yee (1973) states that the many stereotyped perceptions of and prejudices toward Chinese have influenced their self-perceptions to the point that some do not view themselves as having a meaningful identity (p. 99). Yee's study of American social studies textbooks noted the "rising protest and counterresponse to the restrictive perceptions among younger Asian Americans who seek the identity and acceptance they have been denied by others and themselves" (p. 99).

In short, professional literature suggests that Chinese Americans are in search of a new, improved self-image that is self-defined rather than defined by non-Chinese Americans. Ethnic identity, self-pride, and personal identity should be assessed within the sociocultural context of the Chinese-American's experiences.

Chinese-American Culture and Counseling Assistance

The social and psychological variables related to Chinese Americans are important considerations for counselors and other mental health professionals who work with members of this ethnic group. Unfortunately, many professionals lack awareness concerning Chinese Americans and have overlooked problems of adjustment and family (Homma-True, 1976, p. 158). Such problems frequently go unnoticed and are, therefore, perceived by many professionals as nonexistent. Then, too, the Chinese Americans' underuse of counseling and psychiatric facilities has been perceived as an indication that few mental health problems are present among this ethnic group. Yet contemporary advocates, such as Sue and Sue (1972), Sue and Kirk (1972), and Homma-True (1976), maintain that traditional community mental facilities are underused because they lack cultural relevance for Chinese Americans.

Acculturation, Assimilation, and Chinese Americans

Acculturation for many Chinese Americans often involves conflict because of their attraction to their traditional Chinese values and to those of the dominant Anglo society. The transmission of Anglo values comes through participation in educational institutions and exposure to televisions, newspapers, radios, and magazines. Early research findings by Stanley L. M. Fong (1965) indicated that the social and cultural orientations and sentiments of the Chinese shift gradually from those of the ethnic subculture to those of the larger American community. As the American society becomes a positive reference group, its norms begin to guide, as well as modify, the perspectives and behavior of the Chinese. Fong surmises that as an outcome of internalizing Western modes, the Chinese are inevitably losing their traditional values of reticence, formality, and constraint in interpersonal behavior (p. 272).

Such values as individualism, assertiveness, and spontaneity are often in direct conflict with traditional Chinese-American values. Increasing adoption of dominant Anglo values is, in many instances, not easy (Sue and Sue, 1972). Thus, the conflict involved in the acculturative process is an important aspect of the Chinese-American experience. Inability to deal effectively with the conflicts encountered through acculturation results in some individuals experiencing extrapsychic stress and anxiety. Probably one of the most serious problems for Chinese Americans is adapting to a rejecting and prejudicial society. Sue (1977) states:

> Asian Americans are striving to become assimilated and have become quite successful in entering American mainstream in education, occupation, and social relationships. Nevertheless, many feel alienated, anxious, and angry since prejudice and discrimination still exist and structural assimilation is still limited. [P. 386]

Research results support this contention. For example, Sue and Kirk's 1972 research findings about Chinese-American students at the University of California at Berkeley indicate experiences of cultural conflict between traditional Chinese family and Anglo values. Such experiences of cultural conflict and discomfort in relating to persons outside the family often bring on increased emotional distress. In another research report concerning adjustment among Chinese students, Sue and Kirk (1973) found that the students showed higher levels of isolation, anxiety, and loneliness when compared to other students. Sue and Frank (1973) found in their study that Chinese male students experienced more stress than their Anglo counterparts.

Sue (1977) argues, however, that the assimilation theory as suggested by Gordon (1964) is insufficient. First, he says the theory assumes that Asian Americans want to be assimilated and experience anxiety only because of societal limitations. The theory does not consider that many Asian Americans might not want to be assimilated, but might prefer instead to build their own institutions that are representative of the integration of Asian-American and Anglo cultural elements. Second, the theory suggests that assimilation and cultural conflicts are the culprits in fostering the Asian American's feelings of alienation. Asian and Anglo cultural conflicts are thought to result in a lack of choice in identifying with either of the two cultures, which also results in an incongruent self-identity. Whether Asian Americans choose to maintain their identity as Asian Americans or choose to attempt absorption into Anglo mainstream society is a less significant concern. Some Asian Americans prefer to be assimilated into the dominant Anglo culture, yet remain traditionally Chinese or bicultural. Sue argues that perhaps the unnoticed factor within the process of identity is the question of whether there is an available choice between Asian American and Anglo cultures. Additionally, the question includes the degree of control that Asian Americans will have to determine their own lives within either culture. Finally, one theory advocates that as assimilation increases among Asian Americans, there should be a corresponding decrease in alienation.

Sue maintains that the assimilation theory fails to explain why Asian Americans continue to enhance their ethnic identity despite their social and economic gains. He concludes that the assimilation/decreased alienation theory is inadequate to account for the continued ethnic identity of most Asian Americans. Instead, Sue (1977) feels that the "relative deprivation theory" which suggests that alienation is due to gains or standards relative to other groups may, in part, account for this discrepancy between social and economic gains and increased frustration, anxiety, and alienation. Sue contends that Asian Americans' anxiety and alienation may surface as a result of their evaluating their achievement relative to that of Anglo Americans, particularly when the Asian Americans' aspirations exceed their actual achievements. This relative deprivation may be perceived within the framework of the standards established by the dominant Anglo society.

In summary, value conflicts between Chinese Americans and the dominant Anglo society should be considered when counseling Chinese-American clients. The fact that feelings of alienation and anxiety may be associated with a perceived lack of achieved goals relative to goals achieved by those of Anglo society should be taken into consideration.

Perceptions of Mental Health and Mental Illness

The traditional Chinese values and the levels of acculturation discussed earlier may also be associated with Chinese Americans' views of mental health and mental illness. Sue, Sue, and Sue (1975) indicated that many Chinese Americans feel that stable mental health is subject to the individual's willpower and the avoidance of morbid thinking. The avoidance of morbid thinking is considered an essential factor in maintaining sound mental health. Such behavior is encouraged by Chinese with traditional values (Sue, 1978a). Conversely, some modalities of Western therapies encourage nonavoidance of morbid thought, since avoidance of morbid thought is perceived of as repressive or suppressive and harmful to the individual.

In their research, Brown, Stein, Huang, and Harris (1973) state that psychotic behavior among Chinese patients may result from misinterpreting traditional Chinese behavior and overlooking language problems. Such results can occur where psychiatrists lack cultural and language understandings of the Chinese patients. The psychiatrists' interpretations are likely to be based solely on Western therapies and without regard for behavior within traditional Chinese culture. Brown et al. minimized this biasing effect in their research by using bilingual and bicultural Chinese psychiatrists to treat the Chinese patients. Some of the Chinese Americans dropped out of the therapy treatment because they preferred not to be known in the community as mentally ill. Other findings suggested that out-patients attributed the symptoms of their emotional disorders to present rather than previous events.

Reiko Homma-True's (1976) research on Chinese Americans in the Oakland (California) Chinatown indicated that only 2.6 percent were concerned with interpersonal problems within the immediate family. These findings may be related to what Sue and Sue surmised in their 1972 research: Many Chinese are reluctant to self-disclose psychological problems. Much shame is associated with these problems, and Chinese individuals often feel that they are failing their family if they admit their psychological problems to outsiders.

Chinese-Americans' perceptions of mental health and mental illness also vary among individuals. According to Homma-True's (1976) research, differences are linked to the educational levels of the individuals.

Attitudes toward Counselors and Use of Mental Health Facilities

Attitudes that Chinese Americans hold toward counselors, other mental health professionals, and mental health facilities are influenced by traditional Chinese values and the kinds of professional service provided to them. Reiko Homma-True (1976) found that 59.2 percent of the Chinese-American respondents living in the Oakland Chinatown would seek assistance for emotional problems from family members, relatives, and friends. A much lower percentage—14.5—of the respondents indicated that they would seek assistance from social workers at Chinese facilities. About 4 percent of the respondents said that they preferred to attain help from ministers and physicians. Sue, Sue, and Sue (1975) believe that Asian Americans' avoidance of facilities occurs because cultural values inhibit self-referral to such facilities, and because such services are frequently unresponsive to their needs. Asian Americans who do use mental health facilities often prematurely terminate psychiatric services following the first session.

Sue and Frank (1973) suggest that Asian Americans' use of psychiatric facilities is not clearly a direct indication of fewer psychological problems than exist among other groups. Figures representing the use of mental health facilities present the misleading picture that Asian Americans experience little psychopathology (Sue and McKinney, 1975). In short, it appears that Chinese Americans' use of professional services may be influenced by the lack of relevancy of the services provided as well as by cultural factors which interfere with self-referral.

Language and Counseling Services

Language differences between counselor and client often create problems in attaining positive counseling outcomes. Thus, counseling service may prove limited when such problems exist. Homma-True (1976) concludes from research findings that most of her Chinatown (Oakland, California) respondents have problems communicating in English. The communications problem is compounded by the Chinese dialects spoken in the United States.

Even though language differences, which lead to poor communication between counselors and Chinese American clients, may contribute to premature termination of counseling sessions, Pei-Ngor Chen (1970) found that there were few Chinese-speaking professionals in public civil services, as well as few bilingual professional workers in private and public mental health agencies.

Homma-True (1976) maintains that bilingual mental health

professionals are a key factor in encouraging Chinese Americans to use mental health services. Brown, Stein, Huang, and Harris (1973) corroborate Homma-True's statement:

> A bilingual and bicultural Chinese therapist familiar with the local community was of great importance. The extremely limited English language capability of the Chinese-American outpatients made a bilingual therapist an absolute necessity. Moreover, since more than one dialect is spoken in Chinatown, the therapist had to have a multidialect capability. The therapist's bicultural familiarity was equally important to her language abilities. Her familiarity with the life-style in China and Hong Kong permitted her to assist the patients to put their current circumstances into realistic perspective.[P. 225]

Sociocultural Adjustment and Identity Problems

Jung (1976) argues that Chinatown residents in Philadelphia, Pennsylvania encounter many stressful situations such as ineffective mental health services, potential gang conflicts, few opportunities for socioeconomic mobility for recent immigrants, insufficient assistance to the elderly, and poor housing. Other situations that create stress for Chinese Americans include family problems and identity conflicts. Jung feels that many Chinese immigrants are ill-prepared to deal with stressful situations and life-styles in the United States.

Homma-True found in her 1976 study that Chinese immigrants see themselves as experiencing adjustment problems in language and customs and/or life-styles. Other Chinese respondents view themselves as encountering problems in their own families. The largest percentage of the respondents indicated problems with employment, followed by problems with health, interpersonal relations, family relations, psychological stress, and language.

Both Chen (1970) and Jung (1976) found that newly arrived immigrant Chinese youth face adjustment problems in the United States. Many "are overwhelmed by a different culture, and they feel inferior because they see the need for fluency in the English language" (Chen, 1970, p. 594). Also, many of these youth lack enough money to obtain the material goods frequently displayed by the American-born Chinese youth.

Occasionally, immigrant youth must work to assist their families. However, work is not readily available to them because of child labor laws, their lack of marketable skills, and their language problems. Of those who work, many have to work at night and then attempt to function in school during the day. Some, unable to gain entry to higher education, focus on menial work. They settle for less desired kinds of work such as cooks, dishwashers, and waiters in restaurants and custodial and laundry workers in hotels and hospitals.

Those youth who find it difficult to attain employment often become frustrated and may turn to drugs to ease the situation. Also, some American-born Chinese youth become school dropouts and sometimes join gangs that aimlessly roam urban streets (Chen, 1970). Most gang members are searching for identity.

Because many Chinese Americans are ill-equipped with survival skills necessary to function effectively in mainstream American society, sociocultural adjustment and identity crises sometimes lead to psychological discomfort. Inability to adapt to various stressful life situations poses a serious threat to psychological well-being. Such persons often find themselves in a quandry as they strive to circumvent the many obstacles that hinder their efforts to improve their livelihood. Cultural conflict affects the degree to which the individual experiences an identity crisis and further, evokes extrapsychic stress. While many Chinese Americans experience cultural conflict, others do not encounter such conflict, as they tend to form a bicultural orientation (Sue, 1978a, p. 9).

Some predictors of extrapsychic stress related to Chinese Americans' physical and emotional disturbances are language difficulties, poor housing, limited education, social change, and unemployment. According to Sue (1978a), significant sources of extrapsychic stress for many Chinese immigrants include securing employment, cultural change (Chinese to Western society), adapting to unfamiliar surrounding, and adjusting to ethnocentric biases and discrimination. The Chinese Americans' struggle to adapt to these conditions has not been fully recognized, and professional services to assist in resolving such problems are too few and too tradition-bound.

Psychological Characteristics of Chinese-American Students

Several studies indicate that Chinese-American students experience higher degrees of emotional stress than other students on university campuses (Sue and Kirk, 1972, 1973; Sue and Frank, 1973). While many Chinese Americans share similar values, non-Chinese Americans frequently generalize and stereotype these values at the expense of recognizing individual characteristics. According to Sue and Frank (1973), Chinese-American students have been described in such collective terms as *quiet, obedient, studious,* and *industrious.* Further, they are viewed as persons who perform well in physical sciences and engineering and less well in social sciences, linguistic, and in areas that deal with human relations (Sue and Frank, 1973, p. 131). Chinese-American students do, in fact, often pursue the physical sciences and avoid the social sciences but this is probably because the latter require a great deal of verbal communication. Sue and Kirk (1972) maintain that this behavior is linked, in part, to early Chinese immigrants encouraging their children to engage in careers that are economically and socially promising. Nonetheless, the point is that blanket generalizations perpetuate stereotypic and negative views, which, in turn, prevent Chinese-American students from being recognized as individuals.

Traditional family values also contribute to the Chinese-American student's discomfort on campus. Traditional family loyalty and distrust of those outside the family cause these students to appear socially aloof and uninterested in the well-being of outsiders. Cultural conflicts associated with persons outside the family often evoke or enhance emotional stress (Sue and Kirk, 1972).

Then, too, Chinese students who adhere to their traditional values may experience considerable pressure when their academic performance is inconsistent with their family's expectations. Many Chinese-American students experience anxiety because they feel that failure in school will bring shame upon their family. Sue (1973) observed that while appearing autonomous, Asian-American students are actually "less independent from paternal controls and authority figures" (p. 144) than non-Chinese-American university students. Often this seeming autonomy, educational problems, and somatic complaints mask the Chinese student's psychological problems. There is probably a relationship between traditional Chinese family values and the Chinese student's psychological well-being. As Asian Americans perceive the importance of gaining entry into mainstream American society, many Asian university students experience psychological discomfort. The reader, however, should bear in mind that traditional family values differentially affect individual students.

PRACTICAL APPROACHES TO ASSISTING CHINESE AMERICANS

Effective assistance to Chinese Americans will require, in most instances, bicultural and bilingual counselors. Such counselors must be thoroughly familiar with traditional Chinese culture as well as with mainstream Anglo culture. A knowledge base should include identity of those whose cultural orientations are traditional Chinese, marginal, and Asian American. While there are many Chinese dialects spoken in the United States, it is also important that counselors be able to adequately communicate in the client's preferred language.

Sue and Sue (1972) suggest that Chinese students especially may experience cultural conflicts as they attempt to engage in the counseling encounter. Often, students do not volunteer pertinent information; they sometimes answer questions in short, polite statements. Self-disclosure to the counselor may be a difficult task for those who have learned to inhibit expression of their emotions. Direct and indirect strategies used by the counselor to elicit personal information may be interpreted as a personal infringement on privacy. In this type of situation, Sue and Sue advocate that counselors respond initially to the client's superficial concerns, such as educational or somatic conditions. This approach may help clients by providing them with greater freedom to explore threatening data at their own pace. Clients may also be helped to communicate when the counselor deals with psychological material pertaining to career choice or occupational requirements. For example, test interpretations related to concrete material such as the individual's vocational future may also facilitate freedom of verbal expression.

Many Chinese-American students, according to Sue and Sue (1972), are concerned that peers, family members, or persons other than the counselor will learn that they have sought outside assistance. Therefore, when counseling such clients, confidentiality is a serious consideration. A positive working relationship must be developed between the counselor and client in order to assure the client of confidentiality and trust. The counselor should discuss the use of information discussed in couseling sessions with the client. Also, group counseling would likely pose a threat to the individual. Chen (1970) contends that "some Chinese families, however, do respond to family therapy when group sessions are conducted in their homes" (p. 596).

Sue and Sue (1972) maintain that many Chinese-American students feel more at ease during counseling when the counselor has made the setting less ambiguous, that is, when the counselor outlines the structure of the sessions and describes procedures that will occur in the counseling process. Additionally, the student's emotional state and participation may dictate the extent to which the counselor applies approaches to the student's concerns.

Traditional counseling interventions are not necessarily effective with some Chinese-American clients (Sue, 1978a). Nontraditional counseling approaches such as direct cognitive appeals, admonition, advice giving, appeals to shame and guilt may be effective for counseling in certain family settings. Also, according to Sue (1978a), cognitive reasoning and insight counseling approaches to mental health may be relevant, since many Chinese believe that will power and self-control influence the individual's behavior (p. 14). When these counseling approaches are unsuccessful, respected persons within the community (third-party intermediaries) such as friends and elders may intervene to give assistance. As a last resort, family members may seek out traditional counseling help. No single counseling approach will resolve the problems experienced by all Chinese Americans.

Marshall Jung (1976) suggests that professionals who work with Chinese Americans should remember that "(1) the family, not the individual, is the most important unit; (2) the father is the head of the household, and those within the family are subordinate to him; (3) the concept of rugged individualism is not emphasized; and (4) the Chinese have an aversion toward governments and governmental agencies, whether Chinese or American" (p. 153). Jung (1976) also believes that counselors should consider working with some of the traditional organizations in Chinese communities. This approach would enhance counselors' awareness of the problems experienced by Chinatown residents. Moreover, residents would come to know and trust such counselors, as well as seek their assistance when in need of aid.

Ongoing research and surveys might be conducted to attain and maintain current knowledge of the conditions and problems of Chinese-American communities and those communities where Chinese residents are in the minority. For example, information gained concerning changing family structure, cultural patterns, states of assimilation, acculturation, identity, and social behavior will enable counselors to improve their understanding of the problems experienced by Chinese (Chen, 1970). It is assumed that as a result of this knowledge base, counselors will be able to assist Chinese Americans in more effectively attaining their desired goals.

There may be special problems in counseling the elderly. In some cases, it may be necessary to advocate a change in the delivery of public services to elderly Chinese Americans. For example, counselors might encourage counseling agencies to reduce the rigidity of institutional programming by changing office schedules, priorities, and by developing and instituting counseling services that focus on and deal with the clients' perceived needs. Several factors affect the use of services by the elderly persons from ethnic minority groups: differences in socioeconomic backgrounds, cultural factors, differences in eligibility for services, communication and language barriers, and differences in physical and financial access. It seems important that counselors focus on the untapped skills and creativity of elderly Chinese Americans.

Counselors can also be instrumental in helping Chinese youth and immigrants attain the educational opportunities necessary to acquire basic skills and employment. To do this, counselors may need to provide career information and, in some cases, even to make direct contact with potential employers.

Finally, it is essential that counselors encourage higher educational institutions to extend their existing curriculum to include some courses in the training of bilingual Chinese-American students. Also, various social agencies should provide preservice and inservice training of bilingual, multiservice professionals who can employ more than a single intervention of counseling services.

SUMMARY

Counselors and other mental health professionals who provide assistance to Chinese Americans are encouraged to learn about the many psychosocial factors that operate within the Chinese-American culture while remembering that these factors do not equally affect individuals of this ethnic group. Although Chinese Americans are strongly value-oriented as a cultural group, individual members of this ethnic group have diverse values, experiences, and family socialization. Thus, counselors must work with each Chinese American on an individual and a cultural level.

Levels of acculturation among Chinese Americans should be observed to determine which counseling approach may best attain the clients' positive desired outcomes. Meeting the psychosocial needs of Chinese Americans is unlikely until more counselors are trained to become competent bilingual and bicultural professionals.

EXERCISES

The following exercises will help students get acquainted with some of the concerns of Chinese Americans. Another focus of these exercises is to help students begin to conceptualize culturally relevant intervention strategies that best meet the needs of Chinese-American clients.

A. Ask one student in the class to play the role of a Chinese-American university student who is experiencing a great deal of psychological stress. For example, he is not performing as well in his academic studies as he would like, and he fears shame will be brought to his family. Additionally, he is in love with a Chinese-American woman who attends a university in another state. Many of his daily thoughts are focused on her. Another student should play the part of a counselor conducting a ten-minute counseling session with the student. At the end of the session, the client should discuss how he felt during the counseling session and what influence the counselor had on him. The counselor shares his observations of the client as well as his ideas about how effective or ineffective he perceived himself to be during the counseling session. The class may offer feedback and counseling alternatives. Repeat using other students. Try the approaches mentioned in the discussions.

B. Students should read the example below and answer the questions that follow it.

Diane, a Chinese American, is an undergraduate senior majoring in engineering. Diane is a straight "A" student and will graduate in three months with a bachelors' degree in engineering. However, she has elected to pursue graduate work in counseling psychology. Her interest in counseling psychology was gained through readings and through talk with friends who are either students or professionals in the area. Diane's mother is a public school teacher and her father is a psychiatrist. Diane feels that she needs more information pertaining to counseling psychology, institutions offering such a program, and procedures necessary to gain entry into a counseling psychology program either at her present university or other state-wide universities.

The following day, Diane makes an appointment with a counselor in the university counseling center. During the counseling interview, Diane communicates to the middle-class counselor her interests and concerns about a graduate degree in counseling psychology rather than engineering. Her counselor tells her that she should not attempt to go into a field that requires proficient skills in Mainstream American English because her father will likely disapprove and it is essential for her to adhere to their heritage; thus, she should choose a profession in science or mathematics.

1. What are the issues involved in this situation?
2. To what extent is the counselor correct or incorrect in his suggestion?
3. To what degree would the counselor's suggestion be correct or incorrect if Diane's parents were employed as restaurant owners or farm workers?
4. How would you deal with Diane's concern?

C. Divide students into small groups of five or six and ask them to read the example below. After the reading, each group should answer the questions following the example. Discuss the answers with the entire class.

Samuel, a thirty-six-year-old Chinese American who has no experience in being a client in a counseling situation is in his first counseling interview. He infrequently interacts verbally with the counselor. Yet when he does talk, his focus of conversation is on his physical problems which he encounters daily.

1. How do you perceive Samuel's problem?
2. How do you think traditional Chinese values and customs affect Samuel's behavior in this interview?
3. While Samuel's physical complaints may very well be legitimate, what are other factors which might be influencing his physical discomfort?
4. Considering Samuel's traditional culture, other psychological factors contributing to his discomfort, and his lack of counseling experience as a client, how would you plan for this client and facilitate his verbal interaction?

D. Using the example in C, divide students into groups of threes. One student plays the client, one plays the counselor, and another student assumes the role of observer. After about five or ten minutes of role playing, the observer gives feedback to the counselor regarding his performance based on the discussion of answers to questions in C. Repeat with each person shifting to a different role.

REFERENCES

Brown, T. R., K. M. Stein, K. Huang, and D. E. Harris. "Mental Illness and the Role of Mental Health Facilities in Chinatown." In S. Sue and N. N. Wagner (eds.), *Asian-Americans: Psychological Perspectives.* Palo Alto, Calif.: Science and Behavior Books, 1973. Pp. 212–31.

Chen, Pei-Ngor. "The Chinese Community in Los Angeles." *Social Casework,* 1970, *51,* 591–98.

Daniels, R., and H. H. Kitano. *American Racism.* Englewood Cliffs, N. J.: Prentice-Hall, 1970.

Fong, S. L. M. "Assimilation of Chinese in America: Changes in Orientation and Social Perception." *American Journal of Sociology,* 1965, *71,* 265–73.

Gordon, M. M. *Assimilation in American life.* New York: Oxford University Press, 1964.

Ho, M. K. "Social Work with Asian Americans." *Social Casework,* 1976, *57,* 195–201.

Homma-True, R. "Characteristics of Contrasting Chinatowns: Oakland, California." *Social Casework,* 1976, *57,* 155–59.

Hsu, F. "Psychosocial Homeostasis and Jen: Conceptual Tools for Advancing Psychological Anthropology." *American Anthropologist,* 1971, *73,* 23–44.

Jung, M. "Characteristics of Contrasting Chinatowns: Philadelphia, Pennsylvania." *Social Casework,* 1976, *57,* 149–59.

Larkin, R. W. "Class, Race, Sex, and Preadolescent Attitudes." *California Journal of Educational Research,* 1972, *22,* 313–23.

Li, P. S. "Occupational Achievement and Assistance among Chinese Immigrants in Chicago." *The Sociological Quarterly,* 1977, *18,* 478–89.

Lyman, S. M. *Chinese Americans.* New York: Random House, 1974.

Lyman, S. M. *The Asian in North America.* Santa Barbara, Calif.: American Bibliographical Center, Clio Press, 1977.

Moulton, D. M. "The Socioeconomic Status of Asian American Families in Five Major Standard Metropolitan Statistical Areas." In M. M. Evans (ed)., *Summary and Recommendations: Conference on Pacific/Asian American Families and HEW-Related Issues.* Annandale, Va.: JWK International Corp., 1978, B-30-B-117.

Ng, Wing-Cheung. "An Evaluation of the Labor Market Status of Chinese Americans." *Amerasia,* 1977, *4,* 101–22.

Sue, D. "Ethnic Identity: The Impaction of Two Cultures on the Psychological Development of Asians in America." In S. Sue and N. N. Wagner (eds), *Asian-Americans: Psychological Perspectives.* Palo Alto, Calif.: Science and Behavior Books, 1973. Pp. 140–49.

Sue, D. W., and A. C. Frank, "A Typological Approach to the Psychological Study of Chinese and Japanese American College Males." *Journal of Social Issues,* 1973, *29,* 129–48.

Sue, D. W., and B. A. Kirk. "Psychological Characteristics of Chinese-American Students." *Journal of Counseling Psychology, 1972, 19,* 471–78.

Sue, D. W., and B. A. Kirk. "Differential Characteristics of Japanese-American and Chinese-American College Students." *Journal of Counseling Psychology,* 1973, *20,* 142–48.

Sue, D. W., and S. Sue. "Counseling Chinese-Americans." *Personnel and Guidance Journal,* 1972, *50,* 637–44.

Sue, S. "Mental Health Needs as Affected by Historical and Contemporary Experiences." Paper presented at Ethnic Lifestyle and Mental Health Seminar, Oklahoma State University, Stillwater, Okla., March, 1978a.

Sue, S. "The Chinese American Family." *Journal of the Society of Ethnic and Special Studies,* 1978b, *2,* 10–11.

Sue, S. "Psychological Issues, Theory and Implications for Asian Americans." *Personnel and Guidance Journal,* 1977, 55, 381–89.

Sue, S., and H. H. Kitano. "Stereotypes as a measure of success." *Journal of Social Issues,* 1973, *29,* 83–98.

Sue, S., and D. W. Sue. "Chinese American Personality and Mental Health." *Amerasia Journal,* 1971, *1,* 36–49.

Sue, S., D. W. Sue. and D. Sue, "Asian Americans as a Minority Group." *American Psychologist,* 1975, *30,* 906–10.

Sue, S., and H. McKinney. "Asian Americans in the Community Mental Health Care System." *American Journal of Orthopsychiatry*, 1975, *45*, 111–18.

United States Bureau of the Census. *Race of the Population by States: 1980*. Washington, D.C.: Government Printing Office, 1981.

United States Census of Population, 1970, Final Report PC (2)-IG: *Japanese, Chinese, and Filipino in the United States*. Washington, D.C.: U.S. Government Printing Office, 1973.

Wong, P. "The Emergence of the Asian American Movement." *Bridge*, 1972, *2*, 32–39.

Yee, A. H. "Myopic Perceptions and Textbooks: Chinese Americans' Search for Identity." *Journal of Social Issues*, 1973, *29*, 99–113.

7

Vietnamese Americans

MORE THAN 700,000 INDOCHINESE refugees have been forced by war, hunger, and oppression to flee Indochina. The initial wave of Vietnamese, approximately 135,000, departed when the Saigon government fell in 1975. The wave of immigrants from Vietnam offers a unique opportunity for counselors and other mental health professionals to influence the acculturation process of this wave of immigrants.

SOCIAL AND PSYCHOLOGICAL CHARACTERISTICS

Who Are the Vietnamese?

Several terms are used to identify Vietnamese: Indochinese, Vietnamese, Vietnamese American, "boat people," and Southeast Asians. Terms such as Indochinese, ethnic Chinese residents of Vietnam, Southeastern Asians, refugees, Vietnamese refugees, and "boat people" are broad terms which may include other Asian groups, so lack specificity. Therefore, only the terms Vietnamese Americans, Vietnamese, Vietnamese refugees, and Vietnamese "Boat people" will be used throughout this chapter. Although some ethnic Chinese lived in Vietnam, there is a separate chapter on Chinese in this text; therefore, the discussion in this chapter will focus only on Vietnamese.

Location of Vietnamese Americans

Since the fall of the Republic of South Vietnam on April 29, 1975, the United States has taken responsibility for approximately 150,000 Vietnamese refugees. Because of two years of joint efforts by governmental agencies and concerned religious and community organizations, most of these refugees have been resettled in towns and cities across the United States. According to Brower (1980), the total estimated figure of Vietnamese in the United States by January, 1980, was 304,000, and the influx of this ethnic group continues each month. However, the 1980 United States Census report indicates that there were 261,714 Vietnamese Americans residing in various parts of the United States (U.S. Bureau of Census, 1981). Vietnamese refugees are dispersed throughout the United States.

Social Values

Like the social values of other ethnic and cultural groups, traditional Vietnamese values and customs vary from those of mainstream America. The traditional Vietnamese's value system is a significant determinant of his social and individual behavior.

Penner and Tran Anh (1977) investigated the value systems of a randomly selected group of 1,427 Americans and 349 Vietnamese living in South Vietnam shortly prior to the collapse of the Saigon government. The results of this investigation revealed that Vietnamese and Americans varied in regard to their goals in life, and also in their beliefs about how to attain these goals. National security was valued more highly by Vietnamese than by the Americans, while freedom was valued more highly by Americans than by Vietnamese. Social recognition is linked to the Confucian ideology that emphasizes respect and admiration. Penner and Tran Ahn maintain that the respect and admiration of an individual's peers are very important values among Vietnamese. Also, the Vietnamese group considered obedience as more important than did the Americans. Yet ambition was not considered as strong by the Vietnamese as it was by the Americans. Penner and Tran

Anh suggest that this lack of concern for ambition is consistent with the Confucian ideology and the realities of the social structure in Vietnam. Finally, the findings suggested that the college-educated Vietnamese and Americans were more similar in their belief systems than were those Vietnamese and Americans who were less well-educated.

Nguyen Kim Hong (1978) observed several factors of cultural tradition that are important to traditional Vietnamese social values. For example, many Vietnamese perceive life as relaxed and spiritual, in the sense of being guided by religious and metaphysical doctrines. Not much emphasis is placed on punctuality, because time is believed to be elastic. Therefore, a Vietnamese's working conditions are generally relaxed. Also, considerable time is spent in meal preparation. It usually is customary for children to request that their parents eat first, and preferred foods are served first to parents or older persons. These and other values are obviously at odds with some behaviors prized in American society, such as life in a fast-food, fast living, and time-centered world. Most of the Vietnamese refugees who enter the United States suffer varied degrees of cultural shock.

Grognet (1980) contends that most Vietnamese can be characterized as thrifty, industrious, patient, and determined. A love for learning causes Vietnamese to be hard workers. Teachers, too, are accorded high respect; this value orientation may range from "an enlightened and healthy respect for scholarship to a blind veneration of the learned and everything connected with book-learning, an attitude more commonly found among the less-educated masses" (Grognet, 1980, p. A5).

According to Grognet (1980), the interpersonal relations of Vietnamese appear to be more formal than those of Americans. Vietnamese social interactions are couched in protocol where high values are placed on decorum and etiquette. For example, if a teacher requests that a Vietnamese child return a book, the child will invariably return it with both hands, his eyes lightly lowered to show respect. American males are generally addressed as "sir." Kissing in public is frowned on, except for infants.

Vietnamese often observe a degree of formality even within

the confines of the family. For example, family members may practice ancestor worship with annual rituals.

Another interesting traditional value orientation among Vietnamese is their pluralistic approach to life, which does not preclude, for example, identifying oneself as a Buddhist and practicing Christianity at the same time. Members of this ethnic group search out alternative approaches to problems. There is a willingness to accept a range of relative standards as opposed to accepting a single standard.

An important dimension of the pluralistic approach to life is the need to seek harmony in life. This is strongly linked with Taoist belief that through the attainment of emotional harmony and the natural and harmonious growth of all things one finds the self. Vietnamese often avoid conflict-producing situations.

Another traditional value orientation among many Vietnamese hinges on their sense of permanence. This sense of permanence is related to their concept of time. For instance, the everyday pace of life for a Vietnamese person is perhaps more relaxed and less hurried than that of a non-Vietnamese counterpart. According to Grognet (1980), traditions and customs change slowly with many Vietnamese persons. Their sense of permanence is best illustrated, as has already been noted, in the relationship between the deceased and the living through yearly family commemorative rituals conducted for a family member who has died.

These are only a few of the many social factors that influence the behavior of Vietnamese people, and the reader should keep in mind that beliefs vary among individual Vietnamese. Variations in adherence to values are significantly tied to the individual's experiences and socialization processes, which involve such factors as social-class status, education, and family background. Finally, Vietnamese's *prized belief systems* are not static; although the pace of change is slow, these beliefs do change.

Socioeconomic Characteristics

Three categories of Vietnamese people came to the United States as refugees: wealthy upper class who were fearful of persecution because of their fortunes and/or religion; military or government officials and employees; and dependents of American citizens, mainly military personnel (Burmark and Hyung-Chan Kim, 1978).

The official categories of Vietnamese refugees eligible for financial benefits from United States government agencies are families of Americans; Vietnamese who are close relatives of United States citizens or permanent residents in their country; Vietnamese who worked for United States government personnel and their families; and those Vietnamese who were counted as "high risks" for Communist reprisals and/or possible execution, since they were significant political and intelligence figures ("All Those Refugees," U.S. News and World Report, 1975).

Other Vietnamese refugees were described by evacuation officials as middle- and upper-class South Vietnamese. Many were doctors, lawyers, university professors, and technicians. For the less skilled, job training programs have been provided. Also, private organizations have assisted governmental agencies in securing job and resettlement tasks. Today, American Vietnamese can be found in a variety of occupations. Many are employed in industrial and professional capacities and as business owners.

Religion

Closely associated with the Vietnamese value systems are their religious practices and beliefs. The major religious preferences among the Vietnamese are Roman Catholicism, Buddhism, and Confucianism (Rahe, Looney, Ward, Tran Minh Tung, and Liu, 1978). The French occupation of Vietnam led to the introduction of Catholicism in Vietnam (Tate, 1971), but many scholars maintain that the Confucian ideology has continued to prevail as the predominant ideology in Vietnam. Confucianism is not so much a religion as it is a collection of standards dictating how an individual of virtue should live (Penner and Tran Anh, 1977). The ideology of Confucianism suggests that individuals should manifest such virtues as generosity, moderation, politeness, reason, steadfastness, and trust.

As was stated earlier, Vietnamese take a pluralistic approach to life, and therefore, it is not uncommon for some Vietnamese to practice more than one religion simultaneously. In short, Vietnamese vary in their beliefs and religious practices.

Family Characteristics

Nguyen Kim Hong (1978) maintains that a traditional Vietnamese family living in Vietnam often included as many as five families occupying one home. Family socialization patterns between parents and children included teaching the children to respect and obey their parents. Children are given little freedom to meet individual needs. Because of the Confucian ideology, individual achievement is not stressed. An individual's primary responsibility is to the family and society. Nguyen Kim Hong (1978) observes that adult Vietnamese children frequently live with their parents until they marry. The hierarchy for obedient behavior among Vietnamese women is to obey the father, then their husbands, and then the eldest sons, should the father die. This ideology underscores "filial piety and the subservience of women to, first, their fathers, and later in life, their husbands" (Penner and Tran Anh, 1977, p. 189). Because of this expected behavior, it is understandable that Vietnamese women do not value equality as highly as do American women. According to Penner and Tran Anh (1977), some Vietnamese women appear to have "internalized the subservient role assigned to them in the Vietnamese culture" (p. 201). Furthermore, to be obedient seems to be an important behavior among many Vietnamese women, while ambitious behavior is not considered important to either Vietnamese women or men. Perhaps because of the traditional family-oriented roles assigned to women, responsible behavior, such as being dependable and reliable, has greater importance to Vietnamese men than women (Penner and Tran Anh, 1977).

Borrowing from the Chinese, a Vietnamese person's name usually contains three words, although some have four. When a person has a three-word name, the first word represents the family name, the second word represents the middle name, and the last syllable is the given name. The family name is rarely used, and the given name is preferred. In friendly usage, only the given name is used, and to be courteous, the word "Mr." precedes the given name. For example, a Vietnamese named Vo Nguyen Van is known as Van to close acquaintances and Mr. Van to others. In cases where there are four-word names, the last two syllables are the given name (Dinh Phuc Van, 1976; Williams, 1976).

Neither Vietnamese children nor adults look directly at another person when they are talking because this behavior is considered disrespectful. They especially avoid looking directly at an older person or at persons considered to have authority. Instead they look downward and only intermittently glance upward (Vietnamese American Association, 1980; Brower, 1980).

While these traditional Vietnamese family-oriented behaviors still exist, they vary across families as well as within families, due to social status, education, and other experiences. No one should assume a blanket family-socialization pattern across all or even most Vietnamese families. Vietnamese Americans in the United States also are experiencing new and different family-oriented socializations, particularly those who are placed in homes of American families to facilitate their settlement in this country.

Educational Characteristics

Burmark and Hyung-Chan Kim (1978) maintain that nearly 30 percent of the Indochinese refugee population were children less than 12 years of age. According to a United States government report (1976), 42 percent of the population, whose ages ranged from 12 to 17, entered the public education system in the United States. Burmark and Hyung-Chan Kim (1978) state that school systems charged with the task of educating such children encountered difficulties because Vietnamese families with school-aged children were so widely distributed; this meant that many school districts had fewer than one hundred Vietnamese children, which often meant that only two or three Vietnamese might be enrolled in any single school. This contributed to some adjustment problems. Some school districts assign teachers to travel to five to six schools where

Vietnamese children are enrolled. Where feasible, Vietnamese children are transported to centrally located schools where bilingual teachers teach English as a second language, the Vietnamese language, and information pertaining to core courses such as social studies.

Socioeconomic status variations among Vietnamese often create difficulties in the educational setting. Those status-conscious Vietnamese are often resistant to taking part in programs involving other Vietnamese who are of a lower status. Burmark and Hyung-Chan Kim (1978) state that the status-conscious Vietnamese's "seemingly uncooperative attitude is probably due in part to their awareness of the situation in Vietnam where children from lower-class families rarely had the opportunity for formal education" (p. 3). The general attitude felt by these Vietnamese is that the education of their children will be retarded should they attend a homogeneous educational program that lacks consideration for social class and scholastic background differences.

Just as previous discussions on social values, socioeconomic status, family background, and religion have suggested variations among Vietnamese people, the education of this ethnic group contains differences as well. It was stated earlier that, according to Lynell Burmark and Hyung-Chan Kim (1978), three categories of Vietnamese refugees came to the United States: (1) the wealthy upper class, (2) military or government officials and employees, and (3) dependents of American citizens (p. 3). The range of educational achievement among adults includes many college graduates and professionals, persons who have technical skills, and many others at the lower end of the educational continuum.

Language Characteristics

The principal language of the Vietnamese refugees is Vietnamese. The Vietnamese language is, according to Williams (1976), a distant relative of those languages labeled as belonging to the Austro-Asiatic family of Mainland Southeast Asia. Vietnamese language has also been grouped as Sino-Tibetan language (another dominant language family in the Southeast Asian region). The Vietnamese vocabulary "is largely Chinese in origin, in much the same way that English, a Germanic language, is massively indebted to Romance tongues" (Williams, 1976, p. 19). French and English are also spoken by some Vietnamese because of the French and American occupations of South Vietnam.

In short, although several languages including dialects are spoken by the Vietnamese people, the dominant language is Vietnamese. Though English is spoken by some, many Vietamese who have come to the United States lack fluent English; thus, the need to learn a new language was another immediate problem.

Self-Perceptions

Vietnamese war-related traumas and adjustment problems caused by resettlement in the United States have negatively affected most Vietnamese Americans' self-images. Vietnamese with limited English find it difficult to secure employment, and a majority are forced to rely on public assistance. Often, as a result of such financial dependency, which is especially painful to many upper-class Vietnamese (Burmark and Hyung-Chan Kim, 1978, p. 3), a lack of self-respect has emerged. These types of experiences may indeed affect the Vietnamese Americans' behavior and self-perception.

As part of their research investigation at a Vietnamese refugee camp, Rahe, Looney, Ward, Tran Minh Tung, and Liu (1978) studied Vietnamese refugees' perceptions of their life position. The three age groups included people thirteen to nineteen years old, twenty to twenty-nine years old, and forty years old or older. How individuals perceive their position in life was defined as representing how close or how far they are from their worst possible world or best possible world. Vietnamese refugees reported moderately high perceptions for the first and fifth years just prior to their refugee camp period, while the perceptions of their current status during their refugee camp period were significantly low. Their perceptions of their past and future status far exceeded their current or in-camp status. Teenage males reported the lowest perceptions for the past first and fifth years prior to their refugee camp period and the highest perceptions of themselves in the future. Teenage females reported the highest perceived life status over all five-year periods including past, current, and future. The older women reported the lowest perceptions over time. These low perceptions for the older women were significantly different from the higher perceptions reported by men of the same age group for all time periods.

Now that the first wave of Vietnamese refugees have been transported from refugee camps and resettled in communities throughout the United States, new results reported by Rahe et al. (1978) suggest that Vietnamese tend to have a positive outlook about their future. Yet research also indicates variations of self-perception by age and sex groups. Both male and female teenage Vietnamese appear to have higher perceptions of themselves for the future than do older Vietnamese. These perceptions may have important implications for counseling assistance. For instance, the second wave of Vietnamese refugees—referred to as Vietnamese "boat people"—may encounter low perceptions of their world situation similar to the former group during their resettlement in refugee camps. Should this situation occur, this possibility also has counseling implications.

VIETNAMESE AMERICANS' ENCOUNTER WITH SITUATIONAL ADJUSTMENT: AN ACCULTURATION PROCESS

Vietnamese Americans have encountered several problems in the United States as a result of fleeing from a war-torn country and resettling in this country. Many of their problems are related to the difficulty of "leaving home, family, and property probably forever; life in refugee camps; resettlement in nontropical environments; dealing with social welfare agencies; finding a job; learning English; and so on" (Smither and Rodriguez-Giegling, 1979, p. 470). Many of these difficulties are the inevitable conflicts between cultures. The necessity to adjust to new patterns and life-styles frequently evokes varying degrees of psychological frustration and stress.

Institutions such as the schools have been challenged to help resolve the cultural conflicts which Vietnamese students encounter in the learning processes. In addition, families who socialize with Vietnamese are attempting to facilitate Vietnameses' acculturation of American society's attitudes and cultural patterns. The acculturational process has not been an easy one. Although some Vietnamese Americans readily adopt and adjust to the elements of American society, other Vietnamese Americans straddle the two cultures, or refuse to acculturate at all. Research, such as that done by Smither and Rodriguez-Giegling (1979), illustrates the problems that confront Vietnamese Americans as they attempt to heal their scars and make adjustments to a foreign environment. Such efforts often generate psychological stress and anxiety. The ensuing discussion focuses on particular problem areas as identified by Vietnamese and suggests nontraditional and culturally relevant counseling approaches to assist Vietnamese clients in meeting their mental health needs.

Acculturation and Personal Adjustment among Vietnamese Americans

Smither and Rodriguez-Giegling (1979) maintain that Vietnamese refugees in this country are faced with the difficulties of becoming acculturated to a highly modern and industrialized society. They further state that in spite of the much accumulated data on the demographies of acculturation that have been reported (i.e., HEW Refugee Task Force Report to the Congress, 1977), few professionals appear cognizant of the psychological factors of this process. Vietnameses' mental health, personal adjustment and psychosomatic stress rests upon their levels of acculturation. Many behaviors, such as changes in previous levels of linguistic, perceptual, or cognitive abilities, result from Vietnamese individuals' acceptance of and adaptation to the cultural patterns and life-styles of American society.

Some investigations have examined the acculturation process of Vietnamese and other refugees as they attempt to adjust to a modern and industrial society such as the United States. Smither and Rodriguez-Giegling (1979), for example, conducted exploratory research to measure marginality (feelings of being on the edge of a culture rather than integrated into it), modernity (an interpersonal perception that accepts change, diversity, and the inquiry of new experiences), and anxiety in a group of Vietnamese refugees. Their results revealed that compared to a random sampling of Americans, the refugees had higher feelings of being on the edge of both Vietnamese and American cultures, higher feelings of anxiety, and lower interpersonal perceptions than did the Americans. These investigators noted that feelings of marginality seem to be unrelated to the anxiety many Vietnamese experience. Instead, Smither and Rodriguez-Giegling (1979) suggest that the anxiety is more related to job, family, and home than to concerns about marginality.

Harding and Looney (1977) reported similar findings of adjustment problems of Vietnamese children confined to a refugee camp. Their findings suggested that children separated from their families manifested increased emotional vulnerability, and that foster placement of children without families represented a serious emotional problem. Many of these children received strong emotional support from their multigenerational Vietnamese families, and they adapted well to the new environment.

Another study reported by Dao The Xuong (1980) focused on problems related to the mental health of 196 refugees (75 percent Vietnamese and 25 percent Laotian) in the state of Oklahoma. Dao The Xuong states that 50 percent of the refugees who had not adapted to the cultural patterns in the United States were most affected by past problems and appeared significantly more depressed than other refugees. Part of this nonadaptability is associated with the rapid pace in the United States, which was cited most often as the cause for personal dissatisfaction. Eighty-seven percent of these refugees reported that they were depressed; 6 percent were very depressed; and 1 percent attempted suicide. According to Dao The Xuong, these latter behaviors were associated with such factors as increasing age and statements of anxiety and guilt regarding the conditions of relatives in Vietnam, as well as those who were not acculturating to life in American society.

In short, for the Vietnamese, adjustment to American ways of life and concern for relatives who remain in Vietnam are only a few problems which influence their levels of acculturation. Therefore, to assist Vietnamese in relieving their problems, counseling professionals will encounter unique concerns requiring new and different counseling approaches.

Perceptions of Mental Health and Mental Illness

Tran Minh Tung (1978b) states that although community resources in mental health are of high quality and frequently accessible, few Vietnamese use these resources despite their needs. This underutilization of such mental health services is associated with the self-perceptions of individuals who consider themselves mentally healthy even though a problem may exist. While Vietnamese struggle to adjust to life in the United States, few comprehend the benefits to be derived from mental health services such as counseling. These services are effective only if the people perceive the need for assistance. Yet perceived needs and requests for assistance are contingent upon such basic determinants as education and culture. Tran Minh Tung suggests that education will have little effect on Vietnamese culture; yet this culture is considered the major socializing agent that maintains and transmits perceptions, thoughts, and practice of the sociocultural traditions which defines mental health and mental illness of the group. Individual factors, likewise, mediate these perceptions; however, the concepts of mental illness and mental health are generally shared according to the majority of commonly held cultural values.

According to Tran Minh Tung (1978a), the causality of physical and mental problems or diseases is often explained through general categories such as physical agents, supernatural elements, and metaphysical factors. These causal factors may function singularly or collectively.

Although supernatural influences are not a frequent factor in contemporary society, Vietnamese tend to adhere to supernatural phenomena when symptoms appear unclear and inconceivable—as they do in most psychological disorders where specific causal explanations are lacking. The Vietnamese believe that such psychological disorders strike as a result of supernatural powers who convey anger by striking the unfortunate individual, who through some deficiency, accident, or deviation from religious or ethical standards, has provoked their anger. Tran Minh Tung (1978a) states that even those Vietnamese who are Christians or Buddhists use mystical beliefs to explain illness or suffering.

The Vietnamese also use both metaphysical and realistic elements to explain psychological and physical disorders. They consider health an element of life in the universe that works within the standards of a unified, comprehensive plan. They believe, for instance, that an individual's bodily functions maintain a balance between two poles; in medicine, these two poles are hot and cold, with health being the perfect balance between the two and a result of the harmonious functions of the relationship. However, a deviation toward either the hot or cold element creates an imbalance that results in discomfort and illness. Thus, medicines generally contain a mixture of drugs, foods, and other natural properties to help return the equilibrium between the hot and cold condition of the body. According to Tran Minh Tung (1978a), diarrhea results from the individual's cold stomach, while excessive hot elements might be represented through skin rashes or red spots on the skin.

Additionally, Vietnamese perceive that their body illnesses result from explanations of the protagonist *phong* or "wind" theory. It is believed that the wind or *phong* gets into the body and causes, for example, strokes, seizures, or common colds. Some types of foods, such as beef and buffalo meat, are also considered bearers of the *phong*.

These physical, supernatural, and metaphysical Vietnamese beliefs regarding general health and illness of course affect the way in which Vietnamese perceive mental health and mental illness. In the area of mental illness or diseases, the term "psychiatrist," for example, does not have a specific Vietnamese translation (Tran Minh Tung, 1978). Tran Minh Tung (1978a) maintains that the appropriate meaning of psychiatrist is derived from the Chinese literary term suggesting "mental doctor." The term "nerve doctor" is more accepted among the average Vietnamese than the former term. However, a description of the specialist as one who assists "crazy people" is far more comprehensible than either of the two former terms (Tran Minh Tung, 1978a, p. 10).

The Vietnamese view mental illness, then, from two perspectives: (1) a form of medication or cure for the nerves, and (2) a form of medication or cure for the mentally ill. In the organic perspective mental illness is perceived as an impaired nervous system, while from the supernatural perspective, the focus is on mystical and bizarre elements and simplistic explanations are offered for mental conditions.

From the organic perspective, the nervous system is viewed as the source of all human activity. Changes in the level of structure of this activity create dysfunctions in the nervous system, which may be described as "a weakness of the nerves" (neurosis) or "turmoil of the nerves" (psychosis) (Tran Minh Tung, 1978a, p. 10). Weakness of the nerves may range from symptoms of anxiety to depression, as well as mental retardation and mental deterioration.

Mental illness also may be perceived as a supernatural occurrence. In this perspective, an individual's mental illness is attributed to the actions of the individual's shameful character or, perhaps, to his punishment for offensive acts toward god. Mental illness may happen accidentally, because of ignorance, or as a result of bad luck—the hapless individual simply gets in the way of an evil spirit. An individual can be punished for his own wrong doings as well as those committed by family members, simply because of his relationship to them. Nonetheless, through "prayers and offerings or magical countermeasures," the individual suffering mental illness may be forgiven or pardoned for some of his wrongdoings or sins (Tran Minh Tung, 1978a, p. 11).

Most mental illnesses are perceived as negative conditions that mark the family; such illnesses are not usually shared with individuals outside the immediate family. Public knowledge of a family member's mental illness may, by extension, preclude marriage into a mentally healthy family. According to Tran Minh Tung (1978a), psychological factors are seldom considered as the mediators of an individual's mental illnesses.

In conclusion, these perceptions related to mental health and mental illness must be considered when working with Vietnamese-American clients. While the importance of these perceptions is underscored, it is equally important to recognize the diversity—caused by varying acculturation levels—of definitions and practices among Vietnamese Americans regarding mental health and mental illness. Finally, Vietnamese clients' perceptions of mental health and mental illness should be assessed individually as well as culturally. As Vietnamese adjust to the life and behavioral patterns of American society, further variations in their definitions of mental health and mental illness are likely to occur.

Attitudes toward Mental Health Professionals

Few data have been presented to detail the Vietnamese's attitudes toward Western mental health professionals and facilities, but Western mental health practices appear to be inconsistent with traditional Vietnamese beliefs. For example, Tran Minh Tung (1978a) argues that traditional Western-style counseling or psychotherapy places a premium on talk as a method of treatment; this would seldom be applied in Vietnam, or if applied, it would be perceived as nothing more than a partial treatment. Further, he states that sitting down before an outsider and verbalizing problems is not a common practice among most Vietnamese. While verbalization does occur and Vietnamese do talk about their problems, such talk has a different focus and a different point of view from that of Americans. A Vietnamese does not seek professional assistance "with the conscious determination to open himself up to seek relief for his emotional difficulties" (Tran Minh Tung, 1978a, p. 16), but rather, the Vietnamese client expects the mental health professional to apply positive, active intervention and to give direction and guidance. Tran Minh Tung (1978a) asserts that the therapist may be perceived "as the omniscient, omnipotent authority figure which will take over the responsibility of the treatment, asking the patient only to be docile and compliant" (p. 16).

According to Nguyen Duy San (1969), because few Vietnamese are accustomed to Western approaches in psychotherapy, Vietnamese who do experience difficulties tend to seek assistance from older persons, usually members of the immediate family. Others search out help from a healer or a Buddhist monk who has the necessary skill to deal with such conditions. Many monks believe that mental or nervous illnesses and other problems occur as a result of supernatural forces that can be allayed through religious prayers and offerings or magical countermeasures (Hickey, 1964; Tran Minh Tung, 1978a).

At any rate, traditional Vietnamese beliefs and practices regarding mental illness preclude an easy acceptance of Western counselors and therapists and of Western mental health intervention strategies. Many well-educated Vietnamese refugees from upper- or upper-middle socioeconomic levels as well as those who worked with Americans in Vietnam, do exhibit varying degrees of acceptance toward mental health professionals. Mental health professionals need to become aware of Vietnamese cultural and behavioral patterns and skilled in the Vietnamese language to improve the acceptance and effectiveness of their therapeutic assistance.

Communication in Counseling

Communication is emphasized throughout this text as a significant component in the therapeutic relationship between the individual who is to receive assistance and the counselor. Frequently, however, communication barriers prevent the counselor or other mental health professional from productively assisting individuals in need of help (Ivey, 1977). For example, Vietnamese refugees encounter, more often than not, mental health professionals who lack the ability to communicate in the Vietnamese language. Dao The Xuong (1980) reported—from the results of a survey of 196 Vietnamese (75 percent) and Laotian (25 percent) refugees in the United States—that 44 percent of the refugees were experiencing language problems.

Tran Minh Tung (1978b) contends that, in spite of the availability of many physical resources for Vietnamese, personnel rarely included those who could communicate in the refugees' language or understand their sociocultural environment. Even when English-speaking Indochinese were used to translate and provide information to American professionals treating Vietnamese, the simplistic, candid nature of the translation did not reflect the Vietnamese's nonverbal messages and verbal tones. And nonverbal responses frequently underscore an individual's explicit messages and are often incongruent with such verbal messages. Vietnamese, for example, may respond to another person's question by stating yes out of politeness or a fear that a no response would be disrespectful, but the individual's covert feelings are not affirmative. In such a case, the individual's nonverbal cues may indeed be observable behavior that contradicts the verbal messages. For example, a Vietnamese's facial expression may suggest happiness but may often mask emotional anguish, feelings of distress, and isolation (Duong Thanh Binh, 1975). This happy facial expression can also exemplify calm, repressed emotions regarding misfortunes or disguise opposing behavior that may suggest unfriendly perceptions such as hostility (Bourne, 1970).

Linguistic and cultural misinterpretations of Vietnamese prevent positive client outcomes and cause further suffering in the interpersonal relationships between the client and the counselor. For this reason, Tran Minh Tung (1978b) advocates that there is need for a bilingual person who has some exposure to both Vietnamese and American cultures as well as knowledge and experience in the field of mental health.

Adjustment Problems in American Schools

The adjustment to an educational environment is not always an easy task for any individual. This task becomes even more complex when individuals, such as Vietnamese refugee students, are faced with a totally unfamiliar cultural as well as school environment. For instance, most Vietnamese students are not prepared to function in American schools where students illustrate their interests and abilities by asking questions and assuming active participation in the educational process (Burmark & Hyung-Chan Kim, 1978). Traditional Vietnamese learning theories emphasize memorization and recitation of Confucian ethics. As part of these ethics, knowledge is conveyed from teachers to students without any challenge from the latter. Innovation is thought of as secondary to imitation, and students are not encouraged to ask questions or demonstrate creative ability.

Further conflict emerges from different ways of communicating thoughts and feelings. Contrary to the American student's open and direct behavior, Vietnamese students are traditionally taught to rely on more subtle ways of revealing their emotions to others. Therefore, when American students publicly demonstrate affectionate behavior in school, this dismays the Vietnamese student who has been taught that kissing, for example, is equivalent to a marriage proposal. It is not uncommon in Vietnam to see a young male holding hands with another young male, but his behavior is frowned upon should a young male hold hands with a young female. These differences in acceptable behaviors suggest the reluctance of Vietnamese students to engage in coeducational programs involving such activities as dancing and contact sports. (Burmark and Hyung-Chan Kim, 1978, p. 5).

According to Burmark and Hyung-Chan Kim (1978), Vietnamese students also refrain from participating in group activities as a result of racial prejudice conveyed overtly and covertly by some American students. Vietnamese students have begun to establish their own cliques to avoid being called names and to avoid experiencing physical abuse. Obviously, the formation of such a clique further isolates these individuals from the other students.

In short, it appears that few Vietnamese students are able to adjust easily to the American educational environment. Therefore, it is crucial for counselors and educators to take active roles to help ameliorate these students' psychological adjustment. Maladaptive behavior in American educational settings may, of course, lead to poor academic achievement. Over time and with proper counseling help, however, Vietnamese students will improve their adjustment vis-a-vis the educational process as they adopt and adapt to life-styles of American society.

Some Practical Approaches to Working with Vietnamese Americans

It is understandable that a bilingual-bicultural approach to counseling should be the initial consideration when working with Vietnamese Americans since few Vietnamese are able to communicate fluently in English. Therefore, it is necessary for counselors and other mental health professionals who assist these Vietnamese to acquire bilingual and bicultural requisites: fluency in Vietnamese and English and knowledge of both Vietnamese and American cultures. While this statement is certainly justifiable, such requirements appear to be a large order (and rightly so), and most counselors lack Vietnamese language skills and knowledge about the Vietnamese culture. A further consideration here is the extent to which Vietnamese who are suffering with problems of adjustment can afford to defer working on their problems until American counselors are thoroughly trained in Vietnamese language skills and culture. Obviously, the mental health conditions of Vietnamese cannot wait until a massive, arduous, time-consuming counselor training is completed. Therefore, Tran Minh Tung (1978b) advocates that Vietnamese mental health professionals train Vietnamese lay persons to become mental health paraprofessionals. They could provide the necessary communication link between Vietnamese clients and the mental health counselors.

Tran Minh Tung (1978a) contends that the mental health problems of Vietnamese refugees are more varied than the typical "psychiatric symptoms of depression, anxiety, or psychotic breakdown" (p. 7). Many Vietnamese refugees experience problems in social adjustment or interpersonal relationships that involve social behavior, family conflicts, school and job difficulties, isolation, and withdrawal. These problems are extrapsychic rather than intrapsychic.

Mental health paraprofessionals could become involved in many aspects of the resettlement process. As problems arise, paraprofessionals would be responsible for initiating and coordinating the resources necessary to assist refugees in reducing their distress and to apply active techniques to give support and relief to the client. Another function for the paraprofessional would be that of disseminating essential information to Vietnamese refugees. For instance, paraprofessionals could direct clients to appropriate mental health facilities or organizations. Finally, paraprofessionals could interpret information and aid in reports and evaluations by continually evaluating needs and resources and by examining the effectiveness of mental health programs. These functions, as suggested by Tran Minh Tung (1978b), would facilitate the work of counselors and other mental health professionals as well as assist Vietnamese refugees with their adjustment problems.

Because counseling and psychotherapy are virtually unknown to most Vietnamese (Nguyen Duy San, 1969), there are several considerations that counselors should bear in mind as they work with Vietnamese clients. For instance, most Vietnamese are not likely to self-disclose their problems to a counselor in a dyadic relationship. Therefore, self-disclosure as a goal in counseling with such clients may be culturally inappropriate, particularly for recent Vietnamese refugees whose values are grounded in a highly-structured sociocultural context. Like teachers, counselors are considered figures of authority, and it is assumed by Vietnamese that counselors and teachers will be directive and authoritative in their roles. Counselors who function in less than an authoritarian role may be perceived as uninterested in the client's concerns.

Also, most Vietnamese are taught to suppress their anger, stress, and frustration through psychological or physical withdrawal (Nguyen Duy San, 1969). They are expected to accept a humble attitude toward their achievements. Therefore, it may be necessary to explain American society's expectations. For instance, counselors may need to assist Vietnamese in acquiring assertiveness training skills to help facilitate their adjustment to American employment and educational situations. In addition, Tran Minh Tung (1978a) advises that counselors should exercise caution in introducing new concepts that are likely to be interpreted initially as disrespectful and rude behavior. That is, many Western counseling methods used to treat clients are foreign to Vietnamese and will be judged as inappropriate; thus counselors must consider the counseling experiences of Vietnamese clients. As stated earlier, traditional Vietnamese values encourage females to adhere to an obedient role in society, yet the effectiveness of their psychosocial adjustment to American society may be dependent on the degree to which they exercise assertive behavior. Counselors must tread lightly in such matters.

There are also some problems in group work with family

members. Personal concerns communicated in a group format can be harmful and/or embarrassing to the clients as well as other family members. For example, Tran Minh Tung (1978a) observes that family members are typically quick to answer the counselor's questions, but they generally will not discuss their problems in a group situation. Children of the family are reluctant to disclose their negative emotions for fear of being disrespectful, while parents feel ill-at-ease exhibiting their emotions in front of their children. Tran Minh Tung concludes that family group sessions result in a general camouflage, with each member protecting the others and maintaining a respectable reputation as a family unit. Therefore, it appears that more productive assistance for the family will occur through individual contact. The traditional Vietnamese family is patriarchal, so the father is the most important person of the family. Because of this, once a sound rapport or relationship has been established between the counselor and the father, counselors may find it beneficial and more productive to assist the family by working through the father.

Eye contact is another practical consideration when working with Vietnamese. Traditionally, Vietnamese have been taught not to look another person directly in the eye because this behavior exemplifies disrespect toward the other person. Therefore, counselors should not interpret intermittent eye contact as a form of negative, disrespectful, or rude behavior (Nguyen Van Thuan, 1962; Vietnamese American Association, 1980; Brower, 1980).

An equally important consideration is knowing when the counselor should appropriately shake hands with a Vietnamese client. The male counselor's attempt to touch or shake the hand of a Vietnamese female over twelve years of age may be perceived as culturally inappropriate (Vietnamese American Association, 1980). More specifically, this behavior may be seen as a personal insult or threat to the female. Counselors should also be mindful that a Vietnamese female over twelve years old will also experience a degree of anxiety as she sits in a room with the door closed alone with a male who does not have family ties. Counselors who prefer to work with their clients in secluded quarters may have to consider a more open setting to help assure their female clients that the environment is nonthreatening.

In situations where there is language difficulty between the counselor and the Vietnamese client, it is more appropriate to request a Vietnamese adult rather than a child to act as a translator. The rationale is that most Vietnamese expect adult authority in, for example, counseling or school settings (Brower, 1980).

Counselors who work in school settings can play an important function that will assist other school personnel, Vietnamese parents and students, and non-Vietnamese students. Counselors should provide ongoing inservice programs to familiarize teachers and administrators with traditional Vietnamese culture. Included in these programs should be presentations pointing out similarities and differences between Vietnamese and American patterns of school behavior. In addition, with the aid of an interpreter, where needed, workshops for Vietnamese parents should be ongoing to inform parents about the American school system and about other information pertaining to their child's physical, educational, and psychological development. Group activities should be established for non-Vietnamese students to familiarize them with their Vietnamese classmates' traditional culture.

SUMMARY

These suggestions are only a few that might be implemented when dealing with Vietnamese Americans. Probably, the most important consideration is to include traditional Vietnamese values in counseling approaches designed to help facilitate the Vietnamese's adjustment to American society. It must be understood that counselors and other mental health workers can develop other counseling approaches that are culturally relevant to Vietnamese Americans. The perceptions of Vietnamese toward counselors and other mental health professionals are crucial to their use of Western mental health counseling and therapies and mental health facilities. Counselors' misapplication of culturally appropriate counseling intervention strategies with Vietnamese can only cause the therapeutic process to suffer.

Obviously, characteristics discussed here serve only as examples of descriptive behavior among Vietnamese Americans and are far from the total picture of this ethnic group. Counselors are encouraged to obtain more information regarding the Vietnamese and to become more aware of traditional Vietnamese customs in order to derive new, improved, and effective strategies to help the Vietnamese individual adjust to problems.

Finally, Vietnamese Americans consist of a heterogeneous group. Their acculturation levels of cultural patterns and life styles in the United States are varied, and counseling intervention strategies should be adjusted appropriately to these levels.

EXERCISES

The exercises that follow are based on the content discussed in this chapter on Vietnamese Americans. Each example below is typical of one that might be faced by a Vietnamese American who needs some type of counseling assistance; each exercise is designed to give students a practice experience in dealing with Vietnamese.

A. Read the example below and answer the questions that follow it. Then ask the students to role play the example and discuss it in small groups.

> Tung, a forty-one-year-old Vietnamese refugee, has been in the United States less than one year. He is married and living with his wife and two young children in a home provided by a religious group sponsor. Though he is working and maintaining his family, Tung recently has been experiencing difficulties adjusting to the rapid pace and impersonal relations among Americans. Tung has entered counseling for the first time. He is not accustomed to procedures in Western therapies or counseling practices.

1. What are some of the mental health and mental illness factors practiced among traditional Vietnamese?
2. As a counselor, how would you consider these factors in working with Tung?

3. How would you help Tung understand and adjust to the life-styles in the United States?

B. Ask one student to volunteer to play the role of Tran, a thirty-four-year-old, upper-class male Vietnamese refugee.

Tran is well-educated and had a high status in Vietnam. Presently, he is experiencing problems accepting a job that he considers beneath his previous social status. Tran is reluctant to consider any job that requires working with his hands. Because his former position in Vietnam was that of a high ranking government official, he cannot find similar work here. The only jobs available in the local area are those requiring the use of the worker's hands. Tran is unable to state his true feelings about this because it would be perceived by him as a sign of disrespect toward those who are trying to help him.

Another student should volunteer to play the role of counselor. Both volunteers should role play a counseling interview that lasts ten minutes. Following this interview, the client should give the counselor feedback regarding his counseling effectiveness. The counselor should also share his observations concerning the client and his counseling effectiveness. The rest of the class can offer feedback and counseling options for improving subsequent sessions. The counselor and client roles may be repeated with other students using the feedback and new approaches.

C. Ask each student to read and write a brief report answering the following questions. After the reports have been written, students should share their answers with each other and state their rationale for their answers. Discussion may also focus on the similarities and differences among student answers.

1. What are some of the barriers in both verbal and nonverbal communication that may occur between the Vietnamese client and the counselor?
2. What are some social behaviors that may be acceptable with Vietnamese men but unacceptable with Vietnamese women?

3. What are some traditional factors that may inhibit a Vietnamese person's willingness to talk about personal problems?
4. Discuss how these kinds of behaviors might impinge upon the counseling relationship, thus limiting positive, desired outcomes.

D. Ask a student to research and prepare an oral report on nonverbal behavior of Vietnamese persons. (These behaviors should include those extending from traditional Vietnamese culture to the most acculturated of American culture.) The class can discuss what the nonverbal behavior signifies and the effect it may have on interethnic communication in counseling interviews.

REFERENCES

"Agony of the Boat People." *Newsweek*, July 2, 1979, pp. 42–43, 46–48, 50.

"All Those Refugees—Who Are They, Where Are They Going? *U.S. News and World Report*, May 12, 1975, pp. 21–22.

Berry, J., and R. C. Annis. "Acculturative Stress." *Journal of Cross-Cultural Psychology*, 1974, *5*, 382–405.

Bourne, P. G. *Man, Stress and Vietnam*. Boston: Little, Brown, 1970.

Brower, I. C. "Counseling Vietnamese." *Personnel and Guidance Journal*, 1980, *58*, 646–52.

Burmark, L., and Hyung-Chan Kim. "The Challenge of Educating Vietnamese Children in American Schools." *Integrated Education*, 1978, *16*, 2–8.

Dao The Xuong. "Indochinese Refugees Adjustment Problems." In Vietnamese American Association, *Indochinese Refugees Adjustment Problems*. Oklahoma City, Okla.: Vietnamese American Association, 1980, p. F1–F10.

Dinh Phuc Van. "A Vietnamese Child in Your Classroom." *Instructor*, 1976, *85*.

Duong Thanh Binh. *Vietnamese in the U.S.* Arlington, Va.: Center for Applied Linguistics, 1975.

Grognet, A. G. "A Cross-Cultural Glimpse of the Vietnamese People: 1976–77." In Vietnamese American Association,

Indochinese Refugees Adjustment Problems. Oklahoma City, Okla.: Vietnamese American Association, 1980. Pp. A1–A20.

Harding, R. K., and J. G. Looney. "Problems of Southeast Asian Children in Refugee Camp." *American Journal of Psychiatry,* 1977, *134,* 407–410.

Hickey, G. C. *Village in Vietnam.* New Haven, Conn.: Yale University Press, 1964.

Ivey, A. E. Cultural Expertise: "Toward Systematic Outcome Criteria in Counseling and Psychological Education." *Personnel and Guidance Journal,* 1977, *55,* 296–302.

Nguyen Duy San. "Psychiatry in the Army of the Republic of Vietnam." In P. G. Bourne (ed.), *The Psychology and Physiology of Stress.* New York: Academic, 1969, Pp. 45–73.

Nguyen Kim Hong. "The Culture Crunch." *Senior Scholastic,* 1978, *110,* 18–20.

Nguyen Van Thuan. *An Approach to Better Understanding of Vietnamese Society.* Saigon: Michigan State University Advisory Group, 1962.

Penner, L. A., and Tran Anh. "A Comparison of American and Vietnamese Value Systems." *Journal of Social Psychology,* 1977, *101,* 187–204.

Rahe, R. H., J. G. Looney, H. W. Ward, Tran Minh Tung, and W. T. Liu. "Psychiatric Consultation in a Vietnamese Refugee Camp." *American Journal of Psychiatry,* 1978, *135,* 185–90.

Smither, R., and M. Rodriguez-Giegling. "Marginality, Modernity, and Anxiety in Indochinese Refugees. *Journal of Cross-Cultural Psychology,* 1979, *10,* 469–78.

Tate, D. J. M. *The Making of Modern South-East Asia-The European Conquest.* New York: Oxford University Press, 1971.

Tran Minh Tung. "Health and Disease: The Indochinese Perspective." Paper presented at the Health, Education, and Welfare Mental Health Projects Grantee Conferences, Atlanta, Chicago, San Francisco, and Seattle, Nov.–Dec. 1978a.

Tran Minh Tung. "The Indochinese Mental Health Paraprofessional: What Do We Want?" Paper presented at the Health,

Education and Welfare Mental Health Project Grantee Workshops. Atlanta, Chicago, San Francisco, and Seattle, Nov.–Dec. 1978b.

United States Bureau of the Census. *Race of the Population by States: 1980*. Washington, D.C.: U.S. Government Printing Office, 1981.

Vietnamese American Association. *Indochinese Refugees Adjustment Problems*. Oklahoma City, Okla.: Vietnamese American Association, 1980.

Williams, L. E. *Southeast Asia: A History*. New York: Oxford University Press, 1976.

8

Southern Appalachian Anglo Americans

UNLIKE MOST ANGLO AMERICANS in the United States, many Anglo individuals who inhabit the Southern Appalachian region are deprived of certain social, political, and economic opportunities common in American society (Stevic and Uhlig, 1967). Despite these barriers, most Southern Appalachian Anglos continue to struggle to rise above their present conditions and to attain their rightful place in American society. Some have managed to escape the misfortunes of this region by migrating to other locations in the United States, while others remain by choice, because of a lack of marketable employment skills, or because of a fear of cultural conflict. Because of their inability to adjust to a middle-class, rapidly changing, technological society, some of those who do leave the Appalachians to improve their life return. Southern Appalachian Anglos perceive the general American society as foreign to their traditional "folk" society (Killian, 1970).

The psychological discomforts associated with the problems faced by many Southern Appalachian Anglos often require counseling assistance. Counselors, therefore, should attain the cultural and linguistic skills necessary to provide effective counseling services to Southern Appalachian Anglo clients. Thus, this chapter discusses social and psychological characteristics, individual problems, and suggested counseling intervention strategies to assist Southern Appalachian Anglos with their problems.

SOCIAL AND PSYCHOLOGICAL CHARACTERISTICS

Who Are Southern Appalachian Anglos?

Several attempts have been made to describe the people of Southern Appalachia. For example, such labels as "hillbillies," "mountain people," "mountain man," "mountaineer," and "Appalachian mountaineer" have been ascribed to them. A label such as *hillbilly* is perceived by Southern Appalachian Anglos as a negative term (Killian, 1970). Moore states in *Profile of Appalachia* (1974) that most of the people of Appalachia are poor and of Anglo-Saxon descent. Simpkins (1974) points out that early settlers in the Appalachians were Scotch-Irish, English, Dutch, French Huguenots (French Protestants who left France), Portuguese, and Indians. Later, demands for coal from the Southern Appalachians attracted other groups such as Italians, Greeks, Hungarians, Austrians, Poles, and Russians. Blacks also settled in this area.

The primary focus of this chapter, however, centers on those Anglos, or Whites, who live in Southern Appalachia. The discussion throughout the remaining portions of this chapter will refer to the many ethnic groups in this area who consider themselves as White, Southern Appalachian Anglos, or Appalachians. The term "Appalachia," as it is used in this chapter, refers only to a particular geographical location rather than an impoverished, poor, backward, or economically depressed area.

Where Are They Located?

Linkous (1977) maintains that the Appalachian region encompasses a 195,000 square-mile area following the spine of the Appalachian Mountains from southern New York to northern Mississippi. It includes all of West Virginia and parts of twelve other States: Alabama, Georgia, Kentucky, Maryland, Mississippi, New York, North Carolina, Ohio, Pennsylvania, South Carolina, Tennessee, and Virginia. This region is composed of three subregions: (1) Northern Appalachia, (2) Central Appalachia, and (3) Southern Appalachia. According to Linkous, the Appalachian Regional Commission has characterized the topography of these subregions as "old, rugged and rounded mountains, rough mountains and hill lands derived from deeply dissected plateaus, folded mountains forming long ridges enclosing valleys of varying width, high rolling plateaus and valley low-lands and piedmont on the Region's margins" (p. 2).

Southern Appalachia extends from the highlands of Virginia to the Mississippi coastal plain. This subregion is generally where most of the persons discussed here are located.

Social Values

Although there are Anglos of several different ethnic groups in Southern Appalachia, they share common beliefs and social values. The commonalities of these social-value orientations represent a relatively homogeneous cultural population that seems unlike that of any other area of the United States. It has been noted in a survey by Jack Weller (1965) that the people of Southern Appalachia have value orientations toward such beliefs as individualism, traditionalism, and fatalism, and that these people are person-oriented and action-oriented.

Independence was an essential quality brought to this subregion by the early settlers. Weller (1965) states that this trait was necessary because many families live in relative isolation from other families separated by hollows or valleys. Communication and transportation occurred infrequently. This relative, geographic isolation forced these settlers to depend on their own strengths and resources. This trait later shifted to individualism, a trait suggestive of self-centered and self-directed qualities. Increased focus is on the individual himself, although group participation is necessary to attain individual needs. Schwarzweller, Brown, and Mangalam (1971) observed Anglos in three Beech Creek neighborhoods of eastern Kentucky and concluded that individualism is grounded in the philosophy of Puritanism and a democracy that encourages the ultimate rights of individuals. Because all individuals are perceived as God's children, each person has the choice and the responsibility to make decisions about events that will influence the direction of his life. Individuals are also free to place their own interpretations on God's messages. For example, Schwarzweller, Brown, and Mangalam state that "the Puritan creed with its Calvinistic overtones furnished the basis for innumerable quarrels, bickering, family feuds, and neighborhood divisions resulting from different interpretation of the Bible" (p. 65).

Many Southern Appalachian Anglos preserve old traditions that were practiced by earlier Southern Appalachian Anglos. On the basis of these earlier practices, it is assumed that such practices and beliefs are the standards of social behavior.

Significantly enmeshed in traditionalist is personalism. Here, the major concern is to be a person within a group, to be accepted, and to be recognized while responding in kind to such attention. Many believe that because life is a product of participation within a group, their life's goals may best be achieved in relation to other persons. While Appalachians may have individual aspirations and ambitions, they are more concerned with what their peers might think than are persons outside the Southern Appalachian culture. For example, Appalachians may reject a higher work position simply out of fear that acceptance of this position will negatively affect their peer relationships. Weller (1965) contends that personalism causes decision-making difficulty. For instance, Appalachians refrain from stating their mind unless they are sure that other members of the group concur with their feelings.

Fatalism emerged as another method of coping with the lack of material success often experienced by Appalachians. A fatalistic attitude permits these people to unquestioningly accept hardships and setbacks while feeling that life is basically difficult. Their lack of success and their hardships are accepted with a type of religious quality: "That's the way God wants it. He knows what's best. I'll just have to take what comes, I guess."

Another influencing value among Southern Appalachian Anglos is familism (Schwarzweller, Brown and Mangalam, 1971), which emphasizes family life. Each family member is expected to maintain family stability and unity. Family bonds—among immediate family members and other kin—

are important because they provide a sense of emotional and often materialistic support (Looff, 1971). Further discussion of the Southern Appalachian family is presented in a later section of this chapter.

More recent observations of Southern Appalachian Anglos, as noted by Wagner (1977) and Owen (1979), suggest that other value characteristics include a strong emphasis on religion, self-reliance, cultural pride, and family solidarity. Owen contends that self-reliance and individualism became characteristics which were prized because they often indicated success.

None of these social values function in isolation. They are likely to overlap as a dependent operation of social behavior. For example, self-reliance and individualism may overlap, yet these values are not shared equally by all Southern Appalachian Anglos. Although Appalachians hold many similar values, many practice only those of the folk culture; some may practice both those of the folk culture and those of the general American culture; and others practice only those of the general American culture. Southern Appalachian Anglos, like all ethnic groups are heterogeneous.

Socioeconomic Characteristics

Frequently, people think of Southern Appalachia as an economically depressed subregion populated by those who are impoverished, unemployed, illiterate, and isolated. Much of this is true. For instance, early observations of the socioeconomic conditions of Southern Appalachia often confirmed dismal conditions. The people of this subregion have suffered chronic unemployment, lack of educational and cultural facilities, and a tradition of dependency and helplessness (Walls and Stephenson, 1972, p. 227). According to the Appalachian Regional Commission (Linkous, 1977), thousands of workers lost their jobs in the 1950s because of the closing of the coal mines. Because of poor transportation facilities, no new industry came into the area. The cost of building roads over the mountainous terrain was staggering (Moore, 1974). Between 1960 and 1970, Southern Appalachia lost over 100,000 agricultural jobs. These negative economic conditions have often forced people of this subregion to move to urban industrial regions where employment is available (Weller, 1965).

However, in recent years, the people in Southern Appalachia have undergone great change. For example, Southern Appalachia has faced rapid industrial expansion. Since the establishment of the Appalachian Regional Commission and the Tennessee Valley Authority, the area's natural resources have been developed, new industries have moved into the region, and the economy has improved. There was a 22 percent increase in employment between 1965 and 1970 and a 19 percent increase between 1970 and 1974, although the mid-1970s recession has caused a recent decrease. Between 1965 and 1975, the total personal income for each person in Southern Appalachia increased from $2,032 to $4,687, an increase of more than 100 percent. During this same period, the national average increased from 73 percent to 78 percent (Linkous, 1977). However, this increase in personal income during the 1970s dropped below national averages and maintained this status in 1975. Total personal income in 1975 for Southern Appalachia increased by 3 percent, whereas the national average growth rate in income increased by 5 percent.

Manufacturing is a major source of the Southern Appalachian Anglo's income (Linkous, 1977). For instance, the textile industry was responsible for 38 percent of the manufacturing employment during 1974. Other income sources, such as farming, were responsible for a small part of total personal income (2 percent) in this subregion but increased by 8 percent compared to the national average decrease of 0.3 percent. These data suggest that economic conditions have improved for Anglos in Southern Appalachia.

This subregion contains persons whose socioeconomic status is heterogeneous, that is, there are middle, intermediate (combination of low and high class, Schwarzweller, Brown, and Mangalam, 1971), lower-class, and poor families. Some Southern Appalachian Anglos earn their living through farming and mining. Their geographical distribution is diverse: some live in urban areas, others in isolated hollows or valleys. Also, within this subregion, persons can be found in a variety of jobs along the occupational continuum. For example, there are professors, doctors, U.S. senators, scientists, lawyers, sales clerks, secretaries, janitors, unemployed, and underemployed. Some studies (Stevic and Uhlig, 1967) suggest that adolescents of migrant families who leave Southern Appalachia tend to have higher career aspirations than those who stay in this subregion. These differences are a result of variations in personal role models. In some cases, however, individuals consider money important to the extent that they care only to earn enough to sustain themselves and their families (Hansen and Stevic, 1971).

In summary, it is clear that Southern Appalachia has grown significantly over the last fifteen years. During 1970s, this subregion experienced an accelerated population rate; new industry has located in Appalachia; few Anglos migrate to other areas to obtain employment; and the people work at various occupations and levels. Finally, not all Southern Appalachia Anglos are adversely affected by the economic problems of this subregion. The poor as well as the more fortunate continue to persist within their own diverse social and economic structure.

Family Characteristics

Like the heterogeneity of the socioeconomic structure and value orientations found among the people of Southern Appalachia, there are variations in the types of families, too. For example, research results suggest differences among families in childrearing practices, socioeconomic status (Pavenstedt, 1965), work and time orientations, religious perceptions, and value systems (Weller, 1965; Stephenson, 1968; Brown and Schwarzweller, 1970; Schwarzweller, Brown, and Mangalam, 1971; Kaplan, 1971). Therefore, caution has been taken not to suggest that Southern Appalachian Anglo families subscribe to a single set of family attributes.

The two most dominant family types within the Southern Appalachian region appear to be the traditional family system and the modern or contemporary family system. The traditional Southern Appalachian family system is kept together more by standards of obligation than by close affectional ties. While affection may exist within the family unit, a family member is obligated to other members of the family regardless of the degree of that affection (Looff, 1971). Separate studies by Stephenson (1968) and Kaplan (1971) indicate that the modern family system is not one that stresses family closeness or solidarity. Fewer kinfolk live in the close proximity found among those who embrace traditional family systems.

Kaplan (1971) states the youngest child of the traditional family system was expected to stay with and care for the parents as they grew older. As a reward, this child inherited the family home. In the contemporary family system, however, parents or old kin generally live alone, and the children of some parents do not live nearby. According to Kaplan, there does not seem to be a general concensus on a standard set of obligations of the children to their parents today.

In the past, clearly defined sex roles were practiced within the traditional family system: The wife assumed a subordinate position, and the husband maintained his position as authoritarian. For example, women would not sign a petition, because it was believed that this was a man's decision (Kaplan, 1971, p. 64). However, Stephenson (1968) maintains that there is little difference in the values between women and men in the contemporary family system of Southern Appalachia. For instance, both men and women desire much the same things in life and will apply similar methods to attain them. There is a more egalitarian framework for wife-and-husband interaction, yet families still acknowledge the father as the head of the household. According to Brown and Schwarzweller (1970), the family cannot be labeled as patriarchal or even semipatriarchal any longer. Southern Appalachian families are increasingly subscribing to egalitarian values.

Traditionally, Southern Appalachian family members often identify themselves through the family name. For example, a male might identify himself by stating, "I'm a Boone," rather than "I'm James Boone."

Some traditional family members are resigned to many of the unfortunate conditions faced in this subregion. Such conditions are often accepted with the belief that a person has little or no control over his life, anyway. In contrast, contemporary family members are characterized by dissatisfaction with the poor living conditions and these members strive to improve their life conditions. There is motivation to attain "achievement, success . . . money, power, reputation, material goods, and 'higher' style of life" (Stephenson, 1968, p. 135).

Many parents of the traditional family system are stricter with their children than parents of the general American society. The traditional family often strictly controls its young people, and there appears to be less juvenile delinquency in this subregion compared to the rest of the United States (Brown and Schwarzweller, 1970). The children's behavior is sometimes controlled through fear by suggesting to them that certain unpleasant things may happen to them should they not obey (Weller, 1965).

Among some Southern Appalachian families, there is a belief, according to Simpkins (1974), that whenever you talk to someone, you should not look them in the eye. Staring intently, or looking directly into the eyes of another person, is considered impolite. Thus, should another person attempt to look them directly in the eye, some Southern Appalachians may shift their eyes about to maintain politeness.

In conclusion, although there seem to be two dominant family types within the Southern Appalachian region, many families cannot be labeled either traditional or modern. For instance, some families may be a combination of both modern and traditional: the husband, who is modern, wants to migrate to another region, but the wife, who is traditional, fears that leaving this subregion will damage family ties with her kinfolk. Stephenson (1968) has observed that, in addition to traditional and modern family systems in this subregion, there are two middle types that overlap these two family types. Characteristic of one of these middle-family types is the maintenance of a full-time, blue-collar job by the head of household and the favoring of modern ways of life over the traditional ways. The other middle-family type was not committed to either of the extremes (traditional or modern). This latter type accepted and rejected parts of both traditional and modern family characteristics.

Religious Characteristics

Early religious practices are believed to have been relatively homogeneous before the emergence of changes in social patterns, industrialization, and decreased geographical isolation. Southern Appalachians are Christian and many belong to fundamentalist sects. Kaplan (1971) states that revivalism is a feature of religious life characterized by a community that collectively expresses its allegiance to salvation. Fundamentalism emphasizes the belief that words of the Bible should be believed and followed literally. Both revivalism and fundamentalism emerged as a result of economic conditions experienced in Southern Appalachia. According to Kaplan, individuals are to be rewarded in Heaven, not on earth. As a result, there are expressed feelings against those who are assumed to have been rewarded on earth. This practice was quite strong during the 1920s and 1930s, when the economy was very unstable. Among the lower classes, the fundamentalist heritage persists, and Puritan values are still preserved (Gerrard, 1970). Gerrard (1970) also observes that Southern Appalachian people take their religion seriously. In fundamentalism, the Bible is thought to be the sole authority; every word is believed to be divinely inspired and true.

In one part of Southern Appalachia, Stephenson (1968) found that the fundamentalist churches were unaffiliated sect groups, while traditional Protestant churches tended to be affiliated with regular denominational groups such as Baptist, Methodist, and Presbyterian. Fundamentalist church services involve more active participation and emotional expression from the congregation during services than do affiliated churches. In 1968, Stephenson observed that both fundamentalist and affiliated churches were experiencing difficulties in retaining the young as part of their membership.

These two types of churches also differed in terms of women's participation in leadership roles. For example, women tend to hold more leadership roles in affiliated churches than they do in the fundamentalist churches. Stephenson (1968) found that women in fundamentalist churches did not make significant decisions regarding church activities, whereas women in affiliated churches participated in a manner similar to that of the men.

Schwarzweller, Brown, and Mangalam's (1971) investigation of those who left Southern Appalachia suggests that 28 percent identify with the Baptist church; 23 percent identify with the Church of God, Holiness, and similar sect groups; 21

percent identify with the Church of Christ; 20 percent identify with the Christian church, and 8 percent of them identify with Methodists and Presbyterians (p. 135). According to the researchers, these church identifications were similar to the trend found in eastern Kentucky. A similar trend of denominational preference was found between migrants and persons who remained in the subregion; only 43 percent of men continued in the same denomination as their fathers, and only 50 percent of the women continued in the same denomination as their mothers. While the non-migrants of eastern Kentucky tend to be more fundamentalistic in their beliefs, Schwarzweller, Brown, and Mangalam argue that such beliefs are deteriorating among persons who migrate to other regions. During the 1970s and the early 1980s, however, there has been a growing interest and membership of many young and old Southern Appalachian Anglos in fundamentalist churches. This renewed fundamentalism among Appalachians was practiced similarly to earlier practices.

In conclusion, the predominant traditional and fundamentalistic religious orientations found among Anglos in Southern Appalachia, according to Kaplan (1971), have been replaced with a broad spectrum of religious differences extending from denominational acceptance of the secular to renewed emphasis on fundamentalism (p. 120). Also, among the modernists, there may be a decline in religious value commitments and a feeling of apathy toward church membership. Another group consists of both modernists and fundamentalists. There is some conflict between persons of these two orientations because of uncertainty regarding personal religious worth, differences between generations, and lack of a clearcut definition for salvation and membership. The final group, traditionalists, emphasize the move back to old time religion and denounce secular and modern Protestantism (Kaplan, 1971, p. 121).

Educational Characteristics

One of the major factors contributing to Southern Appalachian Anglos' distressed conditions has been poor education and limited marketable employment skills. The Appalachian Regional Committee reported that when compared to national standards there is a significant educational lag in Southern Appalachia. According to Newman (1972), the first priority in Southern Appalachia is toward development of adequate educational facilities that will enable the people to attain skills necessary to help this subregion maintain a labor force competitive with that in the remainder of the United States.

Some studies (Looff, 1971) have reported that the lower educational level of many Southern Appalachian communities is associated with the fact that schools have little holding power; that is, the students' need to be with their family was a much stronger influence than the school personnel's ability to encourage them to remain in school. Other studies (Walls and Stephenson, 1972) suggest that many schools in Southern Appalachia have inadequate educational facilities and materials (i.e., libraries, laboratories, gymnasiums, and culturally relevant textbooks). The number of high school graduates entering higher education was relatively low. The student dropout rate has been high, sometimes as much as 85 percent between first and twelfth grades. Even those students who completed high school attained low reading comprehensive test scores comparable to the tenth-grade level.

Ogletree (1968) states that typical educational programs applicable to many other areas of the United States are irrelevant to the needs of Appalachian students. Also, in many communities, low expectations and evaluations of schools led to low level of financial support for schools.

In his study, Kaplan (1971) outlined Southern Appalachian attitudes toward education. At one end of the spectrum, Kaplan found a group of persons who seemed to encourage education among the young. He found also that a middle group consisting of modern-traditional persons was mostly apathetic toward education, while a traditional group, at the other end of the spectrum, considered education less important than the two former groups did. Furthermore, many adult persons of the middle group felt that not having a high school education would make little if any difference in a person's career, although the youth in this group believed that education was everything. This suggests that children in the traditional group may be caught between their parents' indifference toward education and their teachers' encouragement to complete their high school educations.

Wagner (1977) states that of the many adults and children migrating to urban areas, most believe that education is the single most important commodity that will enhance their chances of attaining social and economic mobility. Schwarzweller, Brown, and Mangalam (1971) report that 14 percent of migrants from an Eastern Kentucky area had dropped out of school before completing high school, and that 22 percent of them had finished high school, a few had gone to college, and one had earned a doctoral degree. Many of these migrants—about 64 percent—completed fewer than eight grades.

In summary, traditional education has not always been a prized commodity in Southern Appalachia. With the many social and technological changes and shifts in family beliefs in this area, improvements are being made in education. Despite the lack of education among some Anglos in this subregion, it is fair to say that many parents now want their children to attain educational skills necessary to reach and maintain desired economic and social levels.

Language Characteristics

American English is the language spoken by Southern Appalachian Anglos, but there are also variations in their usage of the English language largely based on class and education.

Wolfram and Christian (1976) found in their study a type of speech which they refer to as Appalachian English, a particular variety of English language usage among the working class rural population of Southern Appalachia. These researchers noted that there are subregional differences in middle-class speakers of this subregion.

According to Wolfram and Christian (1976), most of the linguistic features of Appalachian English are variable rather than categorical, that is, a Southern Appalachian speaker will not use the dialect consistently in every verbal exchange. For instance, according to Wolfram and Christian, although some Appalachian English speakers use an a-prefix with certain action verbs ending in *ing*, such as "She was a-runnin' up the hill," yet there also are situations when the same speaker will delete the a-prefix in the sentence: "She was runnin' up the hill." Another example of the use of alternate forms is the presence and absence of the relative pronoun: "Here's the garden I made" versus "Here's the garden that I made." Wolfram and Christian maintain that it is impossible to predict which form will be used, but there are studies indicating that social and linguistic factors systematically influence the probability of a certain alternate being applied. The speaker may, for example, shift his style of speech from informal to formal or vice versa depending upon the situation.

In short, Southern Appalachian Anglos use Mainstream American English as well as Appalachian English. In some cases, the two types of speech overlap among the people in the subregion. That is, many persons speak only Mainstream American English, some speak what Wolfram and Christian (1976) refer to as Appalachian English, and others speak both forms, gauging when to use one or the other on the appropriateness of the situation.

Cultural Pride and Self-Concept

Southern Appalachian Anglos are a proud people. Much of this cultural pride and strong sense of self is expressed in their family ties and a growing sense of independence despite the many hardships still present in Southern Appalachia. Also, for many Appalachians, religion is a form of self-expression and a reinforcement of the culture.

Like cultural pride, the self-evaluations of Southern Appalachian Anglos appear relatively positive. For example, Williams and Byars (1968) examined the self-concepts of 310 Anglo and Black high school seniors from a cross-section of rural and urban schools in Georgia. The results suggested that the Anglo seniors evaluated themselves higher than did the Black seniors. In the same period, another study (Wendland, 1968) found that rural Anglo and Black adolescents positively self-evaluated themselves more than did the Anglo and Black urban adolescents. This rural-urban pattern, however, was exhibited, to a lesser extent among Anglo adolescents than Black adolescents. Lawrence (1974) investigated the self-concepts of 170 Anglo and 96 Black high school seniors in a southeastern section of North Carolina. The results also suggested higher self-concepts among the Anglo seniors than among the Black seniors.

Cultural pride and self-evaluations among most Southern Appalachian Anglos may differ from what many outsiders once believed them to be. Conclusions about the manner in which people of this subregion perceive their culture and themselves should be made on an individual basis. Additionally, self-evaluations may vary in degree from one situation to the next. Self-perception stems from such varied sources as family background, values, religion, social and economic conditions, and peers.

PROBLEMS OF SOUTHERN APPALACHIAN ANGLOS AND COUNSELING

The social and psychological problems faced by Southern Appalachian Anglos go virtually unnoticed by many counselors and other mental health professionals. This point is generally valid for most counselors who function outside Southern Appalachia. When Southern Appalachian Anglos migrate to urban and rural settings in other regions of the United States, their cultural attachments and adjustment problems in these sometimes unfamiliar surroundings are major concerns for counselors. It is true that their infrequent use of mental health services is linked to their limited experiences in counseling, yet it can also be attributed to counselors' unfamiliarity of Southern Appalachian culture. Owen (1979) believes counselors must attain a knowledge of the Southern Appalachian Anglos' culture in order to gain insight about the problems these people experience within as well as outside of this subregion and to know which services are needed and which methods are appropriate for delivering them.

Acculturation and Southern Appalachian Anglos

The many economic and social ills found in Southern Appalachia prompt persons to assume residence in other sections of the United States to improve their livelihood, which, in turn, leads to many emotional difficulties.

Kaplan (1971) notes that since the dominant social and cultural trends of communities in Southern Appalachia are in transition, problems may arise in connection with this. For instance, many young Anglos who have embraced the modern modes of the dominant society, such as completing school or even college, find that career choices are then too limited to be realized in the local community. Thus, they feel that they must leave the area to secure employment consistent with their educational skills. Others, however, lack the necessary skills or education to gain employment of their choice. There is an attitude, particularly among the young, of dissatisfaction caused by uncertainty over career futures and the fact that they may need to migrate to improve their economic status. These people are coerced into adopting and accepting the cultural values and life-styles commonly found among the dominant middle-class Anglo society, and this psychological acculturation may have a significant influence on many migrant Southern Appalachian Anglos' problems with self-identification and personality adjustment (Chance, 1965). Although acculturation often encourages positive change among persons involved, a common occurrence is that of cultural disruption which leads to acculturative stress.

Schwarzweller, Brown, and Mangalam (1971) observed in their research of the social and psychological adjustments of migrants from Southern Appalachia that frustration and anxiety are often associated with migrational stages. They noted, too, that transitional adjustment problems are different for men than for women: Migrant women were less dissatisfied with the urban situation than migrant men. It was also found that women seem to have a significant need to display the cultural standards of the place where they live; thus, their socializational needs in urban settings create acculturative stress among them. Because the male migrant's socializational needs were met through their extended family structure, males who were isolated from their kin experienced a high degree of psychological anxiety.

Both migrants of high- and lower-class families tended to have greater contact with urban natives, while migrants of intermediate class families had greater contact with kinfolk in areas of Southern Appalachia. Yet intermediate and lower-class families experienced more feelings of nostalgia for home than did higher-class migrants. However, high-class migrants manifested greater anxiety when they did not have active involvement with a close-knit kin family. This was not found to be the case among lower-class migrants. Schwarzweller, Brown, and Mangalam (1971) speculated that anxiety among the higher class occurred as a result of their aggressive confrontation with urban life, which they believe erodes families' standards.

In short, sociocultural adjustment problems of Southern Appalachian Anglos vary with the degree of an individual's acculturation. As Stephenson (1968) observed, some Southern Appalachian Anglos encounter problems with the rapid social and technological changes within Southern Appalachia as well. While some are able to deal effectively with their psychological stresses, many others do less well.

Perceptions of Mental Health and Mental Illness

The perceptions of mental health and mental illness of Southern Appalachian Anglos vary according to the individual's level of acculturation. Accounts of Southern Appalachian Anglos suggest that there is no single perception or definition of the concept of mental illness. Most who have fully accepted the life-style of the dominant middle-class Anglo society, for example, rely on scientific explanations of mental illness. These people realize and accept that organic and situational factors may contribute to mental illnesses. Observations of some traditional Anglos suggest that mental health and mental illness is explained through superstition (Miles, 1975). In such cases, some persons relied mostly on the supernatural rather than modern science to explain physical and mental conditions. Superstitious sayings often explain such things. For example: "If a bird weaves a hair of your head into its nest, you will have headaches until that nest falls to pieces; and if ever a bird builds a nest in your shoe or pocket, or in any of your clothes, you may prepare to die within the year" (Miles, 1975, p. 99).

Certain herbal medicine practices were designed to protect

against physical and mental illnesses (Miles, 1975). Often, herbs, salves, and other remedies were applied to prevent or heal illnesses.

According to Simpkins (1974), the present-day rural Southern Appalachians' avoidance of staring another person in the eye is based on politeness; however, this behavior stems from an earlier time when strangers were suspect because they were likely to be witches. Witches were perceived as having an evil eye; thus, one would avoid staring at them. A variety of events were expected to result from this intense stare: You could become ill, your cow's milk could dry up, or the milk could get bloody.

Perceptions regarding mental health are influenced by the level of education and how strongly the person identifies with the traditional Southern Appalachian culture or the dominant Anglo culture. Overlap may be found between the two. For example, a Southern Appalachian Anglo may accept modern perceptions of mental health and mental illness and still hold superstitious beliefs about health and illness.

Attitudes toward Mental Health Professionals

How Southern Appalachian Anglos define or perceive mental health and mental illness may affect their attitudes toward counselors and the use of mental health facilities. Cultural attitudes and values may also act as influencing agents regarding professional services. Traditionally, according to Owen (1979), Southern Appalachians have taken care of themselves simply because few services were available to provide assistance. As a result, an independent attitude prevails today regarding health care. Owen contends that persons of rural Southern Appalachia are not likely to seek out assistance from persons outside their families. Appalachian Anglos often tend to their problems by pretending that the problems are nonexistent or less severe than they are. Such Southern Appalachian attributes as individualism, pride, and family solidarity have precluded acceptance of outsiders who have attempted to provide professional assistance. Owen (1979) maintains that many rural Southern Appalachians feel that certain behaviors of outside professionals intensify the Southern Appalachian

Anglos's suspicion—and unacceptance—of such professionals. For instance, the professional's manner of communication or attire may arouse suspicion. Also, the professional intrusions are viewed as an uninvited service. Too often, professionals lack respect for and basic knowldege of the Southern Appalachian culture.

Because of the diversity of attitudes toward mental health professionals and facilities, counselors must consider innovative effective methods of delivering services to the people of Southern Appalachia. Attitudes are changing, though, and Owen (1979), feels that Southern Appalachia presents a different picture of itself today than it did a generation ago. The life patterns, cultural values, and modern pace of life are approaching many of these in general American society.

Communication in Counseling Services

There are many Southern Appalachian Anglos who experience little if any problems in communicating with professional counselors. Their communicative style approximates that of other middle-class Anglos. For some Southern Appalachian Anglos, however, the communicative process is not always a simple one. Some rural Southern Appalachians are suspicious of professionals whose language style is contrary to their own. And also, some of these professionals are often culturally unfamiliar with or intolerant of linguistic patterns found among the people in rural mountain areas (Owen, 1979). Also, there may be barriers of dialect, vocabulary, and expression. For instance, "I don't care to" often really means "Yes, I would be delighted to" (Pearsall, 1974, p. 55). Professionals may find a different rate of verbal interaction than they are used to. Traditional middle-class counselors' expectations often favor insightful clients who speak Mainstream American English well. By contrast, Southern Appalachians speak slowly and are content with long periods of silence (Pearsall, 1974). Also, according to Pearsall (1974), verbal aggression may influence some women to withdraw and some men to become hostile. Looff (1971) found among some Southern Appalachian lower-class people, women are more talkative than men. Both men and women are action-oriented, preferring specific action to the abstraction of the verbal communication that is often found in traditional counseling.

Counselors should not expect to be successful in providing effective services if their communication is not culturally and linguistically appropriate to the individuals whom they are attempting to assist. For counselors to communicate effectively with and help Southern Appalachian Anglos resolve their problems, knowledge of the cultural and linguistic patterns within this subregion is needed.

School Adjustment

It is not always a well-known factor that many Southern Appalachian Anglo students experience difficulty adjusting to the educational environment. Several symptoms or other problems emerge from these adjustment problems: early dropout, separation anxiety from the family, or negative attitudes toward education. The literature reports that, while progress has been made, these problems remain unresolved (Looff, 1971; Wagner, 1977; Selakovich, 1978).

Several factors are linked to Appalachian students' high dropout rate. Wagner (1977) maintains that most schools are middle class in nature, and that they function as one of America's largest socializing agents of such values. Projection of these values in classroom situations often creates psychological conflicts for those Southern Appalachian Anglo students who identify strongly with a traditional and often low-class family background. Few schools have integrated Appalachian culture into curricula and instructional practices. As a result, students are left with feelings of alienation that result in inattentiveness toward classroom instruction, the attitude that education is insignificant, or the eventual dropping out of school.

The students of families who have migrated to cities have special problems. Wagner (1977) contends that urban school instructional personnel fail to meet the social and educational needs of these students. These students, also, do not necessarily hold values of middle-class society. Emphasis on achievement and regular school attendance, for example, is more complex and demanding than is sometimes found in their own culture.

Adjustment is not an easy task for migrant students who are often faced with criticism and ridicule in urban schools. While Appalachian Anglo students may initially be perceived as the same as other Anglo students, they are readily identified as different once they begin to speak. According to Wagner (1977), their mountain "twang" or highlander accent often draws negative criticism and ridicule from instructional personnel and other students. Many Appalachian Anglo students retreat by minimizing their verbal interaction within the educational environment to avoid such negative behavior from others.

Other school-adjustment problems are associated with students' dependency on the family. Looff (1971) has observed that this close intradependent family system has a significant effect on young children who attend school. For example, young children and parents frequently experience separation anxiety or emotional conflict. Separation conflicts occurred frequently in many Southern Appalachian children, for instance, who had acute and chronic school-phobic reactions, those who were excessively dependent on their parents, those with serious learning and behavior difficulties, and in preschool children with deviations in social development.

Many of the problems in adjustment are a result of the behaviors of adults who interact with the youth. It appears that possible modification of the environment to facilitate Appalachian Anglo student's psychosocial development is crucial.

Discrimination and Prejudice

Prejudice has been encountered by most ethnic and cultural groups in the United States, and Appalachians are no exception. Yet few professionals are aware that some Southern Appalachian Anglos continue to face prejudicial attitudes in contemporary society. Prejudice contributes to feelings of humiliation, downtroddenness, and powerlessness.

Killian's (1970) investigation revealed that many migrant Southern Appalachian Anglos in urbanized, industrial settings were discriminated against. Several industrial officials openly expressed that they would not hire Appalachians unless other workers could not be attained. This practice was based on the stereotypic belief "that laziness, lack of education and skills, and an overdeveloped spirit of independence made [Southern Appalachian Anglos] undesirable as employees" (Killian, 1970, p. 109). Although conflict was at a minimum between other Anglos and the migrant Appalachians, conflict often occurred between the two groups when the term "hillbilly" was applied as an epithet. Appalachians were also refused housing once northern Anglos heard their accent. Additionally, according to Killian (1970), intragroup distinctions were made among Southern Appalachian Anglo migrants. The behaviors of some Anglo migrants, e.g., affluent Anglo migrants, were more socially acceptable than those of other Anglo migrants, e.g., lower-class Anglo migrants. It was perceived that some social behaviors of Anglo migrant members brought embarrassment to all members of the group.

Problems of discrimination and prejudice are often counterproductive to Southern Appalachian Anglos' aspirations toward the social and economic gains necessary to improve their life conditions. Limited reception into some social groups and institutions such as industry may hinder their full acceptance of life patterns of mainstream American society. Furthermore, such conditions lead to varying degrees of psychological discomfort such as stress, anxiety, and depression.

Migrants' Adjustment to Initial Entry of Industrial Work Role

Many Southern Appalachian Anglo migrants in industrial settings who are fortunate to find employment find the work demands and expectations are different from those in their familiar subregion. Often, such migrants are accustomed to farm activities, which involve self-directed work and isolation. According to Schwarzweller, Brown, and Mangalam (1971), the transitional period into industrial work poses the greatest problem for many Southern Appalachian migrant workers. Some enter the work world in many urban, industrial settings at an unskilled level. As a result, they must settle for jobs at the unskilled laborer status. The beginning worker often finds the rigid authority system and formal work schedules troublesome. Also, the complicated machinery may be perceived as puzzling and sometimes frightening. Many Appalachian migrants fear their bosses. Others find it difficult to accept kidding from their co-workers. Schwarzweller, Brown, and Mangalam (1971) observed that social relationships with co-workers and their immediate, work supervisors were the source of psychological stress for "the highly individualistic, personalistically-oriented" (p. 160) Southern Appalachian migrants. In some instances, migrants had to be asked to perform job tasks rather than to be told what to do.

In addition, being ill-prepared for urban, industrial work can have a serious effect on an individuals' psychological well-being. However, many Southern Appalachian migrants overcome their psychological discomforts as they become accustomed to the industrial work system. Much of the psychological discomforts are cushioned through contact with other family members, who lend emotional support as well as necessary knowledge about the industrial work system. Schwarzweller, Brown, and Mangalam (1971) maintain that unskilled migrants obtain marketable skills through technical training programs and advanced education.

Some Practical Suggestions for Counseling Southern Appalachian Anglos

It has been stressed throughout this chapter that Southern Appalachian Anglos constitute a heterogeneous group. The diversity of this group requires that counselors and other mental health professionals consider individual differences as well as levels of acculturation. The Southern Appalachian Anglo's ethnic and cultural trappings should dictate counseling approaches that are culturally relevant to attain desired outcomes. The counselor must take into consideration the social, economic, and psychological variations among Southern Appalachian Anglos who range from traditional, rural mountain people to urban, industrial-oriented migrants.

In some cases, effective mental health assistance may require bilingual and bicultural approaches. For instance, some Southern Appalachian Anglos may use Appalachian English. The psychological comfort in Southern Appalachian Anglos' usage of either Appalachian speech, Mainstream English, or a combination of both may indeed determine the quality of the counselor-client relationship as well as the outcome of this relationship. Clients may switch style from Appalachian English to Mainstream American English. For instance, clients who have migrated to urban, industrial settings and have little contact with relatives, infrequent or no visits to Southern Appalachia, and frequently engage in nostalgia of the once-familiar surroundings of this subregion may occasionally shift from Mainstream American English when dealing with personal or emotional material (Looff, 1971). It is not suggested that counselors mimic clients' communicative style; rather they should understand the verbal and nonverbal messages being conveyed. Cultural knowledge is essential to provide effective assistance where bilingual/bicultural intervention strategies are warranted.

While traditional counseling strategies will assist many Southern Appalachian Anglos in reaching resolutions to problems, many nontraditional strategies must also be considered. No single approach to their problems is likely to meet the needs across all Southern Appalachian Anglos. Hence, differential treatment that distinguishes among clients based on their individual and cultural needs may best assist these people in accomplishing solutions to their problems.

Perritt (1979) states that the counselor must go beyond the therapeutic role when providing assistance to Southern Appalachian Anglos. Perritt advocates that counselors might think of themselves in some cases as "teacher, vocational advisor, big sister or brother" (1979, p. 3).

Programs should be developed to assist persons in gaining skills necessary to secure employment and explore careers. Specifically, Appalachians need to be helped to confront the industrial work place. Action-oriented approaches such as role playing may prove to be beneficial.

It may also be helpful for counselors to work directly with the family. For instance, techniques can be offered to assist parents in helping their children adjust to the school environment. Help may be offered to parents to facilitate easing young children's anxiety caused by separation of the family members. With the support and assistance from community members who are respected by others, family-group meetings to provide better understanding of parent-child interactions might be helpful.

Counselors should also provide helpful information concerning child development. For instance, parents might be encouraged to place preschool children in training programs such as Head Start and community day-care programs. These types of programs may help in facilitating the development of personal-social skills, language skills, perceptual-cognitive maturation, and may also lessen the pain of separation from family members.

Counselors who work in schools should be aware that some students may have migrated to urban schools from Southern Appalachia. If the counselor recognizes such a group within the student body, group counseling sessions might be provided to familiarize these students with their new environment. Such groups should include longtime urban students so that students can meet each other. Other provisions should be made to familiarize and sensitize teachers and administrators, through inservice presentations, to the cultural heritage and social values of Southern Appalachian Anglos. They should be encouraged to include Southern Appalachian cultures in school curricula.

Perritt (1979) suggests that the counselor involve the whole family, since many Southern Appalachian Anglos are highly family-oriented. This approach would lend itself to attaining full cooperation of the persons requiring assistance. To minimize the Southern Appalachian Anglo's suspicion of professionals, counselors should refrain from taking notes and administering of tests when possible. It is also important to remember that many tests may be invalid because of the cultural differences between Southern Appalachia and mainstream American society.

Another approach to reduce communities' resistance to mental health delivery services would be the training of community members as paraprofessionals (Perritt, 1979). These persons would be trained to work with Appalachian clients in various locations under the supervision of a professional counselor.

SUMMARY

A variety of perceptions influence the behavior of Southern Appalachian Anglos in social interactions with other individuals. Differences in socialization, religion, and socioeconomic background sometimes present problems in establishing a sound rapport between counselors and Appalachian clients. The distrust of outsiders that some Southern Appalachians have often hinders this rapport and leads to ineffective outcomes for clients. Thus, counselors must be capable of establishing a minimum degree of trust and support with the Appalachian client.

Some Appalachians are strongly suspicious of professionals who are rigid in adhering to appointments and schedules, while other Appalachians are not. Additionally, it may be essential to provide a structured approach in the counseling of some Appalachians, but a less structured approach may be more effective in accomplishing intended outcomes with others.

Not all Southern Appalachian Anglos have the same needs, nor will similar counseling approaches attain positive, desired outcomes. Finally, there is no single-standard counseling approach that meets the needs of all Southern Appalachian Anglos. Because these people are distributed in various other regions of the United States as well as in Appalachia, counselors should be prepared to treat them anywhere they are encountered, and should realize that their environment will influence their needs and levels of acculturation.

EXERCISES

These exercises involve students in dealing with Southern Appalachian Anglos. These exercises are not intended to familiarize students with all of the problems faced by persons of Southern Appalachia, but rather, they are designed to help students begin to realize the traditional and contemporary cultural patterns that must be considered when assisting Southern Appalachian Anglos.

A. Students should read the following description of Southern Appalachians.

Each student should write a brief description of the example as he perceives each situation. A comparison and contrast of the issues involved in both examples can be exchanged among the students. Suggestions may be given to assist the individuals in each example.

1. Wilbur, an eighteen-year-old, high school graduate, lives with his mother and father. Wilbur and his parents live in a hollow surrounded by only a few families. Wilbur's mother is bedridden with illness, and his father is a coal miner temporarily unemployed because of a labor dispute between the miners' union and the mine owners. Wilbur is unable to find employment in the local area. He doesn't have any marketable skills, because his high school program included only a general education. He would really like to have a good job that would help to support his parents, yet Wilbur is indecisive about what he would like to do as a career. There seems to be more time on his hands than activities in which to engage. He is reluctant to migrate to another area away from his family.

2. Mary is a ten-year-old who lives with her parents in a large, urban-industrial area of Ohio. Her family migrated to Ohio from Tennessee about a year ago. Ever since Mary began attending the new local school, she has experienced ridicule from her classmates. Both teachers and students tease her about the use of Appalachian English. She no longer volunteers in class or participates in student-group activities. Her academic performance has deteriorated in the last six months.

B. Students should read the example below. After the reading, they should discuss their answers to the questions that follow.

Most of Bill's family has worked in the coal mines, and they have strongly emphasized that he should get an education and do better than they did. Bill has a strong preference for a white-collar position, and wants to move from the vocational program in which he is presently enrolled. Although he has not shown any ability or interest in scholastic subjects, Bill believes that college is the way to attain economic and social mobility in society. Yet he appears somewhat confused by the disparity between what he seems to enjoy doing in the vocational shop and the values he has learned from the family.

1. How would you define Bill's problem situation?
2. What approaches would you, as a counselor, implement to improve Bill's situation?
3. To what extent should the family members become involved?

C. Students should study the example given below. They then may answer the questions that follow the example.

Saundra is a twenty-two-year-old married woman. She states that she is very angry. Her parents phoned this morning to say they want Saundra and her husband to move back closer to them in the Southern Appalachians because Saundra and her husband have completed college. Saundra claims that she cannot tolerate being around her parents, that moving away from her parents was a good portion of her reason for getting married. She told her mother that they were contemplating moving to San Francisco, California. Her mother wailed and talked about how she and Saundra's father were aging, how they had little time left on this earth, and how everybody was ignoring them, and how her father was too ill to travel.

Saundra is experiencing psychological anxiety, frustration, and guilt. Since talking to her mother, she has not been sleeping well at night, and she cries a lot. Saundra feels that should she and her husband return to Southern Appalachia, her parents would expect them to visit most of the time. She states that this situation is driving her out of her mind, and that she has exceptional guilt feelings. Saundra does not know what to do in this situation.

1. What are the issues involved here?
2. How are cultural factors such as familialism influencing Saundra's psychological discomfort?

3. What approaches should you, as a counselor, implement to help Saundra resolve her problem?

D. Divide students into small groups to work on the following tasks. Each group is to assume responsibility as director of a new community mental-health program to be located in Southern Appalachia. The intent of each program is to assist in meeting Southern Appalachian Anglo's needs. Each group is to develop a program to assist Anglo clients of various socioeconomic levels. In this program, consider the clients' traditional and contemporary practices of mental health and mental illness, distribution of counseling services, clients' previous experience (or lack of it) with counseling, initial steps needed to encourage people to use the services, and the kinds of personnel and facilities needed.

After the groups have developed their programs, each group should present its program to the others. Each presentation should lead to discussion dealing with the advantages and disadvantages of the suggested procedures included in each program.

REFERENCES

Brown, J. S., and H. K. Schwarzweller "The Appalachian Family." In J. D. Photiadis, and H. K. Schwarzweller (eds.), *Change in Rural Appalachia: Implications for Action Programs.* Philadelphia: University of Pennsylvania Press, 1970. Pp. 64–71.

Chance, N. A. "Acculturation, Self-Identification, and Personality Adjustment." *American Anthropologist,* 1965, *67,* 372–93.

Gerrard, N. L. "Churches of the Stationary Poor in Southern Appalachia." In J. D. Photiadis and H. K. Schwarzweller (eds.), *Change in Rural Appalachia: Implications for Action Programs.* Philadelphia: University of Pennsylvania Press, 1970. Pp. 92–98.

Hansen, J. C., and R. R. Stevic. *Appalachian Students and Guidance.* Boston: Houghton Mifflin, 1971.

Kaplan, B. H. *Blue Ridge: An Appalachian Community in Transition.* Morgantown, W. Va.: Office of Research and Development, Appalachia Center, West Virginia University, 1971.

Killian, L. M. *White Southerners.* New York: Random House, 1970.

Lawrence, W. W. "The Relationships of Intelligence, Self-Concept, Socioeconomic Status, Race and Sex to Level of Career Maturity of Twelfth-Grade Students." Doctoral dissertation, University of North Carolina at Chapel Hill, 1974. *Dissertation Abstracts International,* 1974, *35,* 2439A–3939A.

Linkous, J. *Appalachia—An Economic Report.* Washington, D.C.: Appalachian Regional Commission, (Dec.) 1977.

Looff, D. H. *Appalachia's Children—The Challenge of Mental Health.* Lexington: University Press of Kentucky, 1971.

Miles, E. B. *The Spirit of the Mountains.* Knoxville: University of Tennessee Press, 1975.

Moore, J. *Profile of Appalachia.* Washington, D.C.: Day Care and Child Development Center of America, 1974.

Newman, M. *The Political Economy of Appalachia.* Lexington, Mass.: D.C. Heath, 1972.

Ogletree, J. R. *Appalachian Schools—A Case of Consistency.* Morgantown: West Virginia University, Appalachian Center, 1968.

Owen, D. W. "Out of Sight—Out of Mind: Some Thoughts about the Latest Rediscovery of Appalachia and Its People." Paper presented at the American Personnel and Guidance Association 1979 Annual Convention, Las Vegas, Nev. April 2–5, 1979.

Pavenstedt, E. "A Comparison of a Child-Rearing Environment of Upper-Lower and Very Low-Lower-Class Families." *American Journal of Orthopsychiatry,* 1965, *35,* 89–98.

Pearsall, M. "Communication with the Educationally Deprived." In F. S. Riddel (ed.), *Appalachia: Its People, Heritage, and Problems.* Dubuque, Iowa: Kendall/Hunt Pub. Co., 1974,. Pp. 55-62.

Perritt, L. J. "Counseling the Appalachian Youth: Strategies and Techniques." Paper presented at the American Personnel and Guidance Association 1979 Annual Convention, Las Vegas, Nev., April 2–5, 1979.

Schwarzweller, H. K., J. S. Brown, and J. J. Mangalam. *Moun-*

tain Families in Transition—A Case Study of Appalachian Migration. University Park: Pennsylvania State University Press, 1971.

Selakovich, D. "The Learning Styles of Poor Whites." In L. Morris, G. Sather, and S. Scull (eds.), *Extracting Learning Styles from Social/Cultural Diversity: A Study of Five American Minorities.* Washington, D.C.: U.S. Department of Health, Education and Welfare, Office of Education, 1978. Pp. 55–68.

Simpkins, N. "An Informal Incomplete Introduction to Appalachian Culture." In B. B. Maurer, ed., *Mountain Heritage.* Ripley, W. Va.: Mountain State Arts and Craft Fair, 1974. Pp. 29–50.

Stephenson, J. B. *Shiloh.* Lexington: University of Kentucky Press, 1968.

Stevic, R., and G. Uhlig. "Occupational Aspirations of Selected Appalachian Youth." *Personnel and Guidance Journal,* 1967, *45,* 435–39.

Wagner, T. E. "Urban Schools and Appalachia Children." *Urban Education,* 1977, *12,* 283–96.

Walls, D. S., and J. B. Stephenson. *Appalachia in the Sixties.* Lexington: University of Kentucky Press, 1972.

Weller, J. E. *Yesterday's People: Life in Contemporary Appalachia.* Lexington: University Press of Kentucky, 1965.

Wendland, M. M. "Self-Concept in Southern Negro and White Adolescents as Related to Rural-Urban Residence." Doctoral dissertation, University of North Carolina at Chapel Hill, 1968. *Dissertation Abstracts International,* 1969, *29,* 2249B–3143B.

Williams, B. W., and H. Byars. "Negro Self-Esteem in a Transitional Society." *Personnel and Guidance Journal,* 1968, *47,* 120–25.

Wolfram, W., and D. Christian. *Appalachian Speech.* Arlington, Va.: Center for Applied Linguistics, 1976.

Part Three

The Encounter

The therapeutic dyad between counselor and client is examined in Part 3 of this text. Whether the encounter involves counseling or psychotherapy, its success rests heavily on the effectiveness of communication. Equally important are those psychosocial variables of the counselor and client that are brought into the therapeutic milieu.

The following two chapters are a communicative process model that allows for variations to meet the needs of clients from a multicultural society. This model facilitates the communicative process to attain positive counseling outcomes. With culturally different clients, the counselor is encouraged to use culture-specific counseling techniques—unlike other models, where clients are treated similarly.

9

A Communicative Process Approach

IN THIS CHAPTER, LIMITATIONS in counseling practice and some barriers encountered by counseling practitioners are synthesized; salient factors to be considered in cross-cultural counseling dyads are examined; and finally, a comprehensive approach to multicultural counseling that focuses on differential therapeutic interventions is described.

COUNSELING PRACTICE, THEORY, AND PRACTITIONERS

Counseling Practice

Traditionally, counselors and therapists are thought of as communicative experts who relate to clients from varied cultural and ethnic backgrounds. Counselors manifest awareness of themselves and the cultural differentials among their clients, and their professional behavior is conducive to positive outcomes. Yet professional literature on actual counseling practice tells a different tale. A number of critics throughout this book have stated that many cultural and ethnic variables hinder positive counseling outcomes (Walker, 1968; Vontress, 1969; Ayers, 1970; Shuy, 1974; Sue, 1977; Trimble, 1976; De-Blassie, 1976). Because of such variables, results may range from ineffective communication in some areas to a client's complete physical withdrawal from the counseling milieu. Reports reveal an underuse of counseling services, a large percentage of clients who terminate counseling, and high rate of discharge of clients after first interviews (Yamamoto et al., 1968; Warren et al., 1973; Padilla et al., 1975; Jackson, 1975; Sue and Kirk, 1975; Sue, 1977). Such findings point to counselor-client conflicts. Therefore, positive action, however difficult that action may be, must be taken to afford the culturally different client maximum assistance.

Theory

Counselor-client conflicts are perpetuated by outdated and culture-bound theories, which encourage monocultural methods regardless of a client's cultural and ethnic background (Gunnings, 1971; Patterson, 1971; Franklin, 1971). Few traditional theories provide useful linkages between the counselor's communicative skills and the client's personal experiences. Traditional theories tend to have class and cultural limitations (Patterson, 1971). Traditional therapeutic methods such as client-centered (Spang, 1965), group therapy, and psychoanalysis (Trimble, 1976) are ineffective with some cultural group members. Traditional methods place a high degree of responsibility on the client. It must be remembered, for example, that counselors cannot initially expect self-disclosure from some American Indians or Chinese Americans. However, little attention has been given to the fact that some American Indian clients are only listening participants, unlike many Anglo individuals, who may readily express their concerns and become emotionally involved. Also, openness is quite difficult for many Chinese, who have learned to repress emotional expressions (Sue and Sue, 1972; Sue, Sue, and Sue, 1975). The counseling behaviors of American Indians and Chinese Americans are culturally learned behaviors; thus, in these cases, traditional theories are counterproductive. Unfortunately, however, many counselors are trained in traditional programs and apply such methods without consideration for cultural variations (Patterson, 1971).

Counseling Practitioners

Many shortcomings in counseling practice come from the counselor's behavior (Jones and Jones, 1972; Smith, 1973).

Failure to achieve positive outcomes is a direct result of the counselor's misapplication of counseling theories in practice (Smith, 1973). Wrenn (1962) refers to the "culturally incapsulated counselor" as one who disregards his clients' cultural differentials and blindly applies the same strategies and techniques in all counseling situations, adhering to one particular technique. His experiences and professional skills, which may be functional within the limits of a particular culture, are insufficient to assess and assist clients of another social environment. Such indiscriminate mental health interventions can be as biased and unfair as those that provide preferential treatment of the Anglo middle-class group over minority groups. It is evident, then, that sociocultural behaviors and individual needs must dictate counseling strategies, techniques, or actions to be taken by the counselor.

Closely tied to the counselor's professional behavior are his values and attitudes. Some writers, such as Arbuckle (1969) and Ayers (1970) argue that the counselor's attempt to impose his middle-class values on clients is one of the most significant negative factors in multicultural counseling, and one that totally neglects clients' value systems. Too many counselors operate under a halo of prejudices, stereotypes, and myths that limit or negate their effectiveness.

Counseling actions may be based on the client's appearance, sex, social status, or value system as viewed by the counselor. Such actions are colored by the counselor's feelings toward the client. Many counselors avoid anyone of another ethnic group. The acronym YAVIS—young, attractive, verbal, intelligent, and successful—describes the type of client with whom most counselors perfer to work (Schofield, 1964; Ridley, 1978). The counselor's subjective behavior, professional and personal value systems, and attitudes are all interrelated and communicated in numerous ways.

The manner in which the counselor communicates with the culturally different client is of great importance to the outcome of the relationship. The seemingly "foreign" style of a counselor using traditional theory negatively influences communication. For instance, counselors usually communicate in abstractions that describe motivations; they seek to convey change, and refine emotions (Vontress, 1969). The focus is often on a client's improved interpersonal relations or on emotions linked to alienation conveyed in vague terms such as "personal adjustment" and "motivation" (Walker, 1968; Ayers, 1970), when the clients problems may be more concrete. Many counselors seem incapable of moving beyond these language barriers, and thus communicate to the culturally different client as a middle-class neurotic. Little attention is given to the client's real objectives, and no attempt is made to facilitate positive counseling by stating the goals or emotions in operational or concrete terms understood by both participants. Unfortunately, many counselors view the therapeutic interchange as successful only if the client verbalizes his emotions fluently (Bernstein, 1964).

Finally, counselors must be aware that 80 to 90 percent of counselor-client communication is nonverbal (Mehrabian, 1972; Ivey and Gluckstern, 1974a, 1974b). Inattention to and misunderstanding of nonverbal behavior—rhythm of speech, facial expressions, eye contact, body position—limit interchange effectiveness. Attending exclusively to verbalizations about feelings is a refusal to recognize the whole individual and his culture. Communication barriers result when the counselor is not cognizant of cultural variations in styles and patterns of verbal and nonverbal behavior.

Much of the counseling practitioner's success is dependent upon his attitudes, values, subjective behavior, and the application of counseling theories. Many counselors underuse the cultural factors that define a culturally different client. There is a serious need for change in the practitioner's professional behavior and in the counseling curriculum. The identification of a conceptual approach to counseling that acts on the individual needs and experiences of all clients is a good place to begin.

COMMUNICATIVE PROCESS MODEL: A CONCEPTUAL APPROACH

Description of the Model

The communicative process consists of developmental stages involving verbal and nonverbal transactions in the counseling dyad, a process that may include one or more interviews aimed at certain goals as shown in figure 9.1. It provides greater awareness of counseling behaviors as they occur. Any counseling process is effective only if the counselor and client reach their goals. The methods employed should be consistent with the desired goals.

Obviously, the ultimate aim of any counseling approach is to assist the client in achieving an overall goal of functioning adequately and independently in his psychosocial environment. Multicultural counseling goals must be viewed from two frames of reference: (1) they must assist culturally different clients to deal with their psychosocial environment and (2) they must assist these clients to restructure their environment to accommodate their personal and cultural needs. Thus, counseling goals must be consistent with clients' needs, and account must always be taken of whether clients need to modify their behavior or act on the environment that led them to counseling in the first place.

The attainment of goals is contingent upon counseling strategies. These strategies are the counselor's attempts to assist the culturally different client to adapt to or reshape his psychosocial environment. Strategies are viewed as the planning-process phases of the communicative process wherein the culturally competent counselor considers the client's characteristics, counseling goals, and process goals and decides how to approach them. Prior to the implementation of a planned strategy, both parties must make a commitment to it (Delaney and Eisenberg, 1972, pp. 96–97).

Counseling strategies involve verbal and nonverbal skills. Nonverbal behavior is an important area of communication, and it comprises approximately 80 to 90 percent of all communication (Mehrabian, 1972; Ivey and Gluckstern, 1974a).

The Ivey Taxonomy of the effective counselor includes four basic dimensions comprised of verbal and nonverbal skills. These are: (1) basic skills focusing on patterns of culturally specific nonverbal behavior; (2) microcounseling skills focusing on culturally appropriate listening and influencing skills; (3) qualitative skills dealing with subjective dimensions that communicate understanding to the client in his own frame of reference; and (4) focus skills concentrating on the client or

FIG. 9.1.
COMMUNICATIVE PROCESS MODEL IN MULTICULTURAL COUNSELING.

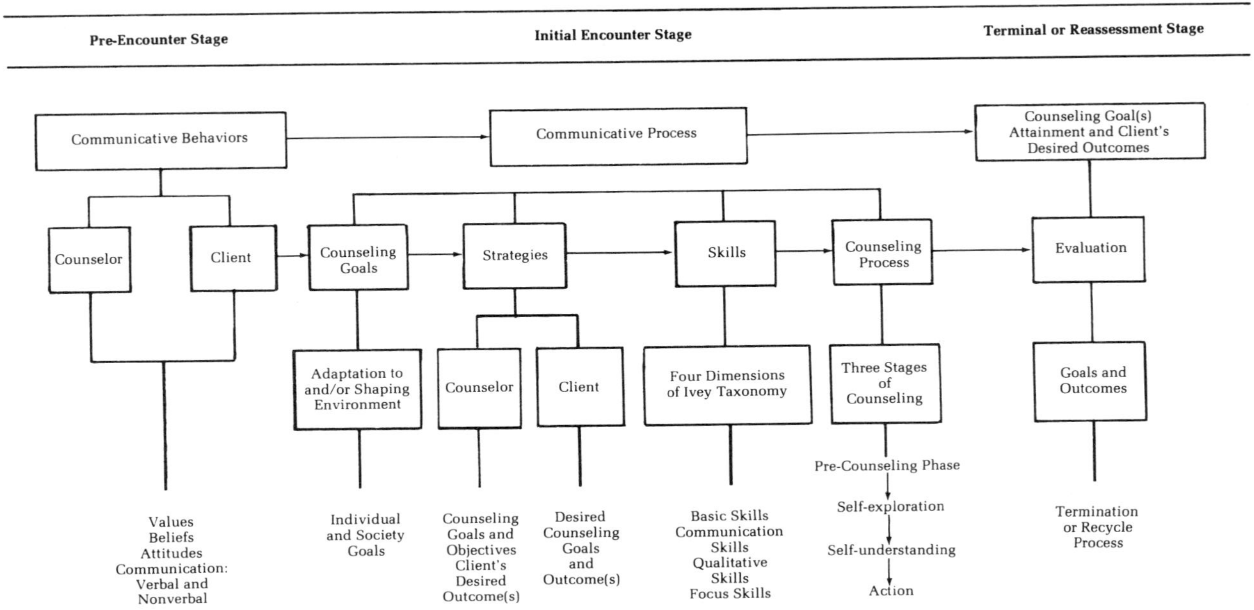

others as the prime subject of conversation. In addition, the effective counselor is capable of discussing a variety of culturally relevant topics (Ivey, 1977).

Basic Skills of Culture

The ability to incorporate culturally appropriate skills is likely to determine effectiveness of the other three Ivey Taxonomy dimensions. The appropriate application of each skill will vary from culture to culture. The basic skills include eye contact, body language, proximity preference, and appropriateness of certain subjects.

Eye contact is an important factor. Usually, the counselor is encouraged to vary eye contact with a client and is urged not to stare at him. A client may feel that something is wrong when a counselor stares too long. Too frequent breaks in eye contact, however, may suggest to the client that the counselor is preoccupied, bored, inattentive, or unconcerned. Patterns of eye contact and the interpretation of it vary across cultures.

Body language is another important factor in counseling because interpretation varies between as well as within cultural groups. The counselor must realize that the client's (and his own) different positions and movements communicate messages. A counselor's personal and educational background may wrongly influence his interpretation of body movements; his awareness should be geared to the cultural background of the client. The counselor's misinterpretation of the client's nonverbal gestures and body movements can lead to serious problems in communication.

Closely linked to body language is the essential consideration of the client's *proximity preference,* or personal space preference. The most comfortable physical distance between the client and the counselor varies within cultures. If the counselor is unaware of these preferences, he may offend the client by adopting a physical distance that is inappropriate to the client's background. This behavior, of course, also may vary depending on the individual.

Effective counseling is also dependent on the counselor's awareness of the *appropriateness of certain subjects* with clients of different cultural backgrounds. Acceptable subjects will vary within as well as between ethnic and cultural groups. To know the acceptable subject range requires extensive knowledge of the different groups. With such knowledge, the counselor can realize the inappropriateness of initiating a discussion on fatherless homes among Blacks or on abortion among Chicanos or Puerto Ricans.

Much of the success of multicultural counseling rests upon the counselor's awareness and application of these fundamental skills. Then, too, the counselor's ability to apply the appropriate skills is likely to determine the effectiveness of the communicative, qualitative, and focus skills that comprise the bulk of the counseling process.

Communication: Attending Skills

Appropriate "attending behavior" tells a client the counselor is carefully listening to him.

Open-ended and *closed-ended questions*, properly employed, can facilitate communication. Open-ended questions give the client the freedom to express relevant information with little direction from the counselor: "How important is completing your education?" or "Tell me more about your getting kicked out of school" or "Would you tell me more about what happened in your discussion with your mother?" Closed-ended questions, on the other hand, allow the counselor to reach for more specific material that is consciously or unconsciously avoided by the client: "How long ago was it that your husband abandoned you and the children?"

Minimal encouragement to the client communicates to him that the counselor is listening, following what he is saying, and waiting to hear more. Verbal cues might include the following:

"Yes."
"I see."
"Tell me more."
"And . . ."
"What else?"
"Mmm-mmm."
"Go on."

Nonverbal cues, such as an occasional head nod or a partial extension of the arm with an open hand, are also effective. They all must be applied with caution, however, because they may be inappropriate to one or another culture.

Reflection of the client's feelings is often used to communicate to him the counselor's understanding of his problem. It is sometimes necessary to reinforce the emotional factors of a client's behavior in order for him to become aware of certain feelings. Mirroring emotions communicates to the client that the counselor is with him and understands his world as he perceives it. "You feel it is rather useless to date her again" or "You're really discouraged right now and feel like giving up school" are both expressions of reflected emotions. Counselors must respond to more than the word content; they must sense and respond to how that content expresses hidden messages or emotions. Joy, happiness, sadness, dismay, laughter, discouragement, enthusiasm—these and other feelings are frequently communicated through nonverbal behavior such as tears, lowering of the head, pauses in speech, erratic speech patterns, or smiling. Reflection of these feelings facilitates the client's awareness and understanding of himself.

On the other hand, one must be aware that the counselor who relies heavily on reflection with some Blacks, American Indians, or Asian American clients may not be successful. Exposure and transmission of personal feeling may be viewed as an invasion of privacy. Thus, it may be necessary for the counselor to respond only to content material until a good rapport has been established.

Generally, though, the reflection of content helps the client to verbalize his ideas more clearly. It is similar to a paraphrase: While a paraphrase states more precisely what the client has said, a reflection of content mirrors in the counselor's own words the main concept that the client is trying to communicate. A client may say, "Occasionally, I do certain things that I'm not sure I understand. I behave in such a way that's not really me." The counselor may reflect the content in this statement by saying, "At times, you act in a particular way that's not the real you, and you don't know why this happens."

Paraphrasing is a basic attending skill. It tells the client that the counselor is actually hearing what he says. It is a direct response to the client's last statement. When a client says, "I had a terrible time with my girl friend last night," the counselor's paraphrase might be, "Things between you and her didn't turn out the way you wanted them to." A counselor's paraphrasing helps the client clarify certain aspects of what he has said, and thus helps him gain a better understanding of the concern. Sundberg (1976) contends that paraphrasing and occasionally checking out perceptions and understandings is important to clients of various ethnic groups where a concrete structure of the counseling process is being provided.

Summarization, the final attending skill, helps clarify and synthesize the client's ideas at various intervals in the interview. This skill incorporates cognitive (content) and affective (emotional) materials to clarify major themes expressed by the client at various points during the interview. Summarizations are usually short, concise statements by the counselor.

For example, the counselor might make a summary statement of the client's series of issues and feelings as:

> Okay, let me take a moment to see if I'm hearing you correctly. Your supervisor at work has really got you going emotionally. And at the same time, you're not too convinced that your skills on the assembly line are as bad as she might have you to believe. This job has a greater importance to you now that your wife is expecting a third child in June.

Communication: Influencing Skills

It is not sufficient to sit back and merely listen to a client. Certain skills also must be employed to influence the client's behavior. These are called influencing skills, and they consist of giving directions, expressions of content, opinions, and advice. The counselor should share himself through self-disclosure, making interpretations, and providing summarizations to help direct the client through his thought process.

Each of these skills may vary across cultures. For example, citing results from Jude Berman's pilot study at the University of Massachusetts, Ivey and McGowan (1977) stated that Third World individuals use such skills as advice giving and interpretation, that Anglo females tend to use reflection and paraphrasing, and that Anglo males ask questions.

The counselor's ability to *give directions* to a client is also an important counseling skill. There are occasions where the client may be assisted through the counselor's directions.

The *expression of content* skill is aimed at teaching the client to express sincerely how she feels about content material (for example, the test results presented by the counselor). Here, the client learns to focus on the "inside" of the total self (Ivey, 1971).

In efforts to facilitate the client's self-exploration—getting the client to open up to express real feelings and concerns and to increase self-understanding—the counselor may use *self-disclosure*, by sharing feelings, content material, or information about himself with the client. However, Ivey and Gluckstern (1976) caution counselors to be sure that they have first effectively attended to the client. By sharing experiences about himself, the counselor places himself in a position to influence the communicative behavior of the client. He must avoid burdening the client with his concerns by controlling the quality and timing of discussion about himself; the goal is to help the client focus more on her problems, thus facilitating greater self-exploration and understanding.

Another influencing skill is *interpretation*, used by the counselor to add something to or to go beyond what the client has stated. This skill allows the counselor to help the client obtain greater awareness of the messages underlying her verbal statements. The counselor provides a new frame of reference by renaming the client's feelings. A client may say, "It hurts when people find out that nobody cares about them." The counselor may interpret this statement with the response, "It's really frightening when you find out your friends don't care for you."

The final skill is *influencing summarization*. This skill is similar to an attending summarization, except that influencing summarization is aimed at what the counselor has conveyed. Influencing summarization may contain cognitive and emotional dimensions. At the end of the session, the counselor summarizes the already stated treatment or suggested steps that the client is to follow. This skill, along with the attending summarization skill, facilitates the counselor's concise and comprehensive account of the counseling session and gives the client directions to follow prior to the subsequent session.

Communication: Qualitative Skills

Qualitative skills, as their description suggests, are an attempt to improve the quality of the counseling relationship, thus producing a high level of communication. These include using immediacy, confrontation, and genuineness. As a counselor communicates in specific rather than vague terms, the client learns concrete terms to help her accurately identify and label emotions and experiences. Respect and warmth convey to the client that the counselor cares about her and accepts her as a unique person without placing a value on her.

At times, it may be culturally appropriate to use skills in immediacy—"direct, mutual talk" or "you-me talk"—to help the client focus on what is occurring in the interview (Carkhuff, 1969; Ivey, 1971; Egan, 1975). Immediacy helps the client gain a better understanding of herself, both in an interpersonal relationship with the counselor and with others outside the counseling setting. Immediacy helps a client deal with behavior as it is occurring. It exhibits to the client, for example, how her behavior is affecting the counselor. The counselor expresses his capability to confront and is also an example of immediacy:

CLIENT: I'm not sure why I'm here. Why should I go on? You're not listening to me. When I leave, I'll feel the same way as when I came in!

COUNSELOR: I hear your anger directed at me as you say that I'm not listening to you, but I feel that I'm being manipulated. This feeling happens whenever I attempt to get you to open up and talk more about yourself.

This example shows the counselor's response to the client's anger; he reveals his feelings of being manipulated by the client. The counselor's disclosure directs the interpersonal communication to the "here-and-now."

Confrontation is a high-level qualitative skill that helps to influence the client's communicative behavior during the interview. In therapy, there are moments when a client needs help in clarifying discrepancies she has conveyed during the interview. At such times, the counselor may use confrontation by responding, "You say you're happy now that you flunked out of school, but you're frowning, and you have tears in your eyes," or "You seem really angry at your supervisor for the three-day work suspension you received, yet you seem satisfied that this suspension did happen."

The final qualitative skill is *genuineness*, or consistency. To develop and maintain trust in cross-cultural situations, openness, authenticity, and honesty must be communicated to the client. This is achieved when the counselor maintains genuineness in confronting issues for the client by saying such things as: "I feel that you would really like to manage your relationship with your wife and children better," "It appears to me that you don't want to work toward resolving the conflict you have with your fellow workers," "I don't understand why you continue to blame yourself for not finding a job during the past few months." When the counselor applies this skill, he conveys a sense of wholeness of self—he is not a "phoney" in the relationship. He is consistent in his feelings and does not hide himself in the transaction with the client. He will always deal with an issue when it arises, thus avoiding the chance that something important slip by undealt with.

Communication: Focusing Skills

The final dimension of the Ivey Taxonomy is the focusing skills, which enable the culturally effective counselor to converse on many topics appropriate to the client and his culture. The goal of focusing skills is to identify the theme of any communication. Examination of the pattern of the relationship indicates what is occurring and directs the counselor to alter or influence the focus of the communication. Of course, the counselor's response to a client's statement may influence the client's next statement. Focus skills include self-focus, focus on other persons, mutual or group focus, focus on various topics, and cultural-environmental-contextual focus.

In *self-focus,* the client is focused on the self as the major theme, and the counselor responds directly: "You feel a little uneasy about facing your case worker right now." The counselor also may focus indirectly on the client through self-disclosure or by discussing experiences about himself: "Sometimes I feel very uptight, too, when I'm pressured into doing something I don't feel good about. Is my feeling something like yours?"

It may be necessary to *focus on other persons* who are the subjects of the client's conversation, persons who are not physically present in the interview. Obviously, focus on other persons detracts from direct-mutual communication (or you-me talk); however, Ivey and Gluckstern (1976) contend that it may be culturally appropriate. Examples of other-person focus might include such comments as, "Who were those people who recently went to your defense?" "Some people wouldn't have defended you," or "Many friends of mine probably would have defended you regardless of the consequences." The counselor's focus on other persons may be of particular importance when he is working with, for example, traditional Puerto Rican clients. Christensen (1977) contends that

> The closeness of the Puerto Rican family is such that rarely is it true that a counselee will not bring it into a discussion with a counselor. Virtually all social interaction with the Puerto Rican culture involves at least a brief discussion of some members of the family. Even if only a brief lapse between contacts has occurred, invariably greetings and farewells include inquiries about certain members of the family. . . . the Puerto Rican extended family includes not only immediate family and other kin but also those related through . . . a joining of families through serving as godparents or close friendships. [P. 413]

While the people in one client's conversation will be family members, those in the conversation of another client may include family members, peers, social case workers, or public health workers. The counselor may at times have to focus on a combination of subjects in the client's conversation.

Mutual or group focus is important in counseling because it tends to give participants a sense of equality. In a one-to-one relationship, the counselor attempts to generate mutual feelings that focus on such words as "you," "I," and "us." In mutual or group focus, the client is drawn into a "we" relationship with the counselor: "We seem to be discussing a topic that's a real concern to you. I feel good that you have talked about his concern. Now we might try to find out where we can go with it." Group focus centers on such terms as "the group," "us," and "we" (Ivey and Gluckstern, 1976, p. 55).

It is equally important to *focus on various topics* to move interpersonal communication in different directions. An example might be: "Swimming is often enjoyable. The water, the competitors, and the atmosphere are fantastic!" While this response gives the client support in this area of interest, it also directs the focus from client involvement to other things or persons involved. Another example might be: "Because your car wasn't working, you bought a new car. What encouraged you to make the purchase?" The counselor's response changes the focus to a topic or area of interest rather than a person. Recognizing that the client's conversation will contain many different topics, Ivey and Gluckstern (1976) suggest that the counselor's focus should be on a mixture of topics brought up by the client. This approach facilitates the communicative process and lends itself to dealing with issues affecting the client.

The last focusing skill, *cultural-environmental-contextual focus*, considers the relationship between the client's concern and societal issues, avoids placing sole responsibility on the client for his behavior. This concept is directly contrary to traditional counseling theories, which emphasize client responsibility. Culture and socioeconomic conditions may be serious concerns to the client. A counselor's appropriate response in such a situation might be: "Were certain nutritional habits dependent on some of your Muslim religion beliefs?" "You stated that your drinking was more of a social or peer-group nature on the reservation than a personal interest," or "Many of our middle-class myths and stereotypes about lower-class ethnic minorities take a dim view on inner-city Blacks."

SUMMARY

Skills within these four dimensions are concrete, observable, and measurable; such skills are likely to be very beneficial in attaining counseling goals. When the counselor and the client are culturally different, these skills work better than traditional methods, yet they can be effective only when they are appropriately applied to clients as individuals within a specific culture.

The Ivey Taxonomy (Ivey, 1977) is closely linked to many traditional counseling theories. The manner in which the Ivey Taxonomy is applied reflects certain aspects of a counselor's orientations. Various counselors and therapists use different microcounseling skills (Ivey, 1977). For example, Rogerian counselors or client-centered therapists use mostly attending dimensions, especially if their counseling is nondirective and relies on minimal encouragers, reflections of feeling, paraphrases, and summarizations. Gestalt counselors, however, communicate content and feelings, provide directions, and make interpretations (Ivey, 1977).

EXERCISES

The purpose of the following exercises is to provide practical experiences using the skills involved in the communicative process model. The first set of exercises is intended to give participants practice in developing a sense for when to use these skills in the precounseling phase. The second set of exercises is intended to facilitate participants' experiential learning of counseling skills in three of the four dimensions in Ivey's Taxonomy.

A. Ask students to form a dyad with one another. In each dyad, one participant will assume the role of a client of an ethnic or cultural group different from that of the counselor. As the two participants verbally interact, the counselor should apply precounseling skills (basic skills of culture) as they appropriately relate to the client. After a period of about five minutes, stop the conversation and discuss the appropriateness of the counselor's precounseling skills. Following this discussion, the counselor-client roles should be reversed and the previous steps repeated.

B. Have all students view a short demonstration of open-ended questions in a simulated counseling dyad. Following this demonstration, students should form triads. One person will be a counselor, one, a client; and the other, an observer.

The counselor asks open-ended questions during a five-minute period. This session might be videotaped if such facilities are available; otherwise, the client or other observers should provide the counselor immediate feedback on his performance. After feedback has been provided and the series of open-ended questions has been reviewed, the same student remains as counselor and attempts an improved demonstration, if necessary. Should this latter step not be needed, students can reverse roles and repeat the demonstration. Once skill has been demonstrated by each student, repeat the procedure using the attending skills, influencing skills, qualitative skills, and focusing skills.

REFERENCES

Arbuckle, D. S. "The Alienated Counselor." *Personnel and Guidance Journal,* 1969, *48,* 18–23.

Ayers, G. E. "The Disadvantaged: An Analysis of Factors Affecting the Counseling Relationship." *Rehabilitation Literature,* 1970, *31,* 194–99.

Bernstein, B. "Social Class, Speech Systems, and Psychotherapy." In F. Riessman, J. Cohen, and A. Pearl (eds.), *Mental Health of the Poor: New Treatment Approaches for Low-Income People.* New York: Free Press. 1964. Pp. 194–204.

Carkhuff, R. R. *Helping and Human Relations: A Primer for Lay and Professional Helpers,* vol. 2. New York: Holt, Rinehart and Winston, 1969.

Christensen, E. W. "When Counseling Puerto Ricans." *Personnel and Guidance Journal,* 1977, *55,* 412–15.

DeBalassie, R. R. *Counseling with the Mexican American Youth.* Austin, Tex.: Learning Concepts, 1976.

Delaney, D. J. and S. Eisenberg. *The Counseling Process.* Chicago: Rand McNally, 1972.

Egan, E. *The Skilled Helper: A Model for Systematic Helping and Interpersonal Relating.* Monterey, Calif.: Brooks/Cole Pub. Co., 1975.

Franklin, A. J. "To Be Young, Gifted and Black with Inappropriate Professional Training: A Critique of Counseling Programs." *Counseling Psychologist,* 1971, *2,* 107–12.

Gunnings, T. S. "Preparing the New Counselor." *Counseling Psychologist,* 1971, *2,* 100–101.

Ho, M. K. "Cross-Cultural Career Counseling." *Vocational Guidance Quarterly,* 1973, *21,* 186–90.

Ivey, A. E. *Microcounseling: Innovations in Interviewing Training.* Springfield, Ill.: Charles C. Thomas, 1971.

Ivey, A. E. "Cultural Expertise: Toward Systematic Outcome Criteria in Counseling and Psychological Education." *Personnel and Guidance Journal,* 1977, *55,* 296–302.

Ivey, A. E., and N. Gluckstern. *Basic Attending Skills, Participant Manual.* North Amherst, Mass.: Microtraining Associates, 1974.

Ivey, A. E. and N. Gluckstern. *Basic Influencing Skills, Leader and Participant Manuals.* North Amherst, Mass.: Microtraining Associates, 1976.

Ivey, A. E. and S. J. McGowan. "Microcounseling: A Systematic Approach for Improving Helping Skills and Teaching-Them to Others." *Focus on Guidance,* 1977, *9,* 1–10.

Jackson, J. H. "Delivery of Mental Health Services to the Black Child as a Model for Mental Health Services to the Larger Black Consuming Public." *School Psychology,* 1975, *13,* 76–81.

Jones, M. H. and M. C. Jones. "The Neglected Client." In A. L. Jones, ed., *Black Psychology.* New York: Harper and Row, 1972. Pp. 195–204.

Mehrabian, A. *Nonverbal Communication.* New York: Aldine-Atherton, 1972.

Padilla, A. M., R. A. Ruiz, and R. Alvarez. "Community Mental Health Services for the Spanish-speaking/Surnamed Population." *American Psychologist,* 1975, *30,* 892-905.

Patterson, C. H. "Counselor Education for Black Counselors and for Counseling Black Clients: Comments." *Counseling Psychologist,* 1971, *2,* 112–13.

Ridley, C. R. "Cross-Cultural Counseling: A Multivariate Analysis" *Viewpoints in Teaching and Learning,* 1978, *54,* 43–50.

Schofield, W. *Psychotherapy: The Purchase of Friendship.* Englewood Cliffs, N. J.: Prentice-Hall, 1964.

Shuy, R. *Problems of Communication in the Cross-Cultural Medical Interview.* Working papers in sociolinguistics, No.

19. Southwest Educational Development Lab., Austin, Tex. 1974. (ED126 691.)

Smith, E. J. *Counseling the Culturally Different Black Youth.* Columbus, Ohio: C. E. Merrill Pub. Co., 1973.

Spang, A. "Counseling the Indian." *Journal of American Indian Education,* 1965, *5,* 10–15.

Sue, D. W. "Counseling the Culturally Different: A Conceptual Analysis." *Personnel and Guidance Journal,* 1977, 55(7), 422–25.

Sue, D. W. and B. A. Kirk. "Asian-Americans: Use of Counseling and Psychiatric Services on a College Campus." *Journal of Counseling Psychology,* 1975, *22,* 84–86.

Sue, D. W. and S. Sue. "Counseling Chinese-Americans." *Personnel and Guidance Journal,* 1972, *50*(8), 637–44.

Sue, S. "Community Mental Health Services to Minority Groups: Some Optimism, Some Pessimism." *American Psychologist,* 1977, *32,* 616–24.

Sue, S., D. W. Sue, and D. Sue. "Asian Americans as a Minority Group." *American Psychologist, 1975, 30,* 906–10.

Sundberg, N. D. "Toward Research Evaluating Intercultural Counseling." In P. Pedersen, W. J. Lonner, and J. G. Draguns (eds.), *Counseling across Cultures.* Honolulu: University Press of Hawaii, 1976, Pp. 139–69.

Trimble, J. E. "Value Differences among American Indians: Concerns for the Concerned Counselor." In P. Pedersen, W. J. Lonner, and J. G. Draguns (eds.), *Counseling across Cultures.* Honolulu: University Press of Hawaii, 1976. Pp. 65–81.

Vontress, C. E. "Cultural Barriers in the Counseling Relationship." *Personnel and Guidance Journal,* 1969, *48,* 11–17.

Walker, R. A. "The Disadvantaged Enter Rehabilitation—Are Both Ready?" *Rehabilitation Literature,* 1968, *9,* 1–4.

Warren, R. C., A. M. Jackson, J. Nugaris, and G. K. Farley. "Differential Attitudes of Black and White Patients Toward Treatment in a Child Guidance Clinic." *American Journal of Orthopsychiatry,* 1973, *43,* 384–93.

Wrenn, G. C. "The Culturally Encapsulated Counselor." *Harvard Educational Review,* 1962, *32,* 444–49.

Yamamoto, J. , Q. C. James, and N. Palley. "Cultural Problems in Psychiatric Therapy." *Archives of General Psychiatry,* 1968, *19,* 45–49.

10

Stages of Counseling

BEFORE THE INTIMATE PORTION of an interview takes place, basic skills of culture relating to the client's culture should be considered to assure that effective movement—exploration, understanding, and action—occurs within each subsequent counseling stage. Many aspects of the client's culture influence the communicative process. How the counselor deals with the individual and cultural aspects of a client determines the outcome of the interview. Therefore, the precounseling phase of the interview focuses on cultural appropriateness of such skills such as eye contact, body language, tone and speech rate, and topics of conversation.

THE PRECOUNSELING STAGE

Eye Contact

Based on the counselor's multicultural experiences and cultural awareness, he should look at his client during the interview in ways that will make the client comfortable and that are culturally suitable to the situation. He should carefully observe the client to determine whether avoidance of direct eye contact is personal or cultural, and then arrange the seating to meet the situation—the counselor and client may sit beside each other in single chairs, on a couch, or at a round table. In some cases, it may not be appropriate to look directly at a client. For example, direct eye contact among some American Indians of the Southwest may be viewed as hostile behavior (Ivey and McGowan, 1977); some Puerto Rican and Black children are expected not to look adults directly in the eye; and some Mexican American and Japanese American families feel that females should not have direct eye contact with males. In such cases, the counselor might be most effective sitting beside the client rather than directly across from him.

Personal Space Preference

Awareness of the client's interpretations of body positions is an essential factor, since interpretations may vary between cultures. The customary procedure is for a counselor to sit directly across from the client, a few feet away, with a slight lean about the head and shoulders toward the client to suggest interest, but this procedure is culturally acceptable to only a few of the clients. Some clients may seek great physical distance between themselves and the counselor. Research indicates that more Chicanos prefer close proximity than do Blacks and Anglos, yet Blacks have a higher preference for close proximity than do Anglos.

These findings have practical implications for the counseling dyad. For instance, it may be necessary to provide a client with great latitude concerning the seating by offering several possibilities. Such facilities allow the client flexibility to where he feels most comfortable and allow him to set the limits of his "personal space."

In some cases, it may be more culturally appropriate to ask the client, "Where do you want to sit?" Once the client has elected where to sit, the counselor might ask, "Do you mind if I sit here?" or "Is it okay with you if I sit here?"

Body Language

The culturally skilled counselor can interpret hand gestures and head and eye movements. A gesture by an Asian American that would typically mean "Come closer," may actually mean "Get away" (Ho, 1973). Another client may give a twist of the head that is interpreted by the counselor as "No," but this actually means "Yes." Understanding these messages means going beyond their interpretation in the dominant culture to see how these messages are interpreted in the client's culture.

Tone of Voice

The counselor's tone of voice is another important factor in the precounseling interview. Although meanings attached to the counselor's words affect the communicative process, the underlying meaning of his communication may be even more important. A client is frequently more attuned to the tone of voice than to the words, thus, the counselor must avoid sounding harassed, condescending, disinterested, or unpleasant. One method of accomplishing this is to adopt a positive tone of voice.

Speech Rate

Obviously, individuals differ in their rate of speech; these differences may be attributed to ethnic and cultural variations, as well as to regional differences. For example, the rate of speech may be slow for some lower-class Black clients from parts of Mississippi, but fast for many lower-class Blacks and Puerto Ricans reared in Harlem, New York, or Boston. Also, many urban Northeastern Anglos are likely to have higher rates of speech than Southern Appalachian Anglos. Yet a client whose rate of speech is slow does not necessarily listen only to slow speech; the counselor should carefully observe his client to determine whether there is a need to adjust his rate of speech to facilitate communication. As the counselor initiates conversation or responds to his client, he can watch for facial expressions such as a frown, a yawn, closed eyes, or activities such as scratching behind the ear (from a Japanese client) that might indicate lack of understanding. If the client's responses contain fragmented sentences or concepts different from those stated by the counselor, this may also suggest a need to adjust the rate of speech. A moderate rate of speech may be most appropriate, at least in the initial contact session. It is essential, however, that any change in the counselor's rate of speech occur out of necessity rather than as a mimicry of the client's speech pattern.

Appropriate Topics

The competence of the counselor to discuss cultural and personal topics must be acceptable to the client. For instance, discussion of his religion would be unacceptable for an Apache from Arizona or New Mexico; he would not wish to share his religion with a non-Apache. Discussion of abortion with an unmarried, pregnant teenager who lives with a traditional Mexican family would also be inappropriate; the concept of abortion is contrary to the teachings of Roman Catholicism.

In summary, skills pertaining to the precounseling phase are ongoing tools that help to energize and move communication into the remaining dimension of the counseling dyad, which involves deeper exploration, understanding, and action. Consideration and application of these skills determines, in part, the development, as well as the outcome, of the counseling interview(s).

THE FIRST COUNSELING STAGE: SELF-EXPLORATION

First Phase—Getting the Client to Open Up

The first stage of the communicative process, self-exploration, focuses on helping the client explore feelings, emotions, and experiences related to her concerns. This phase enables the client to become aware of personally relevant materials—cognitive or content material that provides descriptive information about the problem area and how the client and others are associated with it. A client expressing personally relevant material might say, "I'm not sure what to do. If I go out looking for a job, I'll need to know some kind of trade and to wear presentable clothes to impress the interviewer. If I stay at home and the public social case worker sees me, I'll blow Mary's chances to continue receiving public assistance checks to support her and the children."

Clients bring their concerns to the counseling setting. Many are quite verbal in exploring their concerns, thus they help to sort out their problems. Others are more nonverbal, apprehensive, or unsure of where or how to start the exploration process. Therefore, it becomes essential for clients—especially those in this latter group—to feel a sense of rapport and mutual trust with the counselor before they can explore material and understand and implement alternative actions to their problems. To aid in this process, minimal facilitative skills eventually induce clients to open up and share their concerns.

The counselor communicates his genuineness to the client by being consistent in his behavior. What he says should be consistent with his tone of voice and body language, but the counselor is reminded that the pattern of his verbal and nonverbal behavior must be attuned to the client's culture.

Equally important in establishing a positive relationship is the communication of respect and warmth to the client. A feeling of respect allows each client to differ from another and still feel worthwhile. The counselor expresses respect through his attitude toward the client, valuing her as a person, being accessible, being prepared, being willing to help, and believing that she wants to improve her behavior or her situation. The counselor also expresses respect by not placing a value on the client's behavior and by assisting her in expressing herself.

Gazda (1973) suggests that in establishing warmth toward the client, the counselor should respond in a modulated tone of voice before firm ground is established (pp. 56-57). Warmth and regard for the client further amplifies respect, providing the client with a sense of security and safety. Gazda refers to warmth as "physical expression of empathy and respect. It is generally communicated through a wide variety of nonverbal media such as gestures, posture, tone of voice, touch, or facial expression" (p. 87). Gazda further suggests that the counselor should focus on the client's needs. His attention should be an exhibition of his care for her rather than something that is forced upon her. Gazda cautions the counselor that "initially high levels of warmth can be counterproductive to [clients] who have received little or no warmth or who have been taken advantage of. With certain individuals, initial high levels of warmth may indicate [counselor] weakness" (p. 57). Therefore, it is extremely important for the counselor to attain sufficient understanding concerning the necessity to communicate warmth. The appropriateness of communicating warmth and respect varies with the client's culture and individuality.

The concreteness of the counselor's responses is also an important skill in communicating across cultures during the initial counseling stage. The counselor's statements should focus on the client's specific feelings, behaviors, and experiences. Discussion of vague, intellectual topics may suggest that the counselor is not emotionally involved with the client and is not dealing with her experiences and feelings. The counselor's verbal concreteness attempts to encourage clear language relevant to the client and her problem.

Another qualitative skill that helps the counselor and the client is immediacy. This verbal approach is important in enhancing the client's self-exploration. Immediacy, expressed through the counselor's language, communicates to the client the counselor's intent to deal with issues most "immediate" to the situation—issues of the "here-and-now."

There are four central means by which the counselor conveys immediacy during this stage of counseling. First is the application of verb *tense;* each tense has its own effect on the communication. Statements in the present tense lend assistance to the client in clarifying his concerns. "Right now, your face is flushed and wet with perspiration as you try to talk about the conflict you had with your supervisor." This statement directs the client's attention to the situation in which he now finds himself rather than allowing him to dwell without effect on some behavior in the past or future.

The second verbal approach to immediacy involves the counselor in directing the client to a proactive rather than a reactive role, i.e., involving him in "I" statements in which he takes responsibility for his actions. The client is encouraged toward ("*I* decided to stay home since I didn't feel well" and "I just didn't understand") rather than away from ("My cold had me feeling so bad that I just couldn't go to work" and "They just didn't explain it to me"). The counselor might rephrase a client's statement, putting the client in a proactive role.

A third type of immediacy assists the client in attaining directness of expression. A client often will evade direct questions with vague or indirect responses. To a client's vague statement, such as, "Sometimes people don't want to hide their emotions, but they do because they don't want to embarrass their family," a counselor might respond, "Lawrence, could you say that 'I' want to get away from hiding my emotions from others although 'I' respect the fact that my family doesn't value this kind of behavior?" The client will probably respond, "Yeah, I guess you're right. That's how I feel."

The fourth approach of immediacy teaches the client to avoid the use of vague modifiers such as "sort of," "maybe," "seldom," "perhaps," and "rather" (Ivey and Gluckstern, 1976b, p. 103). Verbal specificity is the aim rather than vague, unclear words that impede recognition of the message. The counselor establishes models for the client, directing her from a vague, "I'm sort of hurt," to the specific, whether it be, "I'm devastated," or "I've been offended by . . ."

The last qualitative skill is confrontation. To maintain open and sincere communication, the counselor deals directly with the issues within the client's experience. Confrontation with a client to point out differences among ideas, emotions, "facts," and verbal and nonverbal behavior is needed. Confrontation gives the client a realistic picture of his behavior and of the situation, placing emphasis on the real point of a discussion and pulling together all the areas covered, especially when they are in conflict. For example, a counselor might say: "You say that you're going to stop being around Bill because he mistreats you, pushes you around, but then you continue to see him" or "You stated that I don't understand you because I haven't lived in a Black ghetto, but I'm a little confused. If I had lived there, would that really make a difference in my understanding of you as an individual?"

The counselor's confrontations assist the client in clarifying discrepancies of behavior or in interpreting a situation, and in developing a realistic view of the situation: The client might say, "I've bought five books with diet plans, and I attended an eight-week diet class, but I go right on eating candy, cake, pie, and anything else that fills me up." The client has confronted the conflicts in her behavior patterns and can now move on to the next stage in her exploration.

The counselor's attending skills—using open-ended and closed-ended questions; minimal encouragement; paraphrasing, reflections of feeling, foci, and summarizations; physical communication of genuineness, respect, warmth; concreteness; immediacy; and confrontation—are used throughout the initial stage. These skills communicate the counselor's attention to the client. The client is taught to evaluate which aspects of his life are problems and then to reassemble these pieces. The initial stage might open with a counselor's invitation for the client to talk in the form of an open-ended question such as, "What would you like to talk about today?" or "Where would you like to start?" Open-ended questions give the client greater latitude to touch on relevant material.

On the other hand, there are times when close-ended questions are needed to give the counselor a clearer view of a statement or a discussion, saying, "I feel like I'm lost" or "I'm pregnant and my boyfriend won't marry me or give our baby his name." At a minimal level of verbal or exploring her areas of concern with such responses as "Go on," "Yes," or "And?" Verbal encouragement conveys to the client that the counselor is listening and wants her to continue. Culturally appropriate gestures may also transmit similar messages to the client.

Second Phase—Exploring Feelings and Emotions

As the client begins to open up and talk more freely, the material disclosed is either cognitive (words and content) or affective (feelings and emotions) material. The second phase of exploration is aimed at exploring feelings and emotions related to personally relevant material. The counselor focuses on the client's emotional investment in his problem area and uses reflection to mirror the client's emotions. An example of self-exploration with a forty-year-old Black male might be:

CLIENT: (pause) I know I'm not good enough to be with some of my Anglo colleagues. That's why they don't invite my wife and me to their home for parties or dinners.

COUNSELOR: You really feel left out as you see some of your colleagues enjoying themselves, and you're frightened, wondering what else will happen to you and your wife since neither of you can change your ethnic background.

This example illustrates the client's close relationship between his emotions and content material. The counselor conveys attention and empathy. The counselor recognizes the client's frame of reference and reflects or mirrors the emotions related to his problem area.

At various intervals during the client's exploration, the counselor might paraphrase the client's message by restating it more precisely. Paraphrasing also allows the counselor to check himself against what the client has tried to communicate, especially when the client's message seems unclear, fragmented, or glossed over. Other applications include the counselor's communicating to the client an understanding of what is being conveyed or emphasizing certain issues or themes. Examples of paraphrasing are:

Example 1

COUNSELOR: It seems that you are saying that you enjoy going to college and having the chance to complete your bachelors' degree to become self-supportive, but it's very demanding and limits activities with your children. Am I hearing you correctly?

Example 2

CLIENT: My brother and sister ganged up on me, and before I realized it, I landed on the kitchen floor.

COUNSELOR: They overpowered you.

Example 3

CLIENT: I'm awfully worried about my son's involvement in gang fighting in the barrio. I'm not sure what to do. The gang's cause is very confusing, and I feel so alone.

COUNSELOR: Right now, you're almost ready to give up in helping your son.
(Alternate paraphrase: You're facing a tough decision, but you've been up against tough decisions at other times, and you've chosen the best alternative.)

In this second phase of the self-exploration process, the counselor also applies focusing skills to attend effectively to and to facilitate the client's self-exploration. The counselor focuses on the client's experience, causing her to explore herself rather than to focus on external factors. Focusing on the client's name or the personal pronoun "you" communicates a sense of concern for the client and keeps her focused in the "I" direction. To the client's statement, "My grade point average has 'bottomed out'. I'm very concerned about whether or not I'll be able to finish out the semester," the counselor may respond, "You haven't done well in your overall grades, and you're worried that your performance may prevent you from remaining in school this semester." Note that the counselor has maintained the focus on the client's personal experience.

Ivey and Gluckstern (1976) have proposed categorizing focusing skills at this stage of counseling into six areas: the client, the counselor, other individuals, various topics, mutual or group, and cultural-environmental-contextual. The following example will help illustrate the various applications of focusing skills within the exploratory stage:

> Gwong, a Chinese-American male, high school student, states to the counselor: My parents are in their late forties—old, you know. They're against dating anyone outside our ethnic group. My two brothers, who are older than me, live with us. It just seems difficult for people to talk to them about anything. It seems like every time anybody attempts to explain how he feels about a situation, my parents and my brothers get really mad and consider him an outcast.
>
> *Focus on the client:* Gwong, *you're* puzzled and not certain how to deal with this situation with *your* family—how to get *your* point across to *your* parents.
>
> *Focus on the counselor: I* was involved in a similar situation with *my* family. It was difficult for *me*, too—made *me* feel that *my* emotions were not important to them.
>
> *Focus on other persons:* Your *brothers* live with you and your parents. How are *they* involved in this situation? What are *their* feelings about all this?

Mutual focus or focus on group: We seem to be saying the same thing. These kinds of emotions are important to *us*. You're sharing your feelings with me makes both of us feel good about the openness between *us*. May *we* continue?

Focus on the topic: Your family's unwillingness to hear you out causes this *frustration*. How might your family's traditional values cause this uncomfortable feeling?

Cultural-environmental-contextual focus: You're saying that where dating is involved your *family* prizes an *ethnic group* similar to its own.

A client's self-analysis may depend on the counselor's ability to use his focusing skills effectively to enhance the therapeutic encounter. A mixture of focusing categories may enhance self-exploration more effectively than a single focus; frequently, areas are difficult to keep separate.

Periodically, the counselor uses *summarization* to check the accuracy of his understanding; he attempts to recapitulate and condense the client's emotions, facts, and ideas. Summarization can also help the client move toward clarity of his problems. The focus of summarization in the first stage is mainly on what the client expresses rather than on the counselor. Ivey and Gluckstern (1974) contend: "By accurately recapitulating, condensing, and crystallizing for [the client], we say we respect and hear what [she is] saying" (p. 48).

A counselor's accurate summarization helps move a client from exploring to understanding and acting on a problem. A summarization of content is similar to a paraphrase and a summarization of feelings is similar to a reflection of feelings, but summarization in both cases includes more verbal and nonverbal material. Furthermore, summarization that integrates feelings and content material may be very effective in moving the client from one stage to another. The summarization may deal with the whole interview or with one or more segments of the interview. The first of these examples illustrates the counselor attempts to verify his perception to avoid distorted understanding of what the client is saying. In the second example, the counselor attempts to help the client tie together her emotions, ideas, and facts.

Example 1

(To a twenty-two-year-old, American Indian woman has left the reservation to attend college and is later confronted by her parents—first interview.)

COUNSELOR: You've expressed several important ideas and feelings in the last few minutes. Let's see if I'm hearing you correctly. You left the reservation to attend a university here in New York City. After finishing your degree, you got married. Both you and your husband have decided to remain here for two more years since you like it so well, and you plan to move west later. But, recently, your parents, who have gotten older now, want you to move closer to them. Yet half your reason for getting married was that you couldn't stand being around them. After hearing your mother crying over the phone and saying that you don't care about them, you feel terrible and guilty. Right now, you feel that you are at a loss and don't know which step to take next.

Example 2

(To a forty-year-old, Southern Appalachian Anglo woman married to a coal miner—after several interviews.)

COUNSELOR: Now you appear to be feeling quite aware that your nagging and the constant demands you made on your husband during his layoff from the mines was one major reason for his drinking. This awareness is different from your feelings of frustration during our first interview when you blamed your husband for his drinking and for not finding work. How do you come to grips with these feelings at this moment?

Summarization, as with other exploratory skills, is viewed as an essential tool that helps the client take action on his own behavior by clearly describing the problem that brought him to counseling.

The counselor uses all these skills during an interview, gauging cultural and time elements as he goes along. Such skills at most will help a client begin to understand his behavior (Egan, 1975). Once the client shows an ability to see the relation between emotional and personally relevant material, the counselor can focus on the next stage—self-understanding—in which additional communicative skills are used.

THE SECOND COUNSELING STAGE: SELF-UNDERSTANDING

A counselor's goal of leading a client to self-understanding involves assisting the culturally different client to reconstruct the communicative process. This allows the client to understand her behavior and the behavior of others as it relates to the problem. To achieve this goal, the skills applied in the previous stage—basic attending, qualitative, and focusing—are continued, and additional new skills are added to assist the client in understanding her behavior or problem. As the client begins to show signs of responding freely during the initial counseling stage, the counselor raises the skill levels to those of influencing and advanced qualitative skills. At this stage, the skilled counselor will help the client clearly understand a problem before exploring alternative courses of action.

Influencing skills move the client into a more active role, helping her assess the relationship between emotional and content material from a different point of view. The influencing skills direct the client to new or improved perceptions of oneself and of others, as well as of the area of concern. They include giving direction, expression of feelings, expression of content, interpretation, and influencing summarization.

Obviously, the counselor gives a certain degree of *direction* to the client before the actual counseling occurs—for example, by politely assisting the client in taking a seat. Ivey and Gluckstern (1976) and Ivey and Authier (1978) consider direction giving an important counseling skill. These authors define direction giving as that which the counselor tells the client to do (Ivey and Authier, 1978, p. 98). High-level directions can be provided within the communicative process of this second counseling stage because the client is more willing to follow the counselor's directions than she was in the first stage.

Four dimensions that accompany effective directions are suggested by Ivey and Gluckstern(1976). The first dimension requires the counselor to provide acceptable and appropriate eye contact, tone of voice, verbalization, and body language that will reinforce the client's desire to follow the directions. The second dimension requires the counselor's directions to be concrete and specific: "You've stated that feeling before. I also saw you cracking your knuckles when you mentioned him. Try saying, 'I feel uptight whenever Garcia's around.' "

The third dimension of effective direction giving involves the importance of structure in the direction when the client's actions may take various forms. The structure must be specific:

> Try keeping a schedule of your study time. Keep a written record of the subjects you study and the time for each, then bring the schedule and record with you to the next meeting.
>
> Let yourself feel your anger and madness.
>
> Tell me about your success on the job. But be sure to say 'I' as you mention each success.

The fourth and final dimension requires that the counselor check to see that his directions are accurately understood. Ivey and Gluckstern (1976, p. 68) suggest two methods of determining if the client has comprehended the directions: (1) request that the client restate directions or (2) simply ask the client if the directions were clear enough to follow. This author suggests caution, however, in applying the first method; some clients may feel offended if they sense the counselor feels they cannot understand or follow simple directions.

Expressions of feelings uses the counselor's feelings as a means of helping the client experience greater interpersonal openness and to direct the client's attention onto the feelings of those around him:

> COUNSELOR: I'd really be upset and angry if I had returned to my apartment and found that my landlord had evicted me and left my furniture and clothes standing on the street!
>
> CLIENT: Damn right! That's exactly how I feel, too! Exactly!

The counselor's expression of her own feelings pertaining to the client's concern enables the client to form a clear understanding of his feelings. Perhaps expression of feelings would prove most effective when the counselor's feelings parallel those of the client.

Expression of content, another influencing skill, includes the counselor's advice, opinions, or information (Ivey, 1977). Expression of content has been defined by Ivey and Authier (1978) as "simply a verbalization from the [counselor] which brings in data from the [counselor's] experience or knowledge which does *not* contain affective words" (p. 104). Recently, suggestions as well as expressions that threaten the client or provide assurance have been added to the category of expression of content (Ivey and Authier, 1978). Before attempting to influence a client's behavior, a counselor must have a good rapport with him. Only then will the client be open to listening to and eventually acting on the counselor's expressions of content. The following example illustrates several expressions of content:

Roy, a forty-five-year-old Southern Appalachian Anglo male, speaks:

> I went to the hospital a few weeks back to go through a series of preliminary tests to determine my condition after a mining accident. When I got there, I was put into a room with an Indian—a full-blooded, red Indian—and I mean *red!* He was recovering from an operation. Mind you, I don't have anything against Indians, but the nurses were never around to help him when he needed it. When they weren't around, I would help him in every way I could. They should have been available to properly assist that man. This same type of situation might happen to me should I need an operation within a week or two.

> Counselor's alternative expressions of content:

> *Giving advice:* Roy, you might consider informing the hospital authorities about the nurses' lack of assistance to the Indian patient. Discuss this situation with your doctor.

> *Expressing opinion:* Having to do the nurses' work while you're a patient yourself doesn't seem to be the best situation

for you. I'm not sure that they are neglecting the gentleman because he's an Indian, but this lack of assistance might happen to you, too, after your operation. The nurses aren't working to help all of the patients.

Offering assistance: I'm sure nursing care will improve for you once you've allowed me to inform the hospital authorities and your doctor of the situation. Everything will turn out okay!

Making suggestion: The next time you see the nurses on your ward you might tell them how you view their services to the Indian patient. Also, mention you're concerned about their assistance to you during your recovery from surgery.

Expressing threat: Should you avoid or neglect inquiring about how the nurses will attend to your needs after your operation, you could end up as helpless as your Indian roommate.

Expressing feelings: I would be terribly angry if I were left to fend for myself as a patient recovering from an operation. But I'd really be worried about what's going to happen to me while recovering from surgery now that I know what happened to that Indian patient.

The appropriate expressions of content will depend upon the cultural and personal experiences of the client. Therefore, it is extremely important for a counselor to be aware of the client's cultural experiences.

Closely linked to expressions of feeling and content is the counselor's *self-disclosure* to the client. Self-disclosure promotes the growth of interpersonal openness between participants, thus leading to mutual trust and better understanding of the problem. In defining self-disclosure, Ivey and Authier (1978) describe its four major dimensions. First, the counselor's self-disclosure should be made from an "I" reference, although such pronouns may be indirectly stated. Second, expressions of feeling or content should be included in self-disclosure. Third, the counselor's self-disclosure should be the central focus of this statement. He might convey his personal experience—"I went through a marriage that was something like yours"—or he could say that his own experience was somewhat similar to the client's but turned out differently—"My experience while living in Chinatown turned out a little differently from yours." Both types of self-disclosure aid in developing a relationship between the participants, and they help the client clearly perceive his own situation. The fourth and final dimension centers on the use of grammatical tense of the counselor's self-disclosure messages. Ivey and Authier (1978) state that a self-disclosure transmitted in the past tense is likely to be safer for the counselor and for the client—"A few years ago" or "Once, my mother and I." However, these authors maintain that self-disclosures communicated in the "here and now" are by far the most effective in helping the client understand his problem.

Interpretation is an invaluable tool for clarifying the client's understanding of his problem. The counselor attempts to move the client's perceptions beyond his present understanding; she provides the client with new frames of reference in which to view his behavior, relabeling the behavior or renaming it from her own advantage. Both verbal content and affective material are integrated into the interpretation, helping the client rethink her perceptions to make sound decisions.

Isolated messages tend to run through the client's conversation. After attending to these, the counselor can make an interpretation by bringing these messages together and attaching her own assessment. The client now may reevaluate his thinking and attain an objective picture of his problem. Thus, he may improve his perception and deal with it more effectively. For instance, once the counselor recognizes that a client experiences a great deal of emotional frustration when he interacts with his mother, social worker, and wife, she might say to the client, "I wonder if you've realized that you tend to become very frustrated whenever you mention your interactions with women who make certain demands on you." The accuracy of the counselor's interpretations is very important to effective communication. Interpretations are appropriate when sufficient information has been presented. Brammer (1979) offers these guidelines for effective interpreting:

1. Look for the client's basic message.
2. Paraphrase this message to him.

3. Add your understanding of what his message means in terms of your theory or your general explanation of motives, defenses, needs, and styles.
4. Keep the language simple and the level close to the client's message. Avoid wild speculation and statements in esoteric words.
5. Introduce your ideas with statements that indicate you are offering tentative ideas on what his words or behaviors mean. Examples are: "Is this a fair statement?" "The way I see it is . . ." "I wonder if . . ." or "Try this one on for size."
6. Solicit client reactions to your interpretations.
7. Teach clients to do their own interpreting. Remember, we can't give insight to others; they must make their own discoveries (pp. 94–95).

With the final influencing skill, *influencing summarization*, a counselor attempts to combine self-expression of content and feeling. During the interview, a counselor may have provided a client with directions, opinions, feelings, and advice, which he then can summarize in a more integrative or combined pattern. The intermittent application summarization aids a client in attaining a clear understanding of the counselor's perceptions of him and his problem. In addition, a summarization assists the client in organizing his perceptions. Influencing summarizations differ from attending summarizations in that attending summarizations are aimed at what the client has expressed, while influencing summarizations allow the counselor to emphasize certain points of his own expression. The following example illustrates a counselor's influencing summarization to a twenty-five-year-old, Puerto Rican woman experiencing problems interacting with co-workers.

> We have discussed several important points the past few minutes, and there are a few things that you need to consider in helping us get a clearer picture of what is happening in your relationship with other people. I have suggested five things that might assist you: (1) selecting three persons on the job with whom you have problems relating, (2) looking at some of the issues that arise as you interact with each person, (3) identifying what happens between you and each of the other persons, (4) identifying those things that led up to the conflict between you and the other person, and (5) meeting here next Tuesday at 11A.M. to talk over what you have found.

THE THIRD COUNSELING STAGE: ACTION

Transition to the next stage of the process can occur when the client has reached a minimum level of understanding and can consistently make statements about herself or himself that mirror a basic understanding of emotions and their meanings. This is the exhibition of awareness of one's explored emotions. The counselor responds to the client's readiness and proceeds to the action stage by assisting the client in acting upon his understanding of the problem.

The ultimate goal of counseling is to bring about behavioral change (Pietrofesa et al., 1978), yet client's thorough exploration and understanding of himself are by no means sufficient to insure that he will take positive steps to alter his behavior or that of others. For instance, the client understands that smoking cigarettes is harmful to his health; he wants to stop, but he continues to smoke. The overweight client understands that his obesity is not organically caused, and the only reason for this condition is his overeating. Or, the Black client may understand that because of his ethnic background, he has been passed up for a managerial promotion, but he has taken no steps toward righting the injury. The counselor's basic aim in the action stage is to assist the client in developing and implementing means of actively altering or effecting his problem situation. A common procedure that helps the client make decisions to resolve his concerns is to establish systematic steps in problem solving.

EFFECTIVE PROBLEM SOLVING

Since the client may enter the counseling setting with one or more problems to be solved, the counselor must be able to lead her to consider several possibilities that might assist her in making a wise decision for an improved life. The ultimate goal in the action stage is not only to help the client resolve her concerns, but to teach approach skills to prevent future problems.

Step One: Defining Concerns

The first step involved in effective problem solving calls for a clear, concrete statement of the client's concern(s). If the counselor has been effective in his communicative skills, the client has been encouraged to define his concern during the self-exploratory and understanding stages. However, it is important for the counselor and client to work toward clarifying the concern and stating it in workable terms so that it can be positively affected. Examples of defining concerns follow:

Example 1

Emanuel is a highly trained computer expert, Puerto Rican, married with sons eight and twelve years old.

> *Client's Concern:* During the past two years, I have been inundated with work at my computer firm—negotiating business contracts, having meetings, traveling, etc. I have allowed myself to take on more responsibilities than I am physically and emotionally capable of handling alone. I have come to the point where I'm frustrated, angry, and often obnoxious. I want to strike out against those around me at work, but I just don't do that. I become so embroiled with my anger by the end of the day that when I reach home I take out my anger on my sons—through verbal and physical abuse, rather than by confronting the source of my anger—my work. My wife just sits passively by and says nothing.

Example 2

Barbara, a Southern Appalachia Anglo, is twenty-eight years old, recently divorced, and lives alone with her children, ages three, five, and fifteen. She has completed one-and-a-half years of college, has never worked outside the home, and does not have substantial marketable work skills.

> *Client's Concern:* I have been divorced one year, but my ex-husband's child-support and alimony payments don't help me meet all of our needs. I would like to get a job, but since I don't have a job skill, it would be unlikely for me to secure one that would pay enough to make up the difference.

These examples illustrate clients' definitions of problems. The first example focuses on the client's inappropriate behavior which interferes with his personal interactions with the family, especially his two sons. The client's statement of concern suggests that he assumes responsibility for his behavior. Example two likewise shows client responsibility for her behavior in the present situation.

Step Two: Selecting Immediate Concerns

The second step deals with assisting the client to discern which concern most needs attention. Egan (1975) suggests four criteria for selecting immediate concerns: (1) provide some priority; (2) deal with easier concerns first; (3) select a concern that, if acted upon, might bring about improvement of other concern; or (4) proceed from less serious concerns to the more serious (pp. 207–9).

For example, Emanuel's concern has two central facets: (1) overwhelming anxiety and frustration with his work, and (2) the anger being misdirected at home as verbal and physical abuse of his sons. His immediate concern is his abusiveness toward his sons; this emergency needs top priority, but since Emanuel's abusive behavior at home occurs as a result of his problems at work, a central concern is also his behavior at work. Emanuel needs to learn to differentiate his interpersonal behaviors at home from those at work.

Step Three: Translating Concerns into Goals

The third step requires the counselor to assist the client in translating concerns into clear, concrete goals. Krumboltz (1970) contends that goals must be (1) designed for the client, (2) related to the client's personal and cultural values, and (3) stated in observable terms. Emanuel's immediate concern and his goal may then be stated as follows:

Immediate Concern: I am verbally and physically abusive to my two sons.

Immediate Goal: I must put a definite halt to my abusive behavior toward my children.

Subconcern: I am allowing myself to take on work responsibilities emotionally and physically greater than I can handle. I am constantly worrying about the work activities at my computer firm even after the work day is over.

Subgoal: I want to reduce my work load and activities so that I will have less responsibility at work.

Whether or not the client's goal is in line with his personal and cultural values depends upon the effectiveness of the counselor's use of focusing skills. The use of the pronoun *I* in goal statements suggests that the client has assumed responsibility for his own behavior.

The goal formulated from Barbara's immediate concern is as follows:

Immediate Concern: I'm not able to meet the economic needs of my four-member family with my ex-husband's child support and alimony payments.

Immediate Goal: I want to attain employment that will help me to be financially independent.

Step Four: Gathering Information and Listing Alternatives

Step four requires the counselor to assist the client in gathering information that will lead to various courses of action. Information gathered from a number of sources, such as reading materials, conversations, or contact with local agencies, may generate alternative courses of action. Emanuel's alternatives might include the following:

1. I can join an organization of parents who have had similar experiences and whose goal is to stop abusing their children.
2. I can place my two sons in a relative's home or in a foster home.
3. I can find a new residence and leave my sons with their mother.
4. I can continue in therapy to improve my work situation which seems strongly related to my inappropriate behavior with my children.
5. I can contact local and state agencies for information about assistance for parents who abuse their children.
6. I can read books, pamphlets, and other materials on child abuse, which describe positive communicative skills between parents and their children.

Barbara's information gathering might include:

1. I can move in with my mother and father and go back to college full-time.
2. I can apply for vocational rehabilitation to attain training.
3. I can remarry.
4. I can find a job, go to school evenings, and have a relative or close friend babysit while I am away.
5. I can place my three children in a foster home, return to college full-time, and get the children after I complete my degree and secure a job.
6. I can take my ex-husband back to court and demand an increase in child support and alimony payments.
7. I can enlist in a branch of the armed forces.
8. I can obtain an apartment management position so I can live free.
9. I can apply for public assistance.
10. I can move in with a friend and share the expenses and enroll in some type of training program.

Obviously, some options may sound rather bizarre, but by gathering all possible information, the client has more courses of action to analyze and choose from. In considering what action to take, the client may need to reevaluate the original goal and consider adoption of another. A new first choice may evolve from his discovery of resources available for a specific program. The client should be assisted in examining options in light of their relationship to personal and cultural factors.

Step Five: Choosing a Course of Action

The fifth step involves the client's choosing a specific course of action. The counselor must consider the cultural appropriateness and the consistency between the client's choice of goal and the proposed actions (Sue, 1977). Focusing skills will help to examine the selection in light of these values. The counselor might respond to Barbara, saying "You feel that you couldn't go on welfare and accept handouts from others, because this just isn't acceptable within your family." Clients must consider how their choice will benefit others—the group, or family member.

Step Six: Taking Action

The sixth step entails the critical stage of applying the action program. If the program is clearly understood and attempts have been made to rehearse portions of the program to simplify procedures, the client's goal may be fairly easily attained. However, there will be times when the client finds procedures are not easy to follow. The counselor may then begin applying expressions of content and expressions of feeling skills to convey reassurance, or it may be necessary to confront the client with the goal and the program, reminding him of his lack of effort.

Step Seven: Assessment of Action Taken

The seventh step centers on assessing the overall action program as implemented by the client. Assessment should continually take place during step six as the counselor and the client constantly evaluate various facets of the program in relationship to the social context in which they are applied.

The transition from exploration to understanding to action is a systematic approach that results in problem resolution. The four dimensions of the Ivey Taxonomy are sets of verbal and nonverbal skills that activate and maintain transition through each stage. These skills always take into account the client's needs and experiences as well as cultural differentials. Figure 10.1 outlines dimensions of each counseling stage of the Ivey Taxonomy.

The counselor who uses these skills must assume an active role in the process of the three stages, remembering as he does so that the skills, as well as the three counseling stages, may need adjustment in their application depending upon the cultural needs of clients. Moreover, clients will not always move through the cycle in an orderly fashion. It may be necessary first to establish self-understanding to enable the client to initiate self-exploration.

Step Eight: Assessment of the Outcome Criteria

The final stage of the communicative process model centers on assessment of outcome criteria. The three stages of counseling

FIG. 10.1.
CULTURAL AND COMMUNICATIVE SKILLS OF THE FOUR DIMENSIONS OF THE IVEY TAXONOMY ACTIVATING THREE COUNSELING STAGES.

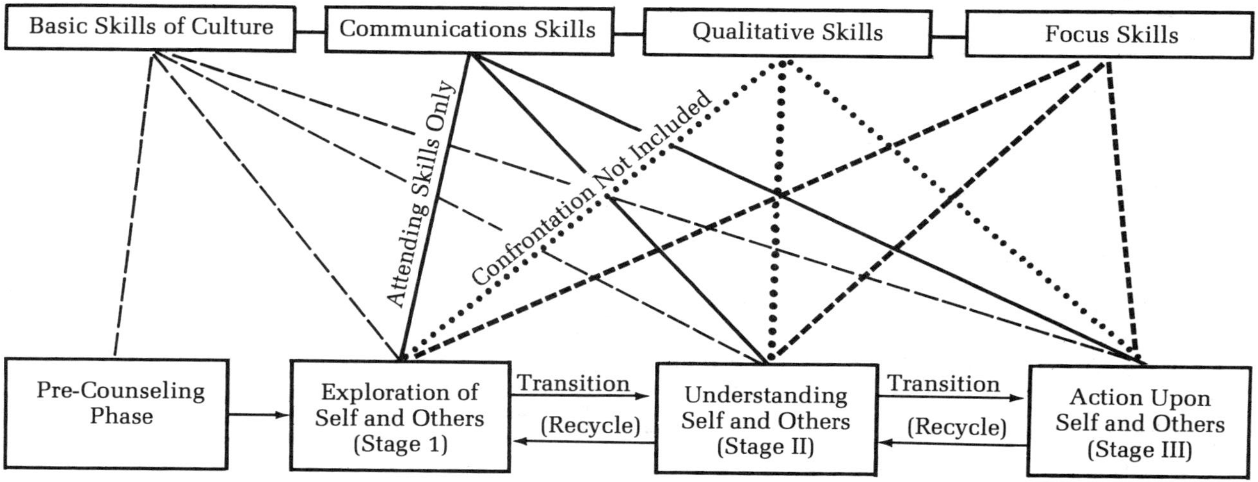

Note: These skills are fluid and dynamic and should not be viewed as fixed.

lend themselves to continuous assessment. The developmental stages contain a built-in mechanism that allows systematic and developmental assessment. Movement from exploration to understanding to action evolves continually both within and between the relevant problem areas (Carkhuff, 1969).

SOME PRACTICAL CONSIDERATIONS OF THE MODEL FOR MULTICULTURAL COUNSELING

Any attempt to provide culturally effective counseling requires a great deal of flexibility in counseling style and model(s). Several practical factors to be considered in applying the communicative process model in multicultural counseling may include (a) structured interviews, (b) cognitive dimensions, (c) goals of shaping as well as adapting to the environment, (d) communication in operational terms, (e) consistency with client's experiences, and (f) use of counseling stages that correspond to desired goals.

Many Black American (Smith, 1973), Chinese American (Sue and Sue, 1972), and American Indian (Spang, 1965) clients enter the counseling dyad knowing little or nothing about what will occur. An unclear counseling process has traditionally been related to anxiety: therefore, the counselor must be flexible and able to provide an unambiguous, well-structured situation to reduce uneasy feelings associated with the communicative process. Explanations of the process must be given to facilitate the clients' awareness of and participation in the process.

The communicative process model focuses on cognitive (content) and emotional (feeling) materials. The cultural experiences of some clients may dictate an adjustment in the model to focus mostly on content instead of emotions. Some cultures' (e.g., Chinese) traditional approaches in providing assistance to a person may include placing greater emphasis on verbal content rather than feelings. According to Sue (1978), cognitive appeals, for example, refer to straightforward statements that demand and direct the individual to apply immediate action upon a particular situation: "You can't allow your grade point average to get any lower. Begin spending at least three hours each night studying up for that course."

An admonition may provide counseling about faults or oversights (Sue, 1978). The counselor might respond, "I think you enjoy your job; you might consider these four alternatives if you want to keep it: (1) complete your evening activities so you can retire earlier than usual; (2) set your alarm early enough to allow yourself time to prepare for work and arrive on time; (3) ask a dependable relative or co-worker to phone you shortly after your alarm clock is scheduled to ring; or (4) request a later work period." Advice giving, on the other hand, is not a command but more prescriptive in nature, resembling the medical (prescriptive) model: "Why don't you try working out a schedule to help you keep track of your time?" The final response, appeal to shame or guilt, might be applied with a child to attain appropriate behavior. For example, "Derald, your grandmother won't come to see you any more if you're disrespectful to her." Obviously, a certain degree of established rapport between the two parties must exist before the client will accept and act upon these forms of cognitive assistance (Sue, 1978).

It is essential that the communicative process model be modified to the client's cultural experiences and expectations. For example, attending to the client's cognitive messages may facilitate attainment of counseling goals. Moreover, the client, on leaving the interview, is likely to feel that he has been given concrete material upon which to act. Likewise, the counselor is perceived as one who has focused on real concerns consistent with the desired outcomes.

Counseling goals must be presented in societal terms (cultural, personal) instead of relating only to the counseling process (genuineness, empathy) or to limited outcome variables (clarifying values, enhancing levels of aspiration) (Adams, 1973; Tucker and Gunnings, 1974).

When formulating goals, two basic assumptions are made by counseling practitioners. The first is that the client is responsible for all behavior and capable of change. Counseling strategies are thus geared to assist the client to understand, survive, cope with, accept, or adjust to his psychological environment (Vexliard, 1968). Conversely, the second assumption is that the client's psychosocial environment or social systems may be responsible for his or her problems (Thomas and

Comer, 1973). Counseling goals consistent with this latter assumption focus on assisting the client to modify, restructure, manipulate, or shape a new cultural environment to accommodate his personal needs (Vexliard, 1968). A middle-of-the-road approach between these two assumptions is valuable in attaining broad goals. For example, a Black male is experiencing marital problems after 20 years of marriage. Contrary to his wishes, he has been forced into early retirement. His wife managed the household chores to his satisfaction before his retirement, but now he finds himself frequently giving unwarranted instructions, and generally being intolerable at times. This situation may require setting goals for the husband and wife to help them adapt to their new situation as well as the husband's seeking other employment or taking legal proceedings to retain his job. The husband's unscheduled retirement is obviously a source of the marital conflict. The goal of adjustment to their new relationship might have been appropriate if the husband had wanted early retirement and a similar marital problem had resulted. But in this case, the counselor also has to cope with the husband's feelings vis-a-vis his environment.

While some culturally different clients will need assistance in adapting to their psychosocial surroundings, others will need to act positively and constructively upon their surroundings to change them. Culturally effective counselors using the communicative process model must base goal formulation on the client's needs and experiences.

Some goals formulated according to the client's individual needs and cultural experiences will not require each of the counseling stages. For example, little or no emphasis on self-exploration and self-understanding will be warranted if the client's greatest need is securing a job. The client might only examine available resources, alternatives, and steps to be taken in securing employment.

Finally, the counselor's ability to communicate with the culturally different client in operational or concrete terms that can be understood by both parties cannot be overemphasized. Verbal transactions should be transmitted in nonabstract terms. For example, a response to the client that, "Maria and

Carlos don't like you," is likely to be understood quickly. On the other hand, an abstract response such as, "You sense a deep feeling of hate from other people," is neither direct nor comprehensible to the client. Thus, awareness of the client's communication patterns provides the counselor with greater latitude in meeting the client's needs.

Summary

Research evidence indicates that the delivery services of traditional counseling have been less than adequate in meeting therapeutic needs of clients who are culturally different from the counselor. Professional literature suggests that a multicultural approach to counseling must be general enough to deal effectively with clients' divergent experiential backgrounds, yet any generalized counseling approach should be delivered systematically. Such an approach hinges on verbal and nonverbal communication; competence is necessary in verbal and nonverbal communicative skills to positively effect communication transactions. The skills of the Ivey Taxonomy are extremely important in influencing communicative behavior between the two parties throughout the three counseling stages. The concreteness of these skills facilitates counselor-client understanding, which, in turn, systematically leads to attainment of positive outcomes.

Exercises

The following exercises are designed to help students conceptualize the communicative skills model.

A. This exercise is intended to help students to examine the appropriateness of applying counseling skills in cross-cultural situations. Ask each student to make a list of skills described in Ivey's Taxonomy, examining each skill separately and writing the advantages and disadvantages of their application with individuals of the following groups: Blacks, Anglos, Southern Appalachian Anglos, American Indians, Chicanos, Puerto Ricans, Chinese Americans, and Vietnamese Americans. Have students share their conclusions with each other.

B. The following exercise is designed to provide students with practice in using the skills in the four dimensions of the Ivey Taxonomy as they might be applied in counseling Stages I and II, self-exploration and self-understanding. Each student should form a dyad with another. In each dyad, one student performs as counselor and the other acts as client. The counselor should attempt to move the client through Stage I with basic, communicative, qualitative, and focusing skills, while the client role plays the situation described below:

> An eleventh-grade, Chicano male, who lives in a barrio and attends school in a middle-class community across town, is experiencing interpersonal problems with students at school.

Stop the role playing frequently so observers can give feedback. At the conclusion, students should reverse their roles. Next, each member of the dyad should redo the role playing but move through the exploratory stage, Stage II, using the skills in the four dimensions of the Ivey Taxonomy. Participants should evaluate the counselor's application of the skills and his efforts to facilitate movement in Stage II.

C. The following exercise gives students practice in developing the skills in the action stage, or Stage III. Students should form dyads with each other. In each dyad, one student assumes the role of counselor and the other assumes the role of client. The counselor should attempt to move the client through Stage III, using the skill in Ivey's Taxonomy and the steps applied in problem solving. The participant acting as the client should role play the following situation:

> I'm bored with the things that I do in the factory. It's so repetitious. I'm worn out. It is physically impossible for me to stack and pack boxes and load trucks. I haven't asked the supervisor for any help. I really don't pack the boxes as well as I should.

Stop the counselor-client interaction in this exercise at various intervals to provide the counselor with feedback concerning her use of the counseling skills and application of problem solving steps. Repeat this exercise with students switching roles.

REFERENCES

Adams, H. J. "Progressive Heritage of Guidance: A View from the Left." *Personnel and Guidance Journal,* 1973, 51, 531–38.

Brammer, L. M. *The Helping Relationship—Process and Skills,* 2d ed. Englewood Cliffs, N.J.: Prentice-Hall, 1979.

Carkhuff, R. R. *Helping and Human Relations: A Primer for Lay and Professional Helpers,* vol. 2. New York: Holt, Rinehart and Winston, 1969.

Egan, E. *The Skilled Helper: A Model for Systematic Helping and Interpersonal Relating.* Monterey, Calif.: Brooks/Cole Pub. Co., 1975.

Gazda, G. M. *Human Relations Development.* Boston: Allyn and Bacon, 1973.

Ho, M. K. "Cross-Cultural Career Counseling." *Vocational Guidance Quarterly,* 1973, *21,* 186–90.

Ivey, A. E. "Cultural Expertise: Toward Systematic Outcome Criteria in Counseling and Psychological Education." *Personnel and Guidance Journal, 1977,* 55, 296–302.

Ivey, A. E. and J. Authier. *Microcounseling,* 2d ed. Springfield, Ill.: Charles C. Thomas, 1978.

Ivey, A. E. and N. Gluckstern. *Basic Influencing Skills, Participant Manuals.* North Amherst, Mass.: Microtraining Associates, 1976.

Ivey, A. E. and N. Gluckstern. *Basic Attending Skills, Leader and Participant Manuals.* North Amherst, Mass.: Microtraining Associates, 1974.

Ivey, A. E. and S. J. McGowan. "Microcounseling: A Systematic Approach for Improving Helping Skills and Teaching Them to Others." *Focus on Guidance,* 1977, 9, 1-10.

Krumboltz, J. D. "Behavioral Goals for Counseling." In S. H. Osipow and W. B. Walsh (eds.), *Behavior Change in Counseling: Readings and Cases.* Englewood Cliffs, N.J.: Prentice-Hall, 1970. Pp. 21–29.

Pietrafesa, J. J., A. Hoffman, H. H. Splete, and D. V. Pinto. *Counseling: Theory, Research and Practice.* Chicago: Rand McNally, 1978.

Smith, E. J. *Counseling the Culturally Different Black Youth.* Columbus, Ohio: C. E. Merrill Pub. Co., 1973.

Spang, A. "Counseling the Indian." *Journal of American Indian Education*, 1965, 5, 10–15.

Sue, D. W. "Counseling the Culturally Different: A Conceptual Analysis." *Personnel and Guidance Journal*, 1977, *55*(7), 422–25.

Sue, S. "Mental Health Needs as Affected by Historical and Contemporary Experiences." Paper presented at Ethnic Lifestyle and Mental Health Seminar, Oklahoma State University, Stillwater, Okla., March 1978.

Sue, D. W. and S. Sue. "Counseling Chinese-Americans." *Personnel and Guidance Journal*, 1972, *50*(8), 637–44.

Thomas, C. S. and J. Comer "Racism and Mental Health Services." In C. Willie, B. Krammer, and B. S. Brown (eds.), *Racism and Mental Health*. Pittsburgh: University of Pittsburgh Press, 1973. Pp. 164–81.

Tucker, R. N., and T. S. Gunnings. "Counseling Black Youth: A Quest for Legitimacy." *Journal of Non-White Concerns*, 1974, 208–16.

Vexliard, A. "Temperament et Modalites d'Adaptation." *Bulletin de Psychologie, 1968, 21*, 1–15.

Part Four

Preparing for the Future

In part 4, the state of counselor training programs is discussed, especially in relation to attempts to recruit and train more persons from ethnic groups. Ethnic minority clients will only use mental health facilities when they can adequately identify with the professionals who provide assistance. There is a pressing need for counselors to acquire skills that can be used in traditional and nontraditional counseling approaches. In addition, clients need to be taught to deal effectively with their problems so that they do not become dependent on the trained professional counselor for assistance.

11

Avoiding Cultural Shock in Counseling: Summary and Conclusions

IN THE PRECEDING CHAPTERS of this book, emphasis has been placed on the idea that traditional counseling approaches are too limited to provide the necessary kinds of assistance across ethnic and cultural groups. While traditional approaches adequately meet the needs of many ethnic and cultural groups in the United States, they fall short for many others because each ethnic and cultural group discussed contains intragroup variations. Furthermore, these groups also contain intergroup variations. And the acculturative patterns, that is, the degree of acceptance and the adoption of middle-class American values, influence the behaviors of counselors and clients during the counseling process.

Ethnic and culturally relevant needs have been described by many counseling proponents. Every group has a unique pattern of social and personal problems and a unique response to traditional counseling intervention strategies. Thus, culturally relevant strategies are required. These strategies may draw on the unity and the strength of the family system, or they have to draw on the sense of individualism that a group fosters. As yet, few professionals are knowledgeable about cultural factors or skilled in counseling various ethnic groups. Thus, there is a great need to develop culturally relevant counseling training programs.

Research strongly suggests that many contemporary counselors have only superficial understanding and knowledge about various ethnic and cultural groups. Clients of such groups are perceived stereotypically rather than realistically. It appears that the educational system has been remiss in providing counseling students with a basis from which to function effectively with clients of diverse cultures.

Recommendations for effective mental health services are directed not only at various counseling strategies but also at the services themselves. There is a need to integrate these services to provide clients of ethnic cultural groups with effective mental health delivery systems. Community mental health agencies, as well as professionals, should perform an ongoing needs assessment prior to establishing and delivering mental health services and it should be continued throughout the life of the program.

The essential focus, then, is not only on counselors, but also on community mental health agencies. Because traditional counseling is often not effective with some persons or groups, counseling that involves nontraditional approaches is necessary. These approaches enable counselors to understand clients from their own sociocultural perspectives and may dictate more action-oriented approaches than traditional approaches. Such approaches might place the emphasis for change on the system itself. For example, they might require counselors to work in the community rather than in their offices. Professionals should locate their facilities in areas easily accessible to persons who will use them. Transportation could be made available to those requiring such services, and flexible hours should be established. The availability of these services can be communicated to the people through the mass media.

PREPARING COUNSELORS FOR A MULTICULTURAL SOCIETY

There is an increasing need for counselors capable of effectively assisting clients of diverse ethnic and cultural groups. Although there is need for more ethnic minority counseling professionals, it is equally important that counselor education and other mental health training programs prepare mainstream Anglo counselors to cross cultural lines so they use counseling skills necessary to deal effectively with persons requiring assistance regardless of their ethnic group.

Graduate programs and training institutions should create programs that address the diverse problems of a multicultural society. There must be a practical link between the counseling orientations of counselors and their intended work sites. Counselor educators and mental health educators must recognize that these orientations may be philosophical, and that they must develop strategies to encourage their application. These orientations should not stand in isolation, but must be translated into observable behaviors that enable prospective counselors to acquire the skills necessary to become culturally skilled and culturally competent within a multicultural society.

An initial step is to develop or modify counselor educational curricula so they can permeate the ethnic and cultural customs and behaviors of people whom counselors will eventually serve. I do not advocate discarding middle-class Anglo counseling theories, but rather, suggest that these theories should be broadened to include the life-styles and patterns of a more diverse American society. For instance, curricula could be designed to provide systematic input of a multicultural perspective. Course readings should include articles and books written by authors of various ethnic and cultural groups. Students should be made aware of the issues involved in drawing conclusions from course work in which little or no significant literature or research is available by authors of varied ethnic minority groups. Courses with ethnic content, such as Chicano psychology, Black psychology, and the sociology of the various ethnic communities should be made available to students. Also, multicultural and cross-cultural counseling strategies could be taught through simulated counseling experiences. Videotape equipment is useful in such a program. Potential counselors should be screened for the human factors necessary to work effectively with persons of other ethnic groups.

As important as curricula modification are provisions for

ethnic and culturally relevant counseling internship experiences for prospective counselors. Internship sites in schools and community agencies where particular ethnic and cultural group members are located should be planned for students. Each student counselor should be teamed with an experienced counselor at the on-site institutions, and these experiences should include work with children and adults. Interning students could be directly supervised by at least one professor and/or an advanced doctoral student who has undergone or is undergoing an internship. Although knowledge and vicarious experiences can also be obtained through professional workshops and in-service workshops, nothing substitutes for real experiences in counseling ethnic minorities.

Another important dimension of revised counseling curricula is the systematic evaluation of counseling skills so as to avoid relying on humanistic rhetoric. Statistical evidence indicates that a systematic counseling skills process accomplishes its intended goals and objectives. Chapters 9 and 10 discussed a systematic approach to using counseling skills; this approach is designed to meet the needs of counselors and clients. In this model, based on Carkhuff's model, which in turn, borrows from the expanded counseling skills advanced by Allen Ivey and his associates, certain steps are implemented in order to attain objectives that are constantly being evaluated to allow for revision of implementation or redefinition of the objectives. However, this systematic process may not meet all needs of some ethnic and cultural group members. Other nontraditional or culturally relevant procedures may have to be implemented as dictated by the individual and the extent of his acculturation. In fact, the individual's needs may require little verbal communication and a high degree of action from the counselor who is attempting to provide effective assistance.

BEYOND THE DYADIC PROCESS—ARMING THE CLIENT WITH THERAPEUTIC SKILLS

While revised counselor education curricula should be concerned with preparing counselors to assist ethnic and cultural group members with immediate needs, there is also a need to focus on training counselors to teach clients skills that will enable them to apply methods to solve their own problems without counselor assistance. This approach is particularly significant for clients who do not have the economic means to continue in counseling for a long time. The counseling practice of the future will require professional counselors to go beyond simple ameliorating the client's immediate problems. The counselor will also have to find methods, approaches, and solutions to environmental and psychological problems; specific approaches to this problem, however, are beyond the scope of this book.

Equally important is the need to teach and train paraprofessionals to work with clients of various ethnic and cultural groups. In this way, many nonprofessionals or laypersons will have greater latitude or persuasion within their own communities.

Any counseling program that trains counselors should strongly consider preparing its students to work with the various ethnic and cultural group members. A combination of nontraditional and traditional intervention strategies can best meet the needs of ethnic and cultural groups. Finally, not only should traditional middle-class persons be trained to function in a multicultural counseling arena, but persons of ethnic groups should be trained to provide necessary assistance to their own and other ethnic and cultural groups.

Index